WALKING HILL
COUNTRY TOWNS

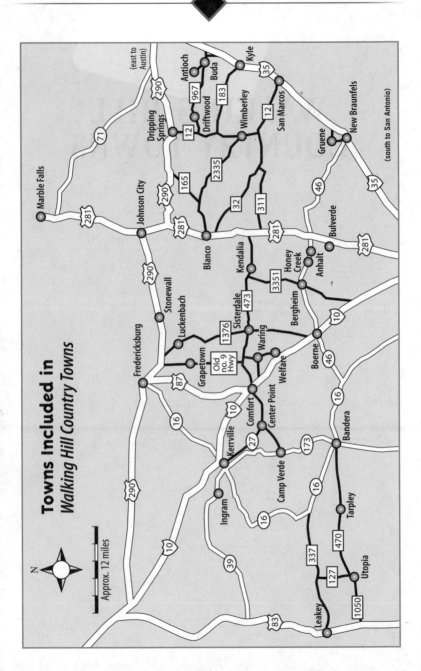

Towns Included in
Walking Hill Country Towns

SECOND EDITION

WALKING HILL COUNTRY TOWNS

41 UNIQUE WALKS IN THE TEXAS HILL COUNTRY

DIANE CAPITO

MAVERICK PUBLISHING COMPANY

MAVERICK PUBLISHING COMPANY
P.O. Box 6355, San Antonio, Texas 78209

Library of Congress Cataloging-in-Publication Data
Capito, Diane.
  Walking Hill Country towns : 41 unique walks in the Texas Hill Country / Diane Capito. –[2nd ed.].
    p. cm.
Includes bibliographical references and index.
ISBN 978-1-893271-55-5 (acid-free paper)
1. Texas Hill Country (Tex.)–Tours. 2. Cities and towns–Texas–Texas Hill Country–Guidebooks.
3. Historic sites–Texas–Texas Hill Country–Guidebooks. 4. Walking–Texas–Texas Hill Country–
Guidebooks. 5. Texas Hill Country (Tex.)–History, Local. I. Title.
  F392.T47C37 2010
  917.6404′64–dc22

                                                          2010016865

5 4 3 2 1

Walk maps by Virginia Ford.
Frontispiece map by Leslie Kell.
Cover, book design and electronic publishing — Nio Graphics, Inc. and Kell Creative, LLC.

Cover photos, clockwise from top left: Faltin Store Comfort; Lyndon B. Johnson Boyhood Home, Johnson City; Bandera County Courthouse, Bandera; old bank building, Comfort.
Back cover photo: Eleventh Street, Bandera.

NOTE: Walking conditions, hours, and other such information reported in this book can change at any time. The author and publisher cannot be held responsible for readers' travel experiences. We urge you to follow the safety suggestions herein and to exercise due care in the course of your travels.

Contents

Preface

This is a book of walks in the Texas Hill Country. It is not intended to be a history book. However, walking in the Hill Country is like walking through history. You don't have to look for it; it reaches out and grabs you.

As I planned this book I listed every town and community I could find on the map or mentioned in Hill Country history. Hill Country boundaries are loosely defined. For the first edition I found myself focusing on a core area of Interstate 35 between Austin on the east, San Antonio on the south, Bandera and Kerrville on the west and Fredericksburg and Johnson City on the north and Highway 46 on the south.

Then I went driving. It was October. The weather was beautiful and the hills were lovely. It was one of my most delightful travel experiences.

Some places yielded two or more walks, others none at all. I found walks where I didn't expect them, and sometimes didn't find them where I hoped they would be. All that is left of Fischer is a new post office and a closed general store, with no place to walk. All that's left of Camp Verde is a general store/ post office and a historical marker down the road. But that road offers a lovely shaded walk along Verde Creek past an old cemetery.

When I began exploring these towns it was their charm and settings that attracted me, not their history. But I found that while all are pleasant places to "just go walking," it's impossible not to wonder, at least a little, about each town's history: When was it established? By whom? Why did they come here? Why are there so many of those small stone houses with the outside staircases? Sometimes a historical marker piqued my curiosity.

Next came the research. It seems that every Hill Country library has a book or two published by the local heritage or genealogical society and compiled by patient people who pored over records and maps, interviewed settlers and their descendants and gathered unique photographs and drawings. Ones with titles like *Solid Lace and Tucks* and *Texas Camel Tales* especially caught my eye.

Reading about early settlers and their adventures whetted my appetite for more. I talked with local historians and with descendants of settlers. Soon I found myself immersed in history, when all I had intended was to take a walk in some charming little town set in the hills. For the first time in my life history became interesting. No longer the stuff of dry textbooks full of names, battles, and dates I could never remember, history became a living story full of ordinary people caught up in the events of their times.

One day while I was scanning a book at the Blanco Library, an elderly woman sat down at the same table to await her husband. As I turned a page she said, "That's my brother," and pointed to a photograph. As we continued through the book she related stories of growing up in Blanco. It was the last time I left my tape recorder at home.

Before long I had to remind myself that I was writing a walk book, not a history book, and that the purpose of the research was simply to add interesting tidbits. Walk books have to be small enough for walkers to hold comfortably. I could not cover all the history nor relate all the stories, no matter how fascinating or entertaining. Nor could I spend countless hours sitting in the library when I was supposed to be outside planning walks. But that time has indeed yielded many tidbits for my sketches of towns and communities. A few of the places have all but disappeared, but since their names kept popping up I include brief summaries of their histories, too. The information for each walk has been read by one or more of that town's historians.

This edition updates some material in the first edition, published in 2001, and expands the coverage area to the north and west, adding walks in Marble Falls and Leakey. Still, it is inevitable that I overlooked something here or there, a walk or even a community. If I missed your favorite, please be understanding.

Using This Book

This book can be used as a trip planner for the Texas Hill Country even if you don't intend to walk. Most walks lend themselves to auto tours. Any can be done by bicycle. Keep in mind, though, that on foot you have time to stop and smell the roses—or at least visually enjoy a garden or an architectural detail you'd miss driving by in a car. So if you are able to walk, or if the walk route is wheelchair accessible, as most are, park the car and really get to know the town. Accessibility for the handicapped is a relative factor, so I suggest driving the route first to judge its accessibility for personal needs.

All town listings include location and a brief history. Walk listings include the main features, distance, parking and restroom availability, walking conditions (flat, hilly, sidewalks), and, in many cases, nearby restaurants.

Walks range from less than a mile to about three miles. When a town has several walks, all start from a central location so they may be combined. To get you oriented toward what is being described, there is often an "L" (left) or "R" (right) after the address.

There are a few things to keep in mind as you walk. When walking along the street, walk on the side facing traffic so you can see approaching cars. Don't depend on the driver seeing you. Be aware at all times. Take care crossing streets and especially crossing highways. When walking at night, wear light-colored or reflective clothing. I prefer not to walk alone at night. Heed low water crossings; never cross flowing water.

As you walk, please respect the property and privacy of people and their homes along the way. Look only from the street or public sidewalk. This book has information on houses with historical plaques. You shouldn't have to go onto someone's property to read the plaque.

Most towns have visitor centers to which you can call ahead or where you can pick up lists of restaurants, accommodations, and schedules of special events. Unfortunately, restaurants, even long established ones, sometimes close. Also, tastes vary, and my idea of a good restaurant may not be yours. So for the most part I simply say, "Several along the route." Sometimes I mention one that's a local favorite, hoping it will still be there when you walk by. As I explored towns I looked at menus and occasionally asked natives for recommendations, but mostly I followed impulse. I've rarely had a bad meal at a Hill Country restaurant.

Since the locator map does not include lesser roads, I recommend *The Roads of Texas* atlas for more detailed overall trip planning. Farm to Market (FM) roads and Ranch Roads (RR) are paved. County Roads (CR) and side roads may or may not be. A word of warning: stay off county and side roads if you have no sense of adventure. These sometimes change from pavement to gravel and seem to go on forever, usually ending at T-intersections with no directional signs. In other words, when you finally reach the dusty end, you don't know where you are. If you're not deterred by this, these roads can offer particularly scenic drives.

I especially like to meander. Sometimes I turn onto a road just to see where it leads. Or I set out with no destination in mind. I might turn off on the first side road that looks inviting and keep turning onto whatever road next catches my fancy. Since I am directionally challenged, I eventually have no idea where I am.

Fortunately, I don't care where I am. I never fail to have a good time meandering. The Hill Country is full of breathtaking vistas, occasional canyons, pastureland and byways that offer an interesting historical marker, general store, or restaurant. Just don't meander without sufficient gas in the tank.

Now please join me on these walks through historic Texas Hill Country towns.

Anhalt

West of U.S. 281 on Hwy. 46 between Boerne and New Braunfels. No walk.

Anhalt translates as "the stopping place." When a loaded supply wagon could travel only about 10 miles a day, Anhalt was one stop between Boerne and New Braunfels where drivers and animals could refresh at the creek and spend the night. In 1875 local farmers under Valentin Fuhrmann formed the Germania Farmers Verein with its own brand, to protect cattle and horses from Indians and rustlers. Buyers knew any animal branded "G" brought to market by other than a Germania Verein member had been rustled. This may be the oldest farmers' cooperative society in Texas.

In 1879 the society built Verein Hall for demonstrations of the newest farming equipment and techniques. Its library of 500 books in German is now at the University of Texas at San Antonio Institute of Texan Cultures. A kitchen was added at the rear and in 1908 a dance hall. As the need for livestock protection declined the Verein evolved into a benevolent society and social center. Many farmers survived rough times in the 1930s with its support.

Although the town is gone, the Farmers Verein hosts a Mayfest and an Octoberfest, announced by a large sign on Hwy. 46 at Anhalt Road. Each begins at noon on the third Sunday of the month, the only time the hall is open to the public. It's a family affair and lots of fun. Food is traditionally pot roast, potato salad, and peaches, served home-style at long tables. Dancing (German music in the afternoon, western in the evening), and, of course, German beer, complete the festivities.

Antioch

West of I-35 between San Marcos and Austin just outside Buda. At Buda's only traffic light, turn from Loop 4 onto FM 967. Go past the school and over Onion Creek. Immediately turn left onto Cole Springs Road, then immediately right onto Old Black Colony Road (CR 147). One walk.

Antioch Colony was established on some of the first land in Hays County held by freedmen. Many of the Hays County settlers were southerners who arrived in the mid-1800s with their families and slaves to plant cotton on the fertile prairie land. After the Civil War, some landowners gave their freed slaves land of their own to farm. Other freedmen opened businesses or worked for wages.

In 1869 an Anglo-American from Missouri, Joseph Rowley, bought 490 acres of good land on Onion Creek for $2.50 an acre. It is not clear whether he took it upon himself to help the former slaves establish themselves or if he was assigned as a freedman's representative. Beginning in 1870, he sold the freedmen land at $5 an acre. Although it seems like he doubled his money, this probably was not the case, since he took care of all paperwork, including stagecoach trips to San Marcos to file deeds. It is said he sold other land to Anglos for $100 an acre to provide himself with working capital. Ten to 15 families lived in the Antioch community.

To protect new landowners from the unscrupulous, Rowley sold deeds with the stipulation that the owner "shall not have the right to sell or cause to be sold this tract of land or any part thereof, without the consent of the said Rowley or his heirs." If the land was sold without his approval, the deed would be invalid. In 1880 Rowley moved back to Missouri, but in 1893 he sent documents back to the colony permitting the landowners to sell their property. Descendants of original Antioch settlers still live here.

Not only was it a beautiful spring day when I took my first walk here, it turned out as a fine example of the pleasures of walking "in the country" where walkers are not the usual passersby. The first car to stop and ask if I needed a ride was along Cole Springs Road. This couple was out for a Sunday drive. We struck up a conversation and were soon busy identifying some of the plants and trees along the road. On Old Black Colony Road a man was closing the gate to a pasture as I walked by. "Do you need a ride?" he asked. After assuring him I was walking on purpose, he told me he had been checking fences and that because of the drought his oats were only high enough to graze half his herd.

Just a few minutes later a family returning from church stopped. They'd spotted my car parked next to the cemetery. Not seeing anyone in the cemetery, and seeing me walking, they thought perhaps I was having car trouble and needed help. Because they were African American I ventured a guess they might be descended from the early settlers. When I got an affirmative answer, I told them about my book and asked if I might interview them for background information. This led to a delightful afternoon around the dining table listening while the six Harper sisters related tales of growing up in Antioch and stories told by their parents and grandparents. They answered some of my questions and added details.

Most of the farms were 40–50 acres on which the farmers raised foodstuffs for their own use and sugar cane, grain, and cotton as cash crops. George Harper sold his cane to Milton Kavenaugh, who had a molasses mill. Minnie Harper's chore as a young girl was to clean and assemble the 21 disks on her father's cream separator. He sold his cream to local dairies for butter and cheese.

During my afternoon with the Harper sisters the conversation turned to ghosts. I finished telling of the ghost at the Baines home in Blanco and reached for my lemonade glass. At that exact moment one of the two ceiling lights went out. My startled look sent everyone into peals of laughter. One sister ventured, "That must be Papa. He was always telling us to turn off unnecessary lights."

My second Antioch walk was with a friend. One car stopped to ask directions, but no one stopped to ask if we needed a ride. This could be coincidence, but our conclusion is that a person walking alone (especially a woman?) equals a need for help, while two people walking are probably local and actually out for a walk.

ANTIOCH WALK

Mostly shady, along Onion Creek and Antioch Cemetery on Old Black Colony Road. 4.5 miles total, 3.5 miles if turning back on Cole Spring Road. Some gradual grades. Most of walk on narrow road with little traffic and grassy shoulders to step onto. For a half-mile on FM 1626 you walk on paved shoulder next to fast traffic. Park at cemetery. No public restrooms. Restaurants in Buda or on I-35.

❶ Starting at cemetery, with back to cemetery, turn left on Old Black Colony Road.

No. 3022L is a 1925 bungalow of the type called Craftsman.

The next house on the left had a gaggle of noisy geese on my first walk. Some horses came to greet me from behind the fence in the pasture next to the house.

Just past there, on the right, are the weathered remains of the Kavenaugh house and barn.

A bit farther on is the tumbled-down house and shed that was the home of the Tom Mullin family.

At the intersection with Cole Springs Road, on the right, is a quarry operation. Behind this enterprise is property owned by the Community Church of Buda. Elias Bunton and his wife, Clarisa, provided religious and educational services to the early community. In 1874 Bunton donated land for a building to be used as school, church, and meeting hall. The community pitched in to build it. The foundation of that early stone building, the Center Union Baptist Church, is still there. The building itself was disassembled and moved over to Goforth Road in the mid-1920s, then later sold to a church in Manchaca. Baptisms still take place in the creek. The church is raising money to rebuild on their property here.

On one walk some wild turkeys crossed the road here.

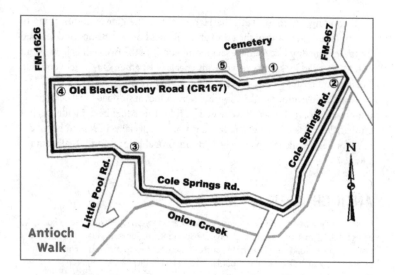

Antioch
Walk

❷ Turn right on Cole Springs Road.

Between heavy rains, Onion Creek has a placid flow, and in times of drought is partially dry. It's possible most trees and plants native to this region can be seen along the banks of the creek and roadway: live oak, hackberry, and Texas persimmon predominate.

Several paths along here lead to the creek. My favorite is the one of exposed limestone. As I reached the creek the book title *Clear Springs and Limestone Ledges* came immediately to mind. There I was on a limestone ledge over a clear creek. Four wild ducks floated off to the right. A flurry of wings to the left proved to be a Great Blue Heron. It landed on a treetop across the creek. We saw a Great Egret on another walk. This is a lovely spot for a picnic.

One day George Harper, when fetching water from the creek, heard a choir up on the bluff singing his favorite hymn, "Wading In the Water." Wondering who could be singing up there, he loaded the mules and led them up. At the top—nothing. As he walked toward the sound it continued to be off somewhere ahead of him, until it finally faded away.

On a hill just past the limestone path is a house with pit bulls, each tied to its own doghouse. They are not a threat but sometimes make a lot of noise. The residents, descendants of original settlers, raise the dogs for sale.

A short way beyond the dogs is a magnificent live oak tree and beyond it another with an exceptionally beautiful gnarled trunk. Where the road makes a right-angle bend, I'm told, there is a heavy growth of the wild onions that gave the creek its name. When these are out in abundance, they say the onion smell is quite evident.

If walking Cole Springs Road only, turn around at this point and retrace your steps back to the beginning.

Beyond the bend, the road turns away from the creek. There are houses along here and a large quarry. Around another bend, sitting on a hill on the left, is a lovely stone and cedar shingle house that dates from 1930.

❸ At the T-intersection turn right, then right again on FM 1626.

FM 1626 was once Burnham Road. It's ironic that originally this road had a name and now has only a number, while the other two roads making up this walk started with only route numbers and now have names.

In one yard on the right we spotted some potbellied pigs eating.

The lovely Victorian house across FM 1626 is new. On my first walk a few cattle grazed near the fence in the pasture to its left. As I approached (remember, I'm across the road), they looked up and stampeded off over a rise. I guess somebody walking along here is too weird even for cattle.

The next house is the Garrison homestead. The Harpers told of sometimes seeing the "jack-o-lantern lights" (ball lightening) rolling just above the Garrisons' field and around the big oak tree in back before disappearing. "Jack-o-lantern lights" is an apt description of these grapefruit-sized fiery balls that glow yellow, orange, or red.

❹ Turn right onto Old Black Colony Road (CR 147).

Along here are a few houses and then some pasture land. A sharp bend in the road brings you back to the cemetery.

❺ Enter the cemetery.

The oldest gravestones I found are dated 1880. Over time some stones have become lost or badly damaged. Among the burials here are those of the Revedes family. The three Revedes brothers, Andreas, Leland, and Dan, were noted masons whose work is seen all around the Buda area.

Bandera

Bandera County seat, between San Antonio and Kerrville at Hwy. 16 and Hwy. 173. FM 1077, 470, and 3240 also lead to Bandera. Population 957. One walk.

The abundance of cypress trees along the Medina River led to the founding of Bandera. In the spring of 1852 three families of settlers—the Milsteads, Odems, and Saners—camped on the river and started a cypress shingles industry. (Trivia bit: A single one of these big trees yielded 30,000 shingles and a good shingle maker produced 1,000 shingles a day.) When Amasa Clark arrived that year he found these three families so friendly he decided to stay awhile. His stay lasted the rest of a long life. He died in 1927 just under 102 years of age.

A few more families settled in the area and the next year, 1853, John James and Charles de Montel surveyed and laid out the town of Bandera in the horseshoe bend of the river. They planned wide streets and a public square where the present courthouse, jail, and library stand. They also built a sawmill on the river, opened a commissary store, and built cabins.

Where did the town get its name? It may have been from Bandera Pass, north of town on State 173, that separates the Medina and Guadalupe valleys. Natives, Spanish conquistadors, settlers, wagon trains, camel caravans, U.S. troops, and Texas rangers used the pass over the years. It is named either for a Spanish general who defeated a band of Apaches there or for a red flag (*bandera*) placed on the highest peak of the pass in 1732 as a reminder of a boundary agreement between Spaniards and Indians.

Several groups of immigrants left their mark on Bandera. In 1854 the Lyman Wight Colony, 250 followers of the Reorganized Church of Latter Day Saints, camped briefly in Bandera before settling about twelve miles down the river and establishing Mountain Valley, popularly known as Morman Camp. They built homes, put in farms, started a furniture factory, and prospered. After Lyman Wight's death, the group, discouraged by constant Indian raids, disbanded and scattered. Among the few who stayed was widow Jesse Hay and her children. Her husband had died before the group left Missouri. Although women could not legally own property in those days, Jesse received the first recorded land deed in Bandera. When the paperwork was sent in, most likely her name fooled them into thinking she was a man.

In 1855 a group of 16 Polish peasant families, escaping hardships of feudal life, arrived at Galveston. They walked to Panna Maria, but that new Polish settlement was still struggling and could offer no jobs. Though skilled craftsmen, with no command of English or German and knowing nothing of frontier life they could find no work, even as farm laborers or domestic servants. Finally, when the families were stranded in Castroville and nearly destitute, James and deMontel heard about them and brought them to Bandera to work in the sawmill. Each family was given land for a home and a garden. The men made cypress shingles and the women built the millrace.

Local historian Margaret Evans, a descendant of Jesse Hay, says her grandmother, Virginia Minear Hay, told of watching Polish women carry rocks in their white aprons as they diverted the Medina River by the sawmill. She was particularly impressed by one woman who carried a baby strapped on her back as she worked.

Bandera was a remote frontier territory with frequent Indian raids until Camp Verde opened in 1856. The County of Bandera, with the town as its seat, formed in 1857. After the Civil War Bandera was a cattle staging area for trail drives. Farm boys turned into cowboys. Ranchers built holding pens. Storekeepers contracted as outfitters.

Sheep and goats, however, proved more profitable than cattle on the thin limestone soil. Andrew Mansfield arrived in 1870 with the first merino sheep, taking them by boat down the Ohio River to the Mississippi, across the Gulf of Mexico to Galveston, then overland to Bandera. The Hill Country became a major wool and mohair producer. In the early 1900s an economic decline was caused by the end of the cattle drives and by a series of floods that destroyed the mills, gins, and other businesses. Bandera remained relatively isolated until the construction of the highway to San Antonio in 1936.

A new image for Bandera, leading to an economic upswing, began in the 1920s when Cora and Ebeneser (Eb) Buck decided to take in summer boarders on their Julian Creek ranch. Other ranchers picked up the idea and by the 1930s Bandera had a growing reputation as dude ranch country. Today, Bandera touts itself as "The Cowboy Capital of the World." Hunters and fisherman fill its campgrounds and cabins. Northerners flock down to enjoy the mild winters. Its dude ranches enjoy a brisk business.

Although tourists are abundant, unlike other Hill Country towns Bandera's Main Street is not a row of antique shops, although there are some. The shops here are filled with western wear and western arts and crafts. The restaurants serve up western food, and for entertainment there are the town's well-known dance halls. Bandera is still a working town with an authentic western feel. Just a few years ago a Longhorn on the way to the veterinarian broke free of his owner and came charging down Main Street. Some local cowboys got a rope on him before he could do any damage.

BANDERA WALK

Historic buildings and neighborhoods, St. Stanislaus Church and Frontier Times Museum. 3.2 miles, mostly flat, some short slight grades. Sidewalks only on Main Street. Start at Main and Cypress (Hwys. 16 and 173 intersection). Public restrooms in Visitor Center, across from the courthouse on Main Street. There are several restaurants along Main. At the OST, standing for Old Spanish Trail, you can "straddle a saddle" to eat at the old bar.

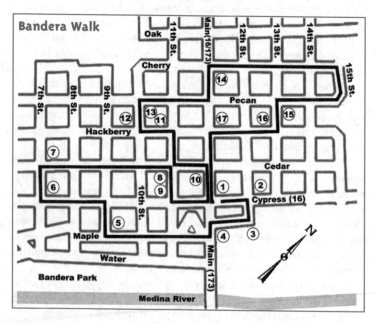

❶ From Main cross to right side of Cypress (Texas 16 South), turn left.

No. 1206 Cypress was built by George Hay for his mother. The first door on the left led to a room with window bars. Legend says it was the jail and courthouse. Not true, says descendent Margaret Evans— it was a pantry and the bars were to keep out both two-legged and four-legged varmints. The center door opened to a schoolroom, the third to the residence, the last to a store–pharmacy–post office–stage stop. Arches added in front in 1935 used rock from the wall surrounding the property.

❷ Turn right on Twelfth Street.

Where the street bends, to the left is the old jail (marker), designed in 1881 by Alfred Giles, one of San Antonio's most noted architects. He was directed to use a new "saw-and-file-proof" material for the "cages." Inside, a heavy iron door leads to the large, limestone block room where prisoners were kept. Evident in the floor are holes where rings were mounted to hold prisoners' leg chains. Among etchings into the soft limestone are "Texas Davy Wayne," "Sad Days," and "Crowbar Hotel." Most noticeable are the initials "DTD" next to good line drawings of horses. The woman who cleans insists a resident ghost turns the lights on and off. This is now a city office but you are welcome to go in and see the jail.

Next to it, the old courthouse (marker), now the Justice of the Peace office, was built as a store about 1868 by Henry White. The Masonic Lodge met on the top floor. Bandera County bought the building in 1877 and used it as a courthouse until the present one was built in 1892.

③ Turn right on the alley (originally a street).

The building on the left side was the 1869 Davenport, Schmidtke and Hay Mercantile Store. H. H. Carmichael later came into the business and Davenport and Schmidtke sold their share. It was in business until 1893.

George Hay had a saloon in the back. In modern times, the city had problems with this alley caving in. It seems Hay had dug a tunnel from the basement of the store to his home across the road so he could carry his money home safely at night. The tunnel came up into a small closet in the house. The day Margaret was showing me around the new owner of the property said he had heard about a tunnel but had no idea where it came into the house. Margaret identified the

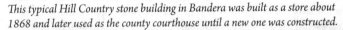

This typical Hill Country stone building in Bandera was built as a store about 1868 and later used as the county courthouse until a new one was constructed.

Kevin Fitzpatrick stands on his horse while doing some trick roping in front of the 1890 courthouse in Bandera, which bills itself as the Cowboy Capital of the World.

PHOTO BY MARY M. FISHER

closet which now had carpeting on the floor. They pulled up the carpeting, and sure enough, there was the trap door to the tunnel.

About 1920 the Bandera County Ranchmen and Farmers Association built their warehouse onto the store. In recent years it was a feed store. That closed in 1998 and the building is now an antique mall. A hand-operated freight elevator to the basement is the only elevator in Bandera and is said to be the oldest west of San Antonio. Jesse Hay once ran a tea room facing the river at the Main Street end of the building where women gathered with their children after shopping while the men got together at the saloon.

❹ Turn left on Main Street (173 South). At driveway to campground turn right, crossing Main (carefully) to Maple.

On the left, Bandera Park runs alongside the Medina River. (Day use only. Admission.)

❺ Turn right on Ninth Street, then left on Cypress.

At Eighth Street, on right, is the St. Stanislaus Catholic Church cemetery.

No. 700 Cypress, built in 1930 with stone from an earlier church building, is where the priests lived at one time.

⑥ Turn right on Seventh Street.

On the left corner of Seventh and Cypress is the 1876 Jureczki-Tobin house. Franz Jureczki, one of the Polish colonists, worked as the church sexton, ringing the bell, lighting the candles, and being general caretaker. When he thought the church should have a steeple, he paid for it. The Jureczkis had a huge wood-burning heater where the parishioners who drove in from the country would warm themselves before services.

St. Stanislaus Catholic Church, established in 1855, is the second-oldest Polish church in Texas, after the one in Panna Maria, southeast of San Antonio. At first a priest based in Panna Maria came on horseback from there once a month to conduct mass in Bandera's 20-by-30-foot log church. Construction began on the present Gothic edifice in 1876. The first sacristy and rectory, of wood, were located at the rear of the present church. A new steeple, sacristy, and altar were added in 1907. A stone monument in front lists the 16 Polish families who settled here. In the cemetery behind the church you will find the burial sites of these pioneers. Many of the headstones are in Polish.

Polish immigrants built Bandera's St. Stanislaus Catholic Church in 1876. The steeple was added in 1907.

Beside the church is the 1874 St. Joseph's Convent for the Sisters of the Immaculate Conception. The sisters also taught school here. This is now a museum, but with no set hours.

Across the street on the left is the two-story limestone St. Joseph's School, built in 1922. It closed in 1968 and is now used as a meeting hall.

⑦ Turn right on Cedar.

Between Eighth and Eleventh Streets are mostly small homes, some dating from the late 1800s to the early 1900s.

⑧ Turn right on Eleventh Street.

Eleventh Street was originally the main street of Bandera. Most streets in Bandera were of caliche and were not paved until the 1950s.

On the corner of Eleventh Street and Cedar is the 1850 First State Bank (marker) on a site bought by John James in 1842. This bank had the rare experience of never being robbed, probably because an operator was always on duty upstairs in the telephone office. Mrs. Mossey ran a school here from 1860 to 1879. In the 1880s it was the Bandera Institute operated by a Professor Ryan, who later was thought by some to be John Wilkes Booth. Rumor had it that Booth had not been killed and there is a distinct resemblance between him and Ryan.

Next to the bank is the 1908 Boyle Grocery and Drygoods Store. The Boyle brothers, Irish immigrants, arrived in 1907.

The stone building next on this side was used by John James and Charles de Montel while they laid out the town. Henry Stevens ran a blacksmith shop here. His wife, Margaret, a devout Methodist, let the congregation use the shop for services until they could build their own church.

To the right, the yard of the blacksmith shop is where the men gathered at the washer ring. This is a game similar to horseshoes, but you toss a flat, 2-1/2-inch metal washer into a cup instead of tossing a horseshoe around a peg. If the

Eleventh Street, Bandera's original main street, now hosts a variety of shops in restored buildings.

women needed to find their men between the hours of 2 p.m. and sunset, they came looking here.

The store across the street was originally Langford Hardware and Furniture. In those days a furniture maker was usually also a coffin maker. Langford opened a funeral home behind the store.

The small wood frame building next to it was first a hat shop, then later the place where you sold your varmint hides. (A varmint is considered any animal that isn't domestic.) You could get 10 to 25 cents a hide during the Depression. The floor was always oily. Some of the old timers got a good laugh when in recent years a restaurant opened here. They wouldn't eat there, insisting they could still smell varmint fat on the floor. The restaurant served good Mexican food and the owner fortunately moved down on the highway.

9 Turn left on Cypress and left on Main Street.

As you turn onto Cypress, the house on the left, built by P. D. Saner, is one of the oldest buildings in town. John Langford later remodeled it as a funeral home. It was used for many years as the home of the town sheriff. Hopefully this historic building will be restored.

On the corner at Main is the old Huffmeyer Store (marker), built in 1873 by B. F. Langford for Emil Huffmeyer. It is Bandera's oldest building.

Across the open space is the 1875 First National Bank building built by W. J. "Short Bill" Davenport. (There was another W. J. Davenport in town. This one was quite tall and appropriately nicknamed "Long Bill.")

Across Main at No. 306 a small red door and neon sign casually mark the famous Arkey Blue's Silver Dollar, the oldest continuously operating honky-tonk bar in Texas. The building dates from 1901. A scene from Peter Fonda's film *Race with the Devil* was shot here in the mid-1970s.

At Cedar, across on the right, are some buildings in a gully. In times of heavy rain the gully becomes a river that divides the town in two. The feed store down there was under water in the 1978 flood.

10 Turn left on Cedar, then right on Eleventh.

The First Methodist Church at the corner of Hackberry is an 1880 stone structure that replaced the original frame church (marker).

11 Turn left on Hackberry.

No. 1007 Hackberry is the imposing two-story stone home built in the 1890s and occupying a spacious 2.6-acre site. The home was purchased by English entrepreneur Stephen Ball and restored as the Mansion in Bandera Bed & Breakfast and Restaurant.

No. 915 Hackberry on the corner of Tenth Street is the 1890 home of H. H. Carmichael. The house was first built outside of Medina, but his wife, Mary Risinger Carmichael, refused to live where the Indians had just raided the white settlement, so they moved all of the building stones from there to Bandera and rebuilt it. Elizabeth Jane (Mayfield) Risinger passed away in this house on May 8, 1900, one of those days when the flooded river had cut the town in two. They had to wait four days before they could get her across the river to the cemetery for interment.

⑫ Turn right on Tenth.

At Pecan Street, up Tenth and to the left of the school gym, is the two-story stone school built in 1913, the first multi-room school in the area.

⑬ Turn right on Pecan. Cross Main Street at the light, then turn left on Main.

We don't walk past it, but up Main from Cherry, just past the Frontier Hotel, is the Cabaret, another Bandera nightspot. Most country western legends have performed there.

⑭ Turn right on Cherry, right on Fifteenth, then right on Pecan.

At the end of Cherry, No. 1501 is a Victorian beauty moved here from San Antonio. French doors replaced the original tall windows. The porch wraps around all four sides.

Coming around onto Pecan, No. 1514 is the 1910 Davenport home, a two-story "washerboard" frame house with a gable bay on the side and Ionic columns. This has recently been restored. The pressed tin roof, resembling shingles, is original.

⑮ Turn left on Thirteenth.

On the corner is the Frontier Times Museum (marker), built in 1933 by journalist-historian J. Marvin Hunter to serve as a museum for his western collection. The display of early pioneer items is augmented with all sorts of "stuff" donated by local residents. The eclectic collection, and the gallery of western art in the back room, is well worth the $2 admission. Open daily 10–4:30 and Sunday 1–4:30.

Outside, note the variety of stones used to build the museum. Most came from an 1878 rock fence salvaged from a nearby homestead. Friends brought pieces of petrified wood, fossils, pieces from cave formations, and one large ammonite (fossil shell) from the Pecos River. A round stone with a hole in the center, used originally as the top of a well, is now a window. A portrait of Geronimo, painted on glass by Hunter's son Warren, is in its center. The entrance was carved from Bear Mountain granite by the Nagel Brothers of Fredericksburg.

Hunter published the local newspaper and a magazine, *Frontier Times*, relating his experiences on the frontier. Although he intended the magazine to be a hobby, it grew in readership throughout the country. People began sending him their frontier stories along with old photographs, tools, and utensils. These soon filled his small 8-by-8-foot office. He enlarged the room, and again it filled. He started thinking in terms of a museum when the Depression came along. Determined to have his museum, Hunter came up with an idea. He printed a limited-edition book, *The Authentic History of Sam Bass and His Gang,* and offered the book and a subscription to the magazine as a package deal. In this way he raised the $1,000 he needed. To thank those who purchased the book, Hunter had their names engraved on the granite pillars at the entrance. Later more rooms were added, financed in the same manner, and the names then placed on bronze tablets.

In 1934 Hunter sold his newspaper and worked fulltime on the museum and magazine. He added yet another room and installed a modern printing plant. Besides the magazine, he continued to publish historical booklets. After his death, the Doane Foundation bought the museum. Later it was deeded to the citizens of Bandera, but the foundation still gives financial support. People continue to contribute artifacts and the museum continues to need more space.

16 Turn right on Hackberry.

At Main is the Bandera County Courthouse, built in 1891–92 in the Second Renaissance Revival style to replace the one you saw at the beginning of the walk. During restoration in 2008 the long-faceless spot for a clock in the tin-roofed cupola was found to have originally had a painted dial and hands, which were restored. There are six (at last count) markers in front of the courthouse, so amble on down for some bits of history.

The library is across the street.

17 Turn left on Main back to the start.

To visit the Bandera Cemetery, the entrance is off FM 173 just north of downtown. The oldest part is on the right just inside the entrance. A medium tall obelisk honors Jesse Hay's husband, Alexander, who is buried in Missouri. Daniel Carmichael, who was only eight years old when he died, has a small iron fence around his burial plot.

Bergheim

Hwy. 46 east of Boerne between U.S. 281 and I-10. No walk.

A marker at the Bergheim General Store tells of the homestead Andreas Engel established in 1903. Though the mill is gone, the store, home, some outbuildings, a cypress water tank, and a windmill still stand. As always, the store is a way station for travelers and a gathering place for locals who come for mail, gossip, and supplies. It is owned and operated by Engel's grandson, Stanley Jones.

Engel was born in Austria in 1864 and orphaned at six. With mandatory military service and few opportunities, he fulfilled his dream of "going to Texas in America" with the help of his foster parents. Arriving in San Antonio in 1885, reportedly with five cents in his pocket and herding his only skill, he found work on a ranch. He was paid in sheep, but he lost his flock in a severe freeze. Next he cut cedar on the Guadalupe River property of Casper Seltenfuss, who sold land to his sons, Paul, and Engel. On it they built a cedar posts and charcoal business. Engel later bought out his partner.

His next venture was an open-air dance hall, but after a young man died of a heart attack on opening night it never gained much popularity. When a season of heavy rain kept the river high and the customers from reaching him, Engel sold the property back to Seltenfuss. His next venture proved more lucrative. In 1903 he bought three acres where two roads crossed and built a cotton gin, store, and home. When boll weevils wiped out cotton in 1926 the Engels converted the gin to a grist mill.

Naming his settlement Bergheim ("House in the Hills") Engel established a post office, first in the cotton gin, later in the store. Three of his six children— Henry, Alfred, and Rudolph—took over in 1916. Alfred bought out the others and ran the store until he retired in 1975. It is said Alfred had the largest cedar yard in the state. Cedar choppers traded posts for groceries. Because he could not turn anyone away he accumulated such a big stock of cedar posts that there are some around even today. Local "cedar choppers" still bring firewood to the store to sell. Cedar continued to be the staple of Bergheim's economy until the stock market crash of 1929, and the Depression that followed, depleted the economy.

A scene from the movie *Sugarland Express*, with Goldie Hawn and Ben Johnson, was shot in Bergheim. While they were on the run they stopped at the service station across the road. As their car pulls away there is a shot of the store, the sign reading "Kilgore."

Blanco

U.S. 281 south of Johnson City. Population 1,505. One walk.

Indians camped along the river here as early as 1150 A.D. Spanish explorer Marques de San Miguel de Aguayo is credited by some for naming the river Blanco (White) in 1721, presumably for its bed of white limestone. (Pronounced BLANK-o in Texas.) Spain began issuing land grants in this area in 1826. Within ten years the Comanches reclaimed all the lands, after which the Lipan Apaches and the Anglo settlers banded together to defeat the Comanches.

In 1853 James H. Callahan, Eli C. Hinds, Billie Trainer, and other early settlers formed the Pittsburg Land Company, named for General John D. Pitts, a member of their group. They bought half a league of an early land grant and laid out the town of Pittsburg on the south side of the river. Three years later, the Pittsburg Land Company donated 120 acres to establish the City and County of Blanco on the river's north side, higher and less prone to flooding. The post office began service that same year. When delivery ceased during the Civil War, citizens raised money to bring the mail once a week from New Braunfels.

The early settlers had few services available. A trip to New Braunfels or San Marcos for milling, mail, and supplies took 4–5 days by oxcart. By 1870 though, the town had grown enough to support four stores, a hotel, and a cotton gin. The Union Church, built in 1871, served for many years as community church, school, and meeting hall.

In 1885, 30 years after Blanco's founding, John W. Speer wrote in his *Blanco City History, 1853–1885,* "Compare their living with ours. We have mills, mail facilities, churches, schools, and most of the conveniences and blessings of an old settled country." Incidentally, the manuscript for Speer's book turned up in 1925 in a washstand drawer. Several chapters are missing, having fallen victim to a mouse that chewed the pages to make a nest. Blanco resident Kathryn Cage McInnis was born in 1892 and lived to age 101. In her 1983 memoir, *Solid Lace and Tucks,* she noted an even wider contrast when she wrote of witnessing "the passing of these pioneer days and the coming of the new era of . . . space exploration and computers."

In 1876 a fire destroyed the old courthouse and the town's records. Ten years later Architect Frederick E. Ruffini designed the present building in the French Second-Empire style.

The county's charter stipulated that its seat could be no more than five miles from the center of the county. Boundary reorganization in 1862 put Blanco at the southern border. With the bulk of the population centered around Blanco this posed no problem at first. But as settlement increased northward, James Polk Johnson established a town on the Pedernales River near the geographic center and petitioned for a change in county seat. It took three hotly contested elections, but Johnson City finally won in 1890.

After the schoolhouse burned down, the courthouse became a school, then was a bank, opera house, union hall, movie theater, library, bakery, and offices. From 1936 to 1970 it was a hospital. A Wild West museum and a restaurant followed. All these resulted in extensive changes to both the interior and exterior, until finally it fell empty and became "a storm-battered hulk."

In 1986 John W. O'Boyle bought the courthouse with the intention of dismantling and rebuilding it on his ranch in East Texas. Local citizens rebelled. They formed the Old County Courthouse Preservation Society, and with help from the LBJ Heartland Council raised $250,000 to buy back and restore the courthouse, considered one of the best examples of the architect's work and of Second-Empire architecture in the state. Inside are original wood wainscoting in the corridors and transom doorways, some with etched glass. A few offices and a gift shop occupy the first floor. In the second-floor courtroom the wooden platforms where the judge and jury sat are still there. It appears that half the jury sat on one side and half on the other. The courthouse is open on weekends.

BLANCO WALK

Historic buildings and homes on and around the square, home of President Lyndon Baines Johnson's grandparents. 1.5 miles, mostly flat; around the square is okay for strollers and wheelchairs, the rest of the walk is not. Park around the square. Restrooms in the courthouse, when open. Restaurant: Blanco Bowling Club Cafe.

❶ Facing Fourth Street, your back to the square, cross Fourth and turn right. (Note: Fourth Street has a lot of traffic and no sidewalk. There is ample grassy shoulder for safe walking.)

Heading down Fourth Street (also FM 165), on the left is the Blanco Bowling Club, a members-only ninepin alley. The Cafe, a local favorite, is open to the public.

No. 302, on the corner of Live Oak, was bought in 1911 by Ben E. Kellam, who ran a boarding house. When the paint fades on the front steps, you can still see "Kellam House" lettered there.

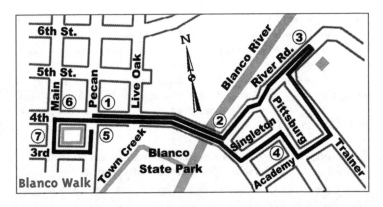

❷ One block past the river, turn left on Singleton, left on Pittsburg, then right on River Road.

Where River Road changes to gravel, No. 819 (marker) is the home Lambert Koeniger built in 1882 for his future bride. The stone, quarried across the river, was too soft and flaky so he applied stucco to protect it, then scored and painted it to look like cut stone. For economy he used plain milled pine for woodwork, then brushed and feathered it to look like more expensive wood. Each of the two floors consisted of two rooms separated by a wide hall.

In 1887 former Texas Secretary of State Joseph Wilson Baines and his wife, Ruth Huffman Baines, bought the house. They named it "Amenthal," "Ament" being a family name. He farmed the property until 1903, when he was elected to the Legislature and the family moved to Fredericksburg. His daughter, Rebekah, met and married Sam Johnson Jr. in 1908. Their son, Lyndon Baines, became the 36th president of the United States.

Several families have owned the house since then. It has seen many modifications both interior and exterior, at one time being covered with shingles. Dell Goeres, owner of the *Blanco County News,* ran her newspaper from the house in 1972. In 1983 William and Mary Godden bought it and restored it to its original configuration, with, Mary says, the assistance of Ruth Huffman Baines' ghost. When Mary first went to see the house, the owner was supposed to be out of town. She entered alone through the kitchen, only to encounter a woman there. Mumbling an apology she quickly went out and asked the real estate agent to please go back in with her and introduce her to the owner. The agent insisted the owner was not there. They went back in but found no one.

During renovation Mary felt a presence while she was in the bedroom measuring. She turned and saw a woman in a long green dress, her hair in a bun.

Mary started toward her, but the woman left. Following her into the hall, Mary saw no one. One other time Mary entered a room and saw the woman looking out a window, and once again she disappeared when Mary tried to approach. Sometimes, when puzzling with a restoration problem, the answer would come to Mary as she slept. After the restoration she never saw the woman again. From research they knew that Ruth Huffman Baines loved the house. Mary feels that once Ruth knew that her beloved home had been properly restored and loved, she was able to leave.

❸ Retrace your steps to the paved road, turning left on Trainer, right on Academy, then right again on Pittsburg.

St. Michael and All Angels Episcopal Church dates from 1956, although it has the feel of an older church.

❹ Turn left on Singleton, then right on Chandler (Loop 163). Stay on the right side of the road.

❺ At Pecan continue ahead on Fourth.

On the site of the Blanco Lumber and Hardware Store was a frame grocery belonging in 1881 to Charles P. Boon, who later took in Robert Crist as a partner. The business grew to include hardware. By 1930 Crist was sole owner, selling dry goods, farm equipment, and leather goods. About that time he added a warehouse in back for lumber and grain. His son, Charles, added another warehouse to store wool and mohair. After the store burned in 1937 it was replaced by the present brick building.

❻ At Main Street (Hwy. 281) turn left, crossing Fourth Street to the square. (Note: You can view the architecture of the buildings on Main Street better from here.)

Looking west, in a block of buildings that recently underwent major renovations, on the south corner of Fourth Street was the Phillip P. Cage and Brothers general mercantile store dating to the 1870s. The present building dates from 1908. The company was in business until the mid-1950s. Then it was Lindeman's until 1997.

Next is the old Blanco Theater. It first housed a cafe. Silent movies played here until 1938, when it was rebuilt as a conventional theater. It closed in the late 1950s and the theater sign was removed in the 1970s.

The next two one-story buildings were built for rentals in 1938.

"The Mercantile" sign is visible on the 1880 Comparet Building. The pressed tin facade and ceiling are by the Berlin Metal Works, today Berlin Motor Works (BMW). It was the post office for a time. After the family sold it in 1931, it became a restaurant. One of the menus is still on the wall. Then it was pool hall and saloon, senior citizen quilting center, and Montgomery Ward catalog store.

Behind the store is the 1877 County Jail, used until 1890 when the county seat moved to Johnson City. This one-room, 18-by-14-foot jail, with its 24-inch-thick walls, can be reached from inside the store.

The two-story building dates from 1907. Various commercial businesses leased the lower floor. Masonic Lodge #216 met upstairs. This was reached by outside metal stairs.

The next building, built about 1909, housed the Palace Barber Shop. It offered an apprenticeship program for barbers. Blanco's first beauty shop was located in the rear, as well as W. C. Byar's tailor shop. For over 50 years it had the only public bath in town. After a fire in 1929 this and all the buildings to its right were rebuilt.

Next is the location of the 1929 Wagner and Weber Store. Felix Lindeman had a general mercantile store at this location earlier. Wagner bought it and took in A. J. Weber as partner. Weber later bought out Wagner and ran the store until he retired in 1956.

Across Third Street is the Henry Beckmann house (marker), dating from 1873. It is thought to be the oldest house still standing in Blanco. Henry Sr. had a mill and gin west of the house, both destroyed by a fire in 1877. Dr. George Edwards also occupied the house. He had a drug store on the corner across Hwy. 281 where the restaurant is now. The Chamber of Commerce used it in the 1960s. Originally it had an outside staircase.

⑦ Turn left on Third Street.

The rock garage dates from 1933. Owners Wayne Smith and Glen Greebon lived with their families on the second floor, which was later removed although the stairway still exists. A blacksmith shop occupied the location starting in 1960. You can see where they tested the branding irons on a pair of double wooden doors on the west side.

Albert Koch had a blacksmith shop between the garage and Barker's Service Station. While repairing wagon and buggy wheels constituted a major portion of a blacksmith's work, he also shoed horses, repaired windmills, sharpened plow points, and made shovels, hinges, pokers, branding irons, and anything else metal that the local folks needed.

⑧ Turn left on Pecan Street.

No. 308, possibly the first business on the square, was originally a general store owned by Phillip Cage and John W. Speer. Cage sold his share and opened one on the north side of the square. After several other owners the building here became the telephone exchange in the early 1880s. Various telephone companies came and went at this site. Sybil Byars lived here starting in 1923 and ran the switchboard until dial phones came in. This continued as the telephone building until the Bell System bought and relocated the local exchange in 1951.

No. 316 was the 1875 location of a general store owned by Cage and John Speer. Then Cage opened his own store, and this became John W. Speer and Son, later Alexander and Speer.

Thomas J. Alexander, as described by his daughter Frances in her unpublished autobiography, "was a real pioneer." In 1867, at age 17, he left his home in Iowa and rode the rails to Austin. He walked from there to Fredericksburg to visit his older brother, only to learn his brother had moved to Blanco. Thomas arrived in Blanco to find his brother planning a move to Mason. But Thomas liked Blanco and decided to stay. He picked up odd jobs for a few years before settling down to clerking in John Speer's general store. There he met and married Speer's niece.

Speer's son Joe and Thomas bought the store, renaming it Alexander and Speer. When an itinerant druggist set up business in their shop, the two entrepreneurs studied pharmacology and became registered druggists. When a photographer set up there, Thomas learned photography. He and Joe built a new drug store next door. Thomas turned the old shop into a studio and became the town's photographer. His daughter says there are undoubtedly more Alexander and Speer photographs of early Blanco and its inhabitants than all other old photographs combined.

Next a jeweler rented space in the drug store. Thomas learned jewelry and watch repair from him and eventually bought out the jeweler.

Besides all these occupations, he gardened, tended his orchards, and kept Jersey cows for milk and hogs for food. "In spring and summer," writes his daughter, "he took a day off now and then to go with us to some pretty river spot to fish and swim."

For more information on the historic buildings, the Blanco Historical Commission has published a detailed book titled *A Portrait of Blanco, Early History and Buildings of an Old Texas Town*. There is a copy at the library or you may purchase it at the gift shop in the courthouse.

After your walk consider a cooling swim or tube in the river, or have a picnic and do a bit of fishing. The paved Towne Creek Nature Trail leads down to the river. Along the way you pass a magnificent live oak tree, second largest in Blanco County.

The Blanco State Recreation Area runs for a mile on both sides of the river and was deeded to the state in 1933. There are fossil clams and oysters in the limestone deposits here and dinosaur tracks in the streambed above and below the park. These are on private property, though. In the early 1980s the first solar heated water system in a state park was installed here. Facilities include campsites, picnic areas, seven miles of trail, swimming, fishing, and wildlife. (Use fee per car.)

Boerne

Kendall County seat, northwest of San Antonio just east of I-10 at Hwy. 46. Population 6,178. Four walks.

As head of the Adelsverein society, Prince Carl of Solms-Braunfels toured the universities of Germany promoting immigration to Texas. In 1847 a group of 40 idealistic young scholars who admired the German poet and political satirist Ludwig Börne, a "radical" writer whose philosophy promoted change without revolution, migrated to Texas. They established a utopian "Latin Colony" along the Llano River, naming it Bettina in honor of Bettina von Arnim, a follower of Börne.

The group's plan was to form a socialistic township where everyone would work and share equally. The Bettina settlement lasted less than a year. As related in Garland Perry's *Historic Images of Boerne, Texas,* although well intentioned, the young scholars were not used to working and had none of the skills for pioneer life. Nor, so they discovered, did they really want to share equally. One settler, Dr. Ferdinand Ludwig Herff, later became one of San Antonio's leading surgeons.

In 1849 five of the Bettina group plus three others created a new, communistic settlement on the north side of Cibolo Creek on what is today Johns Road. They called it Tusculum after Cicero's summer home in Ancient Rome. This settlement also lasted about a year. In the 1999 *150th Anniversary Souvenir Guide to Boerne,* Bettie Edmonds wrote about these intellectuals living the pioneer life, "Think of . . . a Beethoven concert on a grand piano in a log cabin, a bookcase half-filled with classics and the other half with sweet potatoes." The community continued to grow. In 1852 Gustav Theissen and John James laid out a town site and changed the name to Boerne (pronounced locally as BURN-ee) to honor Ludwig Börne. Buildings and industries were typical of the other early settlements. They lived in log cabins with thatched roofs and dirt floors, farmed, especially cotton, raised sheep and cattle, and opened mills, quarries, and cypress and cedar industries. In 1856 August Staffel established the first post office and stage stop.

George Wilkins Kendall published a series of articles and drawings about Boerne in his newspaper, the *New Orleans Picayune*. They were syndicated into newspapers around the country, resulting in an interest in the Hill Country. When the railroad began service from San Antonio the population of Boerne increased rapidly. Kendall was widely traveled in North America and Europe, but it was near Boerne that he decided to settle. At his Post Oak Ranch he imported high-quality wool-bearing merino sheep from Europe and shepherds and their sheep dogs from Scotland to tend the flocks. His domestic animal management techniques made him the foremost authority of sheep raising in the state.

As a Free Thinker community, Boerne did not allow churches. When Kendall in 1860 wanted to build a Catholic church for his wife he had to go outside the town limits. The first church within city limits, St. Helena's Episcopal, dates from 1881.

The Civil War brought a halt to progress here as elsewhere in the South. Without protection of the army, Indian raids increased. The population diminished as people moved to safer places. In 1862, during this low Civil War period, Kendall County was formed, with Boerne as its county seat. Because of the depressed times, a courthouse was not built until 1870. At that time, August Staffel, owner of the only saloon between San Antonio and Fredericksburg, was the most prosperous businessman in town, and citizens approached him for a loan. A simple one-story building designed and built by mason S. F. Stendeback and carpenter Joseph Vincent Phillip was completed in 1870. In 1885 Charles Buckel added a second story and porch and in 1909 architect Alfred Giles made further additions. This was the second-oldest Texas courthouse still used as a courthouse prior to dedication of the new Kendall County Courthouse in 1999.

After the Civil War ended, Boerne's proximity to San Antonio made it a popular Hill Country health resort. It is said that at one time the town had more people sick than well. By 1884 there were five hotels. In the *Texas New Yorker* in January 1873, George Sweet described Boerne as a "romantically situated little town . . . we have of some time past heard a good deal about." He goes on to describe its health attributes saying, it "is for invalids as well as whole families who seek . . . its healing waters. It is especially recommended for dyspeptics, rheumatism, and consumptives. Not a few persons who have gone to Boerne to die are today alive, well, happy and flourishing." He complimented Boerne because all its various cultures—Germans, Americans, Irish, and Polish—"all live happily and prosperously together." Sweet also wrote that "Every married couple whose connubial felicity dates back for a period of seven or eight years rejoices in the possession of an equal number of hale, hearty, rosy boys and girls." He touted it as a safe place to live, as its jail "is now empty and has been for many months."

A trip to Boerne from San Antonio by stagecoach took seven rough hours, an improvement over an all-day journey by horse and buggy or ox wagon. Arrival of the San Antonio and Aransas Pass Railroad reduced travel time to less than three hours, further increasing Boerne's growth and opening new markets for its products. A big celebration awaited on March 17, 1887 when the first train steamed into Boerne from San Antonio, with seven red coaches full of passengers. An article in the *San Antonio Daily Express* headlined "First Train To Boerne" describes Boerne as a place where for "the small sum of ninety-five cents train fare you can enjoy a whiff of the purest air God ever made for man or woman either. The burg is noted for the unlimited quantity and excellent quality of its ozone, whatever that is, its surpassing beauty, its beer, its public spirited citizens, pretty girls, good hotels." After listing "invigerating" things to do, the article goes on about "expanding the lungs with deep draughts of ozone" and describes "the poor consumptive invalid who generally comes when it is everlastingly too late for all the ozone in the world to do him any good."

The Depression almost ended both tourist and farming industries, staples of Boerne's economy. Like other Hill Country towns, its population fell drastically, from more than 2,000 in 1928 to around 1,100 in 1931. Hotels and businesses closed. After that, the population increased minimally until recent times when Interstate 10 brought northward-expanding San Antonio into proximity.

German cultural traditions are still strong in Boerne. The Gesang Verein, the Singing Society established in 1860, was active until 1977. The Schuetzen Verein, the Shooting Society, still exists. The Village Band, organized in 1860, is acclaimed as the oldest continuously organized German band outside of Germany. It received Germany's highest music award in 1996, the first time it was awarded to a band outside of Germany. The town's Berges Fest, celebrating its German heritage, has been held each Father's Day weekend since 1967. Market Days are also held for shoppers.

Walk 3 goes to the Boerne Cemetery. In the old section you'll recognize many historical names encountered in Walks 1 and 2.

The Visitor Center that used to be on the plaza moved to the Menger–Kingsbury–Shumard house south of town adjacent to the Wal-Mart parking lot, and is to move to a new library building on North Main.

The 1880s Dienger Building dominates a corner of Boerne's Main Plaza.

BOERNE WALK I

Historic Main Street (Hauptstrasse), the old courthouse, jail, city hall, and neighborhoods. 2.7 miles, flat except one hill to Kuhlmann-King Museum (open Sunday, 1 to 4 p.m. only). Park on Main Plaza. Restrooms in the parking lot at 179 Main St., in the park at River Road and Main Street and in the courthouse and city hall. Restaurants include the Peach Tree Kitchen in the 400 block of South Main Street and the Limestone Grill in the old Kendall Inn on the plaza. Many shops.

❶ The Plaza.

When John James surveyed and platted the town of Boerne, he gave the city several parcels of land, among them this piece for the Main Plaza, where Boerne still holds its many special events. Summer evening concerts feature the Boerne Village Band.

On the northwest corner of the Plaza (Main and Blanco) is the 1884–85 Dienger Building. Karl Dienger, Boerne's first schoolteacher, arrived in 1855. He helped organize the Gesang Verein and Village Band. This was his general store with living quarters upstairs. In 1969 his son Joseph opened the Antlers Restaurant here, displaying his many sets of trophy antlers. Bill and Paige Ramsey-Palmer restored it as an office building, and in 1991 it became the

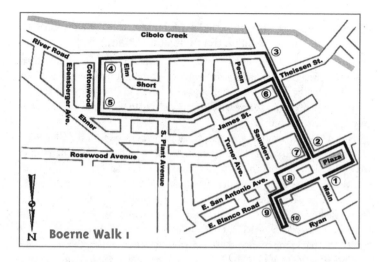

Boerne Public Library, scheduled to move to a larger, new building down the street.

The library's treasure is a rare, illustrated 1614 Low German version of the Martin Luther bible, one of only seven known to exist. It lay for years in a closet at the high school. The library's Texana/Genealogy Room, where knowledgeable volunteers are always ready to help with research projects, is known for its extensive collection of archival material.

Walk around the plaza to the right from the library.

Since the first edition of this book, the parking area between the Dienger Building/Library and Ye Kendall Inn has been invaded by a three-story office building out of scale and context with its location. Scattered around the parking area are small cottages moved in from elsewhere. They are now part of Ye Kendall Inn, serving as offices and guest rooms.

The central portion of the inn is the 1859 residence Erastus and Mary Reed built, which served also as the local stage stop. The Reeds rented out their spare rooms to overnighters. Thus began the hotel tradition on this site. In 1878 C. J. Rountree and W. L. Wadsworth added the two long wings to accommodate the growing number of persons coming to Boerne for their health. It remained a stagecoach inn throughout the 1880s. When Dr. H. D. Barnitz bought it in 1909 he gave it the name Ye Kendall Inn. The inn is reputed to have a ghost or two. A guest once reported seeing a woman in old-fashioned dress who told him her name was Sarah. A previous owner's wife was named Sarah. Along the far side of the plaza a bank is on the site of another early hotel, the Sunnyside.

❷ From the plaza turn right on South Main. (Note: The buildings described here are all on the right side of Main.)

No. 106 is the 1901 Rudolph Carstanjen Building, first a livery stable, then Levyson's Drug Store. It had several owners before Erhard Ebner bought it in 1941. He kept the drug store open from 7 a.m. to 11 p.m. The soda fountain and the ever-present domino game were both popular with the town folks. A toot of your horn brought curb service.

Nos. 112–146, a series of one-story shops on both sides of the alley, were built by Ardon Gilliat in 1910. His father, Alfred G. Gilliat, was an Englishman who arrived in Boerne in 1879 at the age of 19. Deaf from birth due to scarlet fever, he learned lip reading in special schools around Europe. He first immigrated to Mexico, then came up the Butterfield Trail with a cattle drive. He worked on a Cibolo Creek ranch for ten years. When the owner decided to return to Germany in 1892, Gilliat bought the ranch. He was a high-tech farmer, the first in the county to use a tractor, cultivator, and combine.

No. 152 is the Vogt Building. The Vogt brothers, August and William, came to Boerne in 1856 with their families. August ran freight to San Antonio. He also had a hotel where the Benefit Planners office is now.

No. 194, Benefit Planners, incorporates local limestone and design elements from earlier times. Rather than tear down the 1887 Fabra smokehouse (marker), architects wrapped the south side of the building around it. Julius Fabra arrived in Boerne in 1854. The outside stairs of the smokehouse were used for ease of placing meat on the upper racks. Animals were kept in a corral behind the shop. Fabra's grandson, Henry, hauled meat through the neighborhoods in a two-wheeled horse cart.

No. 210, the Adams Building, dates from the early 1900s. Hugo Adams was a butcher like his father. A description of him says he was "the picture of a small town butcher [with a] huge pot belly, white handlebar mustache, rosy cheeks, dressed in a white apron and hat." When kids came into his shop he always cut a wiener off a long string and gave it to them free.

No. 222 was the Adams home. His wife baked cakes for all of Boerne's special occasions. When not in the kitchen she sat at the dining room window facing on Main Street crocheting or playing solitaire.

No. 236, the H. O. Adler Building, was both general store and home to the Adler family in 1911. Bergmann Lumber Company bought it in 1957.

No. 248, at Newton Alley, was originally the Theis blacksmith shop. Behind it is the 1858 Phillip Jacob Theis House, one of the oldest structures in Boerne. The Theis family owned the house for over 100 years and in its 140-year history it has had only two other owners. It grew from one room to a two-room dogtrot, and finally to its present size. It is now a privately owned museum and is open on special occasions or for group tours.

Newton Alley was used for river access by the fire bucket brigade. When the town acquired pumping equipment they ran the fire hoses from the creek.

No. 302 was the Wendler house begun in1860. Henry August Wendler's cabinet shop and general store was next door with a campground in back for convenience of out-of-town customers. He also ran a saloon and dance hall next door. His sons, Adolph and Henry, worked in San Antonio but returned to Boerne to run the family store which they renamed A. and H. Wendler. It closed in 1928. The brothers had other businesses, including the first telephone exchange. Adolph also ran a mail service between Boerne and Bandera.

No. 308 was another Wendler house dating from 1860. No. 322 is the former Louis Vollbrecht Tin Shop, established by his father-in-law, Henry A. Wendler Sr. Many standing seam tin roofs on older homes were fabricated here. The house was added later. It has a well and pump in the back room. Inside water systems were rare before 1900.

No. 334 is the 1875 Staffel/Schumard Building. August Staffel, Boerne's first postmaster, ran a post office and telegraph office from here. Out back was a livery stable, stage stop, and campsite.

No. 404, across Theissen, is an impressive building of pressed tin and stone-filled Fachwerk, currently a shop named The Landmark. This wonderfully old-looking building is not a landmark but was built in the early 1990s.

Nos. 424, 438, and 448, all the work of master craftsman Ed Clemens, date from around 1900. Originally all three had picket fences. Note especially the bracketing and turned columns.

No. 421 (across on the left) was built as a residence in 1890. After being a general store, a barbershop, and a clinic, Dr. Jack Diamond converted it into a hospital in 1949. Some operating-room lights still hang from its ceiling. The hospital closed in 1954.

No. 470 was Sach's Garage, one of the first automobile garages in Boerne. The family lived upstairs.

No. 518, a fashion store, is a former International and Great Northern Railroad depot moved from Encinal.

❸ At River Road (Cibolo Creek), turn left, crossing Main Street at the light.

There is no sidewalk here. You can walk on the grassy shoulder or inside the white line curbside. At Elm Street, if you cross over to the river, you are on the site of the Dietert saw and gristmill, the first business in Boerne. The rocks on the lower side of the reconstructed dam are part of the original.

No. 604, on the corner of Elm Street, is the nicely renovated 1860s William Dietert home. He and his brothers came to the Hill Country in the early 1850s: one to Comfort, one to Kerrville, and one here.

④ Turn left on Cottonwood.

No. 136 Cottonwood is the 1925 Berthold "Pat" Ebensberger home. He ran his father's lumber company on Main Street.

No. 116 is the first Ebensberger home, built by Ed Clemens in 1914 for Carl Oscar Ebensberger, a carpenter who established Ebensberger Lumber Company.

Cabinetmakers also made caskets, which led to Ebensberger also running a funeral business. He learned embalming, although little of that was done then. In 1907 his son, Edmund Walter, took over that business. The first motorized hearse also served as an ambulance.

⑤ Turn left on Theissen.

No. 608 Thiessen is an older home. Most of the others along here are newly built.

No. 228, after you cross Plant Street, is the 1910 Davis-Kidwell home. Jefferson Daniel Davis, charcoal burner by trade, was popularly known as the "Old Time Fiddler."

No. 221, at Turner Street, is the Boerne Turnverien, organized in 1890.

No. 208 (marker) is another Clemens home, built in 1890 for Reinhold Kutzer and now the Methodist Parsonage. Kutzer owned the first cotton gin and feed mill, located next to this house.

No. 106, a small stone house, is the 1887 Gottlieb Weiss home. His blacksmith shop faced on Main Street. The porch was added later.

⑥ Turn right on Main.

No. 401, on the corner at Main, is the Joe Vogt Building, originally a grocery and dry goods business.

No. 325 was a livery stable. The brothers Lawrence and Christian Schrader had a livery stable behind this one in 1898. They ran ten-cent buggy rides between the train depot and the hotels.

No. 265, on the north corner of James, was the Albert Kutzer Garage. He sold wagons and buggies until the auto age and then had the first gasoline distributorship in Boerne.

No. 259 (past the driveway) was at first Ort's Saloon and then the Krause Bar. In the ten years I've been visiting Boerne it has changed names at least three times, but the cozy interior remains basically the same.

No. 231 was the C. O. Ebensberger and Son Lumber yard in the 1880s. After several other owners, Edgar Bergmann, who had worked for Ebensberger, bought it in 1957. In 1968, when property across the street at No. 236 became available, he moved the business there.

No. 195, at Rosewood, was the Kuhlmann Apothecary back in the 1880s. It remained a pharmacy until fairly recently, although it had several owners.

No. 179, the 1900 William Ziegler building, was a hardware store and residence.

No. 143 was Max's Place, a saloon owned by Max Beseler who moved to Boerne in 1891 from Welfare, where his father ran the general store. Max built the Metropolitan Opera House and Saloon, ran a cotton gin and a haberdashery, and was a member of the singing and shooting societies and the Village Band. When Prohibition came he sold the saloon, which became an ice cream parlor. After Prohibition Max bought it back and reopened his saloon. The cherrywood bar from Max's Place, later the Plaza Theater, went to the Antlers Restaurant in the Dienger Building in 1975 and is now on the second floor of Frost Bank at Main and Hwy. 46.

Nos. 129–133 is another Gilliat block of buildings. The original was destroyed and then rebuilt after a fire in 1908. After walking past, look back to see the arched brickwork over the windows.

❼ Turn right on San Antonio.

The 200 block of East San Antonio is Courthouse Square, on land given to the county by John James. The 1909 Kendall County Courthouse (marker), its front section designed by Alfred Giles, sits on the site of an earlier 1870 courthouse. Beside it is the 1884 jail, in use until 1986.

Across on the right, the new courthouse, dedicated in 1999, reflects the architecture of the original.

❽ Turn left on Saunders. Cross Blanco and turn right.

At Hill Street is the Boerne City Hall (marker) in the 1910 Boerne High School building designed by Alfred Giles. Behind (marker) is Boerne's 1870s first public schoolhouse, now city offices and not open to the public.

❾ From the City Hall parking lot walk up the hill to the Kuhlmann-King House (open only on Sunday from 1–4 p.m.).

William Kuhlmann, a pharmacist, built this house with a separate kitchen in 1885. Salina King lived here next. From 1920 to 1951 it served as extra classrooms and a lunchroom for the school.

The Boerne Area Historical Preservation Society now runs the Hullmann-King House as a museum.

Behind it is the H. J. Graham Building, Boerne's first bank, built in 1891 on the 100 block of South Main. Among its many other uses, including being the telephone exchange, it served as a beauty parlor from 1938 to 1978. It was moved to another location before finally coming to rest here in 1984.

⑩ Retrace your steps to parking lot. Turn right on Blanco back to plaza.

BOERNE WALK 2

Benedictine Sisters Monastery, St. Peter's Catholic Church, old and new neighborhoods. 2.2 miles, mostly flat or downhill, one short uphill grade. Few sidewalks, but little traffic and good shoulders, with the exception of School Street, Step 3. This is a gradual hill with traffic and a rough shoulder, okay to walk but not recommended for wheelchairs or strollers. Park on Evergreen west of South Main. Public restrooms at Monastery, Step 5.

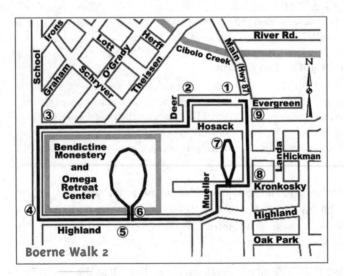

Boerne Walk 2

❶ Walk up Evergreen.

No. 109L Evergreen is an older home. The rest of the block is newer, mostly designed in styles representative of earlier days. Particularly noticeable is the use of native limestone and Victorian-era scrollwork.

❷ Turn left on Deer, then right on Hosack.

The property on the left along Hosack is part of the monastery.

❸ Turn left on School.

This .2-mile hill is two-thirds gradual and one-third a little steep.

❹ Turn left on Highland.

On the right is the new (1998) First Baptist Church, an imposing edifice. The spire of the older church on School Street is visible from here.

❺ On Highland, the first gate on the left leads to the Mother House of the Benedictine Sisters Monastery. *Do not enter here.* Continue to the second gate. Enter at the second gate with the sign reading Benedictine Hill Country Ministries. This is the Omega Retreat Center.

The sisters grant permission to enter the monastery grounds. To continue this privilege, please respect the privacy of the sisters and those on retreat by walking quietly. Please stay on the route as described. You are requested especially not to go by the day care center.

Benedictine Sisters purchased the Albert Kronkosky estate from his son in 1961. After 25 years of vacancy, the grounds were so overgrown that doors of the buildings could not be opened. As they cleared the grounds the sisters found the old flowerbeds, walkways, ponds, and fountains.

Because his property did not have potable water, Albert Kronkosky Sr. had water piped to a tank from a well near where I-10 intersects with Highway 46. He built a stone tower around the tank, the lower part housing a generator used to supply some of his electricity. The sisters removed the generator and tank and renovated the tower for multipurpose use.

A native of New Braunfels, Kronkosky moved to San Antonio, where he founded the San Antonio Drug Company and invested successfully in other enterprises. The family moved to Boerne when Albert Jr. was a child. The estate dates from 1911. Impressed with oriental architecture seen on his travels, he adorned the houses and tower with pagoda-like rooflines. The family invited neighbors to enjoy the recreational facilities on their estate and during World War I entertained the military. The Kronkosky Foundation carries on the family's philanthropic tradition.

The sisters operate a kindergarten and day care program on the grounds. The nearby Omega Center now serves as a retreat for approximately 5,000 guests

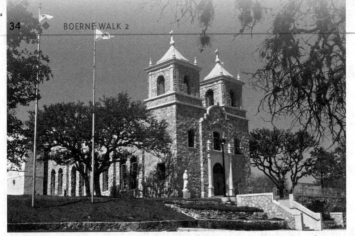

Boerne's 1923 St. Peter's Catholic Church was built in a Spanish mission style.

each year. Through it the sisters teach the values of Benedictine hospitality, stewardship, and spirituality.

From the second gate, walk straight ahead to the Kronkosky Tower.

The sisters dedicated the tower as a memorial to Albert Kronkosky Sr. on November 15, 1961, on the feast of St. Albert the Great. (Do not enter the tower.)

Turn right on the path to the tower, walk alongside the tower, and go left on the walkway to the cliff.

The view across the valley is terrific from here. It's easy to see why Kronkosky created this garden spot. Unfortunately, at the time of this writing it was not being maintained.

Passing through the pagoda, turn left on the next path. Turn right past the statue of Mary. At the driveway turn left and at the next driveway right to Hilltop Treasures, Books and Gifts.

The shop is open 9 a.m.–4 p.m. on Monday through Friday and 11 a.m.–3 p.m. on Saturday. It has a good selection of cards, gifts, and books, many of the latter of a spiritual nature or on women's affairs. Past the shop is the area used for retreats; this area is off limits. (The restroom door is on the outside of the Health and Wholeness Center. Look for the sign that reads, "Please Keep This Door Closed.")

Follow the road back to Highland. Please go around the circle drive.

❻ Turn left on Highland, left again on Mueller, then right on Kronkosky.

On Kronkosky, as you approach Main Street, about halfway up the block on your right, look for a wagon-wheel stained-glass window inset into a former garage. This is the back portion of the J. Hester Studio and Gallery, a particularly charming complex of buildings and rock garden.

On the left is St. Peter's Roman Catholic Church. The front portion dates from 1923; the back was added in 1999. The controversy between those who wanted to tear down the older church and the preservationists who wanted to keep it ended as a Supreme Court case in 1997.

Past this is the original St. Peter's, built in 1867. A Texas Historical Landmark plaque gives details.

❼ Retrace your steps to Kronkosky. Turn left

At Main, looking across and to the right, you can see the Sunday House Inn on the corner. Behind it is a little house built in 1852 by Johannes Stendebach, noted for his rock masonry. He passed on his talents to his sons. One son, John Frank, a rancher-farmer and stonemason, built the original portion of the Kendall Inn, the Kendall County Jail, and the northern portion of the courthouse. Another son, William P., at the age of 75, did the rockwork on PoPo's restaurant in Welfare.

❽ Turn left on Main.

No. 714 S. Main, the 1879 Weyrick Beissner Building of rough cut lime-stone, was a grocery store until 1910.

Next on the left, across from the Country Spirit, is the 1860 Phillip Manor House. It has been expanded several times from the original structure. At the turn of the century Boerne had six two-story hotels. This and Ye Kendall Inn are the only two left. Besides an inn it has been an athletic club, shooting club, and dance hall.

No. 707 S. Main, the Country Spirit, was the 1876 home built by Frenchman Frank LaMotte. Rudolph Carstanjen bought it in 1886. In 1893 Phillips bought it as an annex to his hotel. August Phillip renovated it back to a private residence known as the Gilman Hall Mansion from 1953 to 1978. Sue Martin opened the Country Spirit in 1984.

Legend says it's haunted by David, an orphan the cook would feed. He died in the 1890s after a fall in the driveway while playing with the Carstanjen children. I met a cousin of Augusta Phillip Graham's who thought Augusta would be horrified at stories of a ghost in her house.

Across on the right at Evergreen, the Robert E. Lee House is one of several cabins that were part of the O'Grady Inn. Irish-born John O'Grady came to Boerne from Boston and opened a boarding house and inn along the Cibolo. General Lee came through Boerne several times between 1856 and 1861 when he was stationed at Ft. Sam Houston in San Antonio as liaison officer to the forts in the Hill Country. He is said to have spent the night of March 20, 1856, in this cabin. You might be thinking, "Big deal." But had it not been for that one night, this cabin would have been torn down with the rest of them and we would not have this example of an early "motel."

⑨ Turn left on Evergreen back to the start.

BOERNE WALK 3

North Main Street, Boerne Cemetery. 1.8 miles, longer if you meander around the cemetery. Flat. Park at Plaza. Public Restrooms: at beginning if library is open, in parking lot middle of 100 block of South Main.

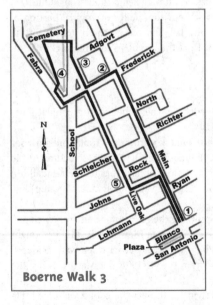

Boerne Walk 3

❶ From plaza turn left on North Main Street.

No. 265R North Main, the small stone house on the first block, is the 1860 Luckenbach-Carstanjen house.

No. 410L (across at Johns Road) is St. Helena's Episcopal Church (marker), founded in 1881 by English settlers. The original church was replaced by this Gothic building in 1929.

Across Main Street from St. Helena's is the planned location of the new Boerne Public Library.

No. 508L is the Hagemann-McGinnis house. Later additions to this 1890s three-room house reflect the original architecture.

No. 515R is the 1865 F. W. Schweppe house. This lawyer and teacher either worked for or owned the *Boerne Advance,* an early newspaper that is now the *Boerne Star.* The house was used as the courthouse and clerk's office in 1868–69.

No. 518L (marker) is the 1903 home of Max Beseler, a master woodworker, civic leader, and businessman. He owned a haberdashery but was best known as the proprietor of the Metropolitan Opera House and Saloon. His son, Carl, loved to write. His poetry was published in the *Boerne Star,* and his story of pioneer life in the 1850s was published in the *New Braunfels Herald Zeitung* in 1972.

No. 612L was the 1894 home of Arnold S. Toepperwein. His furniture, carrying the "Ring Tail Rino" logo, is still prized today.

No. 717R is the Foote-Hawkins house, which dates from 1879. Avery Foote was the town's undertaker.

No. 720L is the Edith Gray home, built around 1908. It housed a private library from 1949–75.

② Turn left at Frederick (by the fire station), then right on Live Oak.

As you turn onto Live Oak, at the time of this writing a small herd of goats grazed in the field on the left. At the rate of development in this part of town, however, they may no longer be there.

③ At School Street turn right. Enter the cemetery at the second entrance (the stone gate) and walk straight ahead.

A state historical marker to the right of the entrance relates the history of the cemetery, which in 2001 was designated a Texas Historical Cemetery. On Memorial Day 2008 the city dedicated the new urn garden next to the pavilion. Gravesites other than those noted in this book can be found in the Cemetery Foundation's self-guided tour brochure available at the library.

This cemetery was established in 1867 when Adam Vogt donated the land and paid to have a graveyard built for Precinct 1 of Kendall County. The original one-plus acre was enlarged in 1881 and again in 1926. The cemetery is now owned and maintained by the City of Boerne. Approximately 4,000 burial sites have been identified.

Many tombstones have German inscriptions. The cemetery has recently been restored and has a state historical designation. Two funding sources ensure its perpetual care. Col. Bettie Edmonds (Ret.) has computerized the burial records, including available genealogical data, for the library's Historical and Genealogical Room. I wish to thank Bettie for taking time to give me a tour.

The road from the entrance faces west. To visit the burial sites of some of Boerne's earliest settlers, walk ahead to the old cemetery (Section I).

Part of the rock wall that once ran along the north side is still visible. Although rows of trees once delineated the east and west borders, they are not as distinct now.

As in most cemeteries, the gravestones mostly face east. The easiest way to identify the beginning of the four quadrants that make up Section I is to look

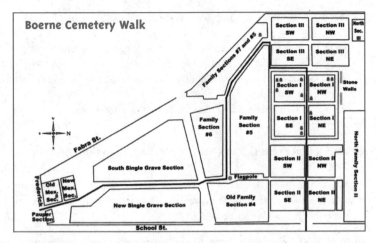

for a row of gravestones facing west. Sometimes boundaries of old cemeteries were delineated by facing the tombstones inward. The markers face inward along the north and south boundaries of Section I also. Once you find the western boundary, with the aid of the map, you should be able to identify the burial sites mentioned.

In the first row of Section I SE on your left is the Kingsbury family plot. The tallest marker is that of an Englishman, Dr. W. G. Kingsbury. He kept an office in London and recruited many Britons to come to Boerne.

If you turn around, directly across from Kingsbury is the multiple grave of four settlers killed in an Indian raid in 1868.

On the right, toward the end of Section I NE, are three shell graves. Terry Jordan discusses this practice extensively in his book, *Texas Graveyards: A Cultural Legacy.*

It seems the practice is too widespread to be merely decoration. Some say it stems from pagan times in Mediterranean Europe, possibly as early as the Cro-Magnon era 30,000 years ago. In the United States it is a southern folk custom. All three of the major cultural groups that shaped southern culture used shells in this manner on their gravesites. Shell-covered graves are found in Africa. Although the custom may have been brought from Spain, it is not found south of the border in Mexico. Although found among the German graves here in Texas, it is not found in Germany.

Just beyond, on the far right, is the first of two remaining sections of the stone wall of the north boundary. This is the beginning of Section I NW. Note that the gravestones face inward along the wall. If you look to the far left you will see the same along the southern boundary.

In the lower corner of the NW section, by the road, is the burial site of Rudolph Carstanjen, one of the founders of Tusculum.

Just beyond, on the left in the SW section, is the grave of Max Beseler.

Walk to the lower end of the second section of stone wall. There, with a historical marker, is the resting place of George Wilkins Kendall, for whom the county is named. This is the Valcourt family plot of his wife. To the left of the Valcourt plot is the gravesite of Adam Vogt, who arrived at Indianola in 1849, financed the expedition that founded Tusculum, and gave the first tract of land for this cemetery.

Directly across the road on the left, in the SW section, is the marker for Henry Wendler Sr. He settled in Sisterdale first, then moved to Boerne and opened one of the first general stores and a dance hall. He also contributed to the founding of this cemetery.

Continue along this row. In the Vogt family plot is the marker for Wilhelm Vogt, who came from Prussia in 1852. He lost everything to the Indians, then came to Boerne during the Civil War.

Turn left to the in-facing row of gravestones along the southern boundary. The pink granite marker is the gravesite of Karl Dienger, Boerne's first school teacher and organizer of the Village Band and singing society.

Further down the side is the marker for William Dietert, who operated the first business in Boerne, a saw mill and grist mill, and built the first dam on the Cibolo.

From here, facing south, turn right, walk up to the road, and turn left. On the right, where the road bends, is a black granite cowboy boot marker commemorating a 17-year-old killed in an auto accident. His friends and family have decorated his monument with memorabilia of his life.

At the fork go left toward the flagpole, which is not visible until you're at the end of the road. Turn right and stay straight ahead. About where the road bends, on the right, you begin to see more Spanish surnames mingled with the Anglo and German names. At one time Mexican burials were segregated from Anglo burials.

At the next bend, in the old Mexican section, are two pink granite markers, one in front of the other. Both Francisco Garcia's second wife and his daughter by his first wife insisted on placing markers on his grave.

On the left at the fence line is the Pauper Cemetery. At the present time there are three markers, two placed by the VFW and the other honoring Indian John Ruth. Some mystery surrounds his early years. Most likely he was born around 1900 in Globe, Arizona. He came to Boerne for wedding festivities on the Schoope Ranch and stayed. While working on local ranches he gained a reputation for his ability with animals. It is said he could even heal them by not much more than talk. When rancher Edwin Houston shipped his fine breeding bulls to South America, he sent Indian John along as caretaker.

4 **Exit cemetery on Frederick Street. Turn left and continue up Frederick to Live Oak. Turn right on Live Oak. Along here are several early homes.**

No. 108 Rock Street is the Vogt-Janensch-Ellis home, built of native rock. The center portion is the original two-room house built between 1870–80. Joseph Vogt lived here in 1884. He sold it to Helena Janensch, who passed it on to her children. It is still referred to as the Janensch house.

5 **Turn left at Johns Road, then right on Main back to the plaza.**

BOERNE WALK 4

The Cibolo Nature Center trails are open daily for hiking. The office is open 9–5 Monday–Saturday and sometimes on Sunday. A map can be found outside the office showing the well-defined trails, which vary from flat and easy to slightly rugged. Stay on the trails, keep dogs on leash. Restrooms are in the pavilion. To reach the center, take River Road to City Park Road.

In the mid-1800s this property was part of the farmland of Dr. Ferdinand Herff. The City of Boerne bought it from the family in 1964, turning the northern end into a park with pool, ball fields, picnic areas, and an agricultural museum. The rest was left undeveloped. Herff's great-granddaughter Carolyn Chipman-Evans watched as the marsh became a stagnant dumping ground. Remembering how it looked when she played here as a child, she wondered if an almost extinct marshland could be restored. The naturalists she consulted said yes.

With gentle persuasion, the city agreed to the project. Carolyn formed Friends of the Cibolo Wilderness. After years of accumulated tires and other junk were dredged from the marsh, water returned, and eventually the grasses and other native plants. "It was wonderful watching it come back," she said. With the return of the plants came the return of wildlife. The Friends of the Cibolo Wilderness have purchased the rest of the Herff family farm and plan to develop the farm area.

Today little of the Hill Country is preserved in its virgin state. Cedar and mesquite growths replace the native grasses and wildflowers. Here along the Wilderness Trail you can see a glimpse of what the Native Americans and early pioneers saw. The various trails pass through grassland, creek bed, marshland,

and woodland environments, allowing views of native flora and fauna. Incidentally, Cibolo means "buffalo" in Tonakawan.

Nature Center Office. This late 1800s building was moved here in 1992 and renovated for the Nature Center. Inside are educational displays and exhibits, and a library. Special programs and school activities are held here. A wildscape garden, planted to attract butterflies and hummingbirds, surrounds the center.

Marshland Trail–1/2 mile: The trail begins near springs that feed the marshland. A boardwalk gives access for wheelchairs, strollers and walkers. Look for tracks of the animals that come for food and water. Peer into the water to view life in these shallow pools. Birds nest in the grasses.

Prairie Trail–1/4 mile: Here you get a glimpse of the typical native grassland prairies that once covered a large part of Texas. Small animals make their home here. Deer graze its food supply.

Creekside Trail–1/3 mile: Huge cypresses hung with moss shade the creek bed. Sheer rock walls bordering the trail provide habitat for a variety of trees and bushes (including poison ivy!). The threatened Sycamore Leaf Snowbell can be seen near the second set of rustic stairs off the trail. Check the water's edge for mosses and creek life. A large cypress log is a bridge across the creek for those daring enough to risk it. It leads to the next trail.

Historic Farm Trail–1 mile: This trail runs the whole distance of the park on the other side of the creek.

Woodland Trail–1/2 mile: This runs parallel to the Creekside Trail. Hundreds of varieties of birds nest in the trees bordering the trail. Deer, rabbit, armadillo, and other woodland animals live here.

The Cibolo Wilderness Trail has a flagstone walk across a cypress-shaded creek.

Buda

West of I-35 between San Marcos and Austin. Population 2,404. Two walks.

Buda is small. Main Street is about four blocks long. Businesses line one side and railroad tracks the other. The city hall, library, and a gazebo dot the railroad right-of-way, and three residential blocks extend on either side of Main and the tracks. That, basically, is it—unless you count the subdivisions sprouting in the fields around the town.

Buda (that's pronounced BEW-da, as in beauty) came into existence in 1881 when the International and Great Northern Railroad began to extend its line south from Austin toward San Antonio. The railroad built a depot here, bypassing the already established town of Mountain City to the west. Mrs. Cornelia Trimble donated land for streets and public places so a town could be established, then sold the rest of her land as lots. Not to be left behind, many Mountain City residents jacked up their homes and businesses and moved them here or farther south to the other new railroad depot at Kyle.

Originally Buda had the name DuPre. However, another DuPre existed up in East Texas, resulting in both passengers and mail sometimes being routed to the wrong destination. There are several theories about how the town came to be named Buda. The favorite says it evolved from the Spanish word *viuda,* meaning widow. Two widows had been hired by the railroad to cook for the workers building the bridge over Onion Creek. The Spanish-speaking workers fondly referred to the two women as las vuidas. When train service began, hotel owners L. D. and Sarah Carrington arranged to make the town a meal stop. Hotel ads claimed an " elegant table, attentive waiters, and moderate prices" in its dining room. It once served 1,000 people headed to a cattlemen's convention in San Antonio. The hotel soon gained a reputation as "the best meal stop between St. Louis and San Antonio." Some stories say the Carringtons hired *las viudas* to cook for them; others say las viudas ran a little food stand alongside the tracks that was popular with passengers and locals who could not afford the expensive hotel meals. Whichever is true, or maybe both are, it is said that when the town had to choose a new name they called it Buda to honor these fine cooks.

The railroad basically followed the old stagecoach route. In its turn, the San Antonio road (now FM 2770), the interstate of its day, went the same way. Begun around 1915, it is believed to be the first paved rural road in Texas and the first paving project of the newly created Texas Highway Department. This tar-covered road was such an improvement over the gravel roads that automobiles could comfortably reach speeds of 20 to 30 miles an hour.

Samuel Ealy Johnson Jr., Lyndon's father, was born in Buda in 1877. The family moved to Stonewall about 1889. During Sam Jr.'s term in the Texas House of Representatives, instead of riding directly into Austin he rode to Buda, stabled his horse there, and took the train up to Austin. He claimed the Buda stables took better care of his horse than those in Austin. Local historian Barbara Barton Younts's grandfather, Henry Barton, a descendant of one of the early pioneer families, was a longtime friend of Sam Johnson. Her grandfather liked to say, "If I hadn't lent Sam Johnson enough money to buy a marriage license we would never have had a Lyndon Johnson."

Cotton was the basis of Buda's early economy. The rich soil of the blacklands to the east was ideal for this as well as grain crops. The town prospered. Then, in 1913, a severe flood washed away much of the topsoil. A 1925 attack by boll weevils, followed closely by a drought, brought an end to cotton as a profitable crop. With an abundance of good grass in its fields, Buda's entrepreneurs turned to dairy cattle. That led to a cheese factory. It was successful until a shipment of coal, used to fire the machinery, caught fire and burned down the factory. The dairymen then sold their milk to Austin companies until rising costs ended profits. The Depression of the 1930s was the final blow. Buda's population plunged from 600 in 1929 to 300 by 1933. The passenger train quit running in the 1940s. Better automobiles and improved roadways bypassed Buda and added to the town's steady decline.

When Jeanette and Carl Chelf happened into Buda in the 1970s they found most shops along Main Street boarded up. Chelf was a geologist and anthropologist from Austin and an avid collector of just about everything. He fell in love with an 1898 limestone building that had been the Birdwell General Store, bought it, and moved in the rocks, antiques, and miscellaneous stuff he had accumulated. When Chelf decided to open a store and sell some of his stuff he named it simply The 1898 Store. After acquiring a partner, he bought up the rest of the buildings along that stretch of Main and leased them to artists and craftspersons. Buda became "the arts and crafts town." Gradually that current staple of Hill Country economy, antiques and collectibles, took over from crafts.

When a fire destroyed half a block of Main Street in 1993, Chelf and his partner, Mary Ogden, rebuilt them. Scattered among the antique stores are a grocery store, feed store, laundry, florist, real estate office, and restaurants serving everyday needs of the townspeople. Subdivisions grow on the fields around Buda these days as its close proximity to Austin and the excellent Hays County schools attract commuters and new businesses. Both Jardine and Nighthawk moved their food processing plants here from Austin in recent years.

The population jumped from 597 in 1980 to 1,795 in 1990, and by 2000 was 2,400 and growing. Hopefully growth will not spoil the charm of this delightful little town.

BUDA WALK I

Main Street and neighborhoods on one side of the tracks. 1.4 miles, flat, no sidewalks in residential areas but light traffic. Park in library or City Hall lot. Public restrooms in Library and City Park at San Antonio and Austin Streets. Main Street restaurants include the Main Street Cafe and Garcia's Mexican Restaurant.

❶ From the library walk to the gazebo. Cross Main Street and turn left.

No. 320 Main (at Elm Street) was the Carrington Hotel. Leonidas Davis Carrington, a wealthy Austinite, moved here with his wife, Sarah, and their family in 1882. After L. D.'s death, Sarah returned to Austin and Minnie Birdwell, who ran a grocery store on the corner of Main and Live Oak, bought the hotel as a private residence. They say the spring bluebonnets bloom in the side yard here before anywhere else in town.

No. 312 is the former Farmer's State Bank building. The bank, established in 1910, changed its name to Farmer's National in 1922. The all-time favorite local story recalls the great bank robbery of 1926. It's not the amount of money the thief took, but who the thief was that has the town still talking. On December 11, 1926, a 22-year-old secretary in the office of Attorney General Dan Moody and a University of Texas student, held up the bank at gun point. She took $1,000, then locked the two employees in the vault. She was apprehended the same day by the Hays County sheriff. It seems she had borrowed money from her boyfriend and needed to pay it back. After a series of sensational trials she was convicted and given a 14-year sentence. This was later reversed on appeal. Later she and the boyfriend married and had a family. It was not until after their parents' deaths that the children learned their mother had robbed a bank.

No. 300 is the former 1914 Carrington Drug Company. W. D. Carrington, son of L. D. and Sarah, had his pharmacy downstairs and Drs. Holtzclaw and Lauderdale had offices upstairs, reached by metal steps on the outside. W. D. never learned to drive. His wife did. But she had such a bad reputation as a driver that one of the old-time residents says, "Whenever Mrs. Carrington offered us a ride we would make some excuse why we couldn't accept." It is said that W. D., without the opportunity to make excuses, rode with the car door open so he could jump out in case of an impending accident.

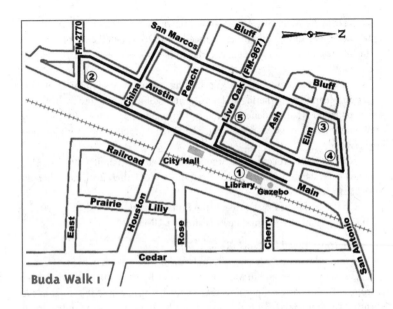

The filling station that stood on the corner of Ash was not rebuilt after the 1993 fire. The yellow brick building behind the vacant lot was a blacksmith shop.

Nos. 218, 216, and 214 have been home to such diverse businesses as Labinski's Meat Market, Nivens Confectionery, doctors' offices, and Mollie's Cafe.

No. 212, Buda's three-story "high-rise," dates from 1915. At various times it has been a cafe, post office, Phoebe Martin's Hat Shop, and the town's silent movie theater run by Lindsey Carter. His sister Elsie accompanied the movies on the piano. Lindsay also ran a skating rink.

No. 210 is another former bank. It opened in 1928 just in time for the stock market crash, closing in 1931.

On the corner of Live Oak Street is the delightful 1898 Store, originally the Buda Mercantile Company and in 1914 W. S. Birdwell and Company, Buda's largest and most prosperous general store. In those days there were stables behind where they sold wagons and farming equipment. The present 1898 Store, run by Jeanette Chelf since her husband's death, is part retail store and part museum. Not everything is for sale.

Across Live Oak is the last of Buda's former filling stations, now a real estate office and antique store.

Next is the Main Street Cafe (good down-home cooking). G. A. Moore and his son, Clifton, built this as a grocery in 1926. When the Moores retired the Whites bought it and opened a Red and White Grocery, an early grocery chain.

The barber shop was originally a cleaning and pressing shop run by Arthur Tatton. He took up barbering and ran a combination cleaning and barber shop. His daughter Mattie opened a beauty shop next door in the 1940s. Under different management there has been a barber and beauty shop at this location ever since.

No. 108 was a grocery and dry goods store before becoming the Casa Alde Mexican Restaurant run by Helen Rodriquez. Her father, Juan, came here in 1913 as a tenant farmer.

On the corner of Peach Street is the Buda Grocery, established in 1909 by cotton buyer and two-term state legislator E. J. Cleveland.

Continue ahead to Ranch Road 2770.

A few older homes and magnificent trees line this section of Main Street.

Farther up, at the end of Main, is the former Barton Cotton Gin that dates from 1914. The original portions may be seen at the back of the store. In the early days cotton was fed into the gin by hand. Seeds were removed and returned to the farmer for next year's crop. Then the cotton was compressed by a large wooden mule-driven press into bales weighing 450–500 pounds. All this took time. While the farmers waited for their cotton to be processed they played dominos with Barton. Barton's granddaughter says that when people asked her what her grandfather did for a living she would say, "He plays dominoes." A game of hide-and-seek among the bales scattered around the gin yard kept the children occupied.

2 Turn right on 2770, right on Austin, left on China, right on San Marcos.

Where China Street turns into San Marcos Street the land on the left drops down to Onion Creek.

At Peach is the First Baptist Church established in 1882 (marker). The original church is now on the grounds of the Buda Elementary School. Across on the left corner of Live Oak, the Mission Fellowship Church, organized in 1893, holds its services in the historic Buda Christian Church. Its first church, built on this site in 1903, was lost in a 1909 storm. This 1913 Gothic had beautiful stained-glass windows over the altar and along the sides. After the congregation disbanded in the 1950s, the church sat empty. During Lyndon Johnson's term in the White House, when tourists were flocking to Johnson

Buda's Mission Fellowship Church occupies the former Buda Christian Church, built in 1913.

City, a friend of LBJ decided the windows would be seen by more people if they were moved to the Christian church there. The altar window had been installed but the side windows were leaning against the building when a hail storm hit and destroyed them.

On the right, at the corner of Ash, is a string of apartments, hardly recognizable now as the former Army barracks moved here after World War II by Dr. McCormack to serve as a birthing hospital. This was the only hospital Buda ever had.

On the left, between Ash and Elm, is the 1928 school (center portion with arches), designed by San Marcos architect Roy L. Thomas and built on the site of earlier schools dating from 1885. The school served all grades. You started kindergarten on the left side and graduated from high school on the right side. The auditorium is in the center. R. C. Barton, grandson of Robert C. Barton, was superintendent of the school from 1931 to 1945. During the Depression years he drove the school bus, fired up the furnace, coached the football team, substituted for the janitor, and taught classes.

Across Elm on the left is the Methodist Church (marker), established in 1880, the first church in DuPre. Reverend Thomas Garrett, a Methodist circuit rider, held services here. It served as a place of worship for all denominations until each built its own church.

Although altered now, like many of the older homes it is constructed with square nails and wooden pegs. Jennie learned to play the fiddle and with her sister Mary, who played piano, formed a local band. They always performed at the Confederate reunions at Camp Ben McCulloch. For these occasions Jennie made herself a Confederate uniform. The veterans appointed her their mascot.

Scenic Hill Country vistas include this of the sunset on Verde Creek at Camp Verde (Page 53).

❸ Turn right on San Antonio Street.

On the left, along San Antonio Street, is the Buda City Park. Onion Creek runs behind it.

❹ Turn right on Austin.

On Austin, just past Elm, the one-room shack behind the Carrington house was where the Carringtons' servant, Clint, lived.

Just past Ash, on the left, is a tin-roofed room whose walls are made of old windows. Great recycling idea for a sun room or greenhouse!

❺ Turn left on 967, then left on Main.

Follow Main back to the start. With all the shops, it may take a while.

BUDA WALK 2

Neighborhood on the other side of the tracks. 1.0 mile.

❶ From the gazebo, walk down Main to San Antonio Street. Cross tracks to Railroad Street. Turn right.

When the town got a bit more prosperous, the move began to "the other side of the tracks." Just across the tracks is the former Severn house, until a few years ago a falling-down ruin. A Severn story tells how in 1912 the school needed a new sports field. Trustees asked the Buda Ladies Aid to help raise funds. When the women asked Elmer Severn for a donation, instead of money he offered them a section of cotton to pick. They picked two bales, sold them, and donated the rewards of their labor for the field.

❷ Turn left onto Cherry, then right on Cedar.

On the left at Cherry and Cedar is the home of the druggist, W. D. Carrington.

No. 211 Cedar is the 1925 tan brick home of William M. Woods, farmer, dairyman, part owner of a cotton gin, and one who established the Buda Cheese Factory.

No. 100, on the corner across Houston, belonged to Mr. Puckett, a Civil War veteran who proudly donned his uniform for all the city parades.

❸ Turn right on East Street, then right on Prairie.

No. 200 East, on the left at Prairie, was the home of John Howe, reputedly the tightest man in town. When Methodists were building a church the preacher went asking for donations. Howe was in the barn milking when he came by. As the preacher approached the barn, the cow kicked over the bucket. Howe used his "best language" on the cow, then discovered the preacher behind him, well within earshot. He gave the preacher a big donation.

❹ Turn left on Houston, then right on Main back to start.

At the corner of Railroad, the red brick house on the left was the 1937 Clifton Moore home. This, and much of the rock work around Buda, is the work of the Revedas, an African American family who lived in Antioch. See Walk 1 for information on Main Street.

8 Bulverde

U.S. 281 north of San Antonio toward Blanco. Population 3,761. One walk.

Today Bulverde is mostly new subdivisions, but a walk down Bulverde Lane leads to Cibolo Creek and across it to the stone remnants of an early homestead.

August Anton Pieper (pronounced PEEP-er) came to Texas in 1845 as a single man of 21. He and his friends Johann Kabelmacher and Heinrich Voges were wagoneers, hauling freight between New Braunfels and Fredericksburg. They always stopped at the Cibolo watering hole and eventually decided to settle there. Pieper married Kabelmacher's stepdaughter Johanna in 1851. He built a rock barn and a two-story house with a cellar on the south side of the creek in what is now Bexar County, dragging rocks from the creek by oxen and cutting oak trees for beams. Both buildings still stand. The well bears the date 1851. From the well he built a *wasser schlucht* that carried water to the barn.

When travelers between New Braunfels and Fredericksburg stopped by, Johanna always had big pots of food ready. Two sleeping rooms in the barn served overnighters. Johanna also served as community "doctor," making medicines from roots and herbs. Indians also stopped at Pieper's Settlement. They came to drink coffee, smoke tobacco, and be treated by the doctor. When Johanna died from an injury sustained from carrying a sack of corn, as many Indians as settlers attended her funeral. Pieper never bothered to file a claim for his land. When, years after he established his homestead somebody else did file for that land, he had to buy it back. Pieper lived to be 89, though he developed Parkinson's disease in later years.

As the settlement grew it spread across the creek. The section on the north side became the town of Bulverde in 1879, probably named for Lorenzo Bulverda, an early landowner believed to be Italian, not Spanish. His name shows up in several early documents with several different spellings including Balverdo, Lorenzo Bulverde, and Luciano Bulverde. Whatever the correct spelling, he helped survey the first road from San Antonio to California in exchange for 320 acres of land. His homestead still exists, but cannot be seen from the road.

BULVERDE WALK

Original Pieper Homestead. 2.4 miles plus optional 5.6 mile-side trip to Specht's, mostly flat, one slight grade at creek, some traffic on Bulverde Lane but ample grassy shoulder. Park at Downtown Bulverde Emporium complex. No public restrooms. Restaurants come and go in Bulverde. There's usually one at the Emporium. A popular option is Specht's, down Obst Road.

The Emporium was a ninepin bowling alley when Jane and Charles Wood, along with his parents, Laura and Charles Sr., bought 150 acres of property in 1956 that included a rock store and frame home. Charles served as Justice of the Peace and Laura ran the store. In 1958 the bowling alley moved to a new building. The Woods gave the bowling club the lanes in exchange for a new floor.

After the conversion, the building was used for the Baptist church's youth program, a feed store, and a storage-rehearsal hall for the local theater group. Eventually Jane opened an antique shop, leasing part of the building for a restaurant.

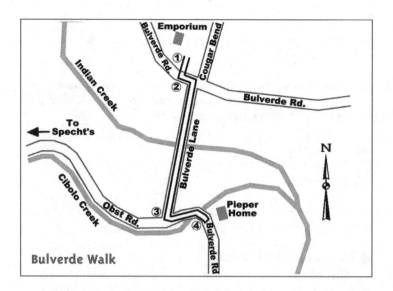

Bulverde Walk

There were few old buildings left in Bulverde when the Woods arrived. Their 1895 home is the white frame house across the parking lot from the store. The small stone building alongside it was a smokehouse. The stone store burned down in 1969.

❶ From the parking lot walk down to Bulverde Road.

Across the street, starting from the left, is an early home that in recent years has served as either a bakery or a candy store.

To the right of this building is the former Justice of the Peace (J.P.) Court. The new Comal County J.P. Court is next in line.

Farther to the right is a stone house dating from the 1880s. It belonged to the parents of Harry Wehe, whose house is the two-story frame farther on to the right. That's about all that's left of "old" Bulverde.

❷ Turn left on Bulverde Road, then right on Bulverde Lane.

On the right at the beginning of the walk is the post office, located in a house dating from the turn of the century and moved from New Braunfels.

As you continue down Bulverde Lane you cross over Indian Creek. Off to the left is an old stone wall with drainage pipes in assorted sizes. It supports the runway for the Bulverde Airport. Up ahead you can see the metal hangers for private planes.

Further down is a house with a miniature church in the yard. Although this looks like it might be the property of some religious group, I was told it is simply "the whimsy of the owner."

❸ At the T-intersection, Obst Road, turn left. The road bears right and crosses Cibolo Creek. Do not go onto the low-water crossing if there is moving water on it.

As you walk along Obst note the wood and barbed-wire fence on the left. I first walked here shortly after the 1998 flood when debris still clung to the barbed wire and posts of the uppermost portion of this fence, giving an indication of how high the water rose. Awesome!

Across the creek and up the short rise is the Pieper homestead. This is private property. Please do not enter. The front building is the barn. The two-story house is now a ruin.

❹ Reverse steps back to town.

At Bulverde Lane, Obst Road continues ahead along Cibolo Creek. Farther up, it bends left to become Specht Road and leads to Specht's Store. This former way station from the 1890s is now a restaurant. For those who want a longer walk, the distance from this point to Specht's is 2.8 miles (5.6 miles roundtrip). Good food and, frequently, music, awaits you for your effort. (For those who can't walk it, this is also a lovely drive.)

Fred Hans built the way station back in 1897. In 1907 he sold it to William Specht, a carpenter. As a carpenter Specht was also the local coffin maker. He included six pairs of white gloves for the pallbearers with each coffin. Specht's was actually a small settlement that included a cotton gin. When the price of cotton dropped in the late 1920s, the gin closed.

Specht's Store served as post office and telephone exchange for the small community. The telephone switchboard remained in use until 1956. The old Specht's Store was in bad shape when Kate Mangold came along. Kate had always wanted to run a cafe-store. With the help of friends she repaired the store and adjoining homes. The restaurant opened on Thanksgiving Day 1985. A large, covered back patio is where most people gather for good food, beer, and on Friday and Saturday nights, and Sunday evenings, music. (Closed Monday.)

Camp Verde

Between Bandera and Kerrville, near junction of Hwys. 173 and FM 480.
Population 41. One walk.

Camp Verde is where the U. S. Army conducted its experiment using camels as pack animals in the desert Southwest. Major George Crosman first urged the War Department to use camels in 1836. Also interested in such a project was Major Henry Wayne. He talked to then Senator Jefferson Davis about this possibility, suggesting the camels would be useful because they could travel faster with little need for water. When Davis became Secretary of War in 1853 he convinced President Franklin Pierce and Congress to appropriate money for the experiment. The money was approved in March 1855, and in May an expedition commanded by Wayne and Porter set out for the Middle East to secure the camels.

The men thought they would go buy some camels and bring them back. It proved not that easy. Their adventures are recounted in Chris Emmett's *Texas Camel Tales*. A year later, in May 1856, they arrived back in the United States, landing near the port of Indianola with 32 adult camels, one baby camel, and native handlers and caretakers. For the townspeople, "A free circus had come to town." During their stay in Indianola to allow the camels to recover from their long voyage, the camels had opportunities to show off. Caretakers loaded two bales totaling 613 pounds on a camel's back. The crowed doubted the camel could rise. When it did the handlers put on two more bales, for a total of 1,256 pounds. Again the camel rose and walked off. The crowd "was incredulous."

As the group headed overland to their new home, a caretaker had to ride ahead calling, "The camels are coming," because the sight and the smell of them terrified horses and mules, but not oxen. Another problem was keeping camels fenced in. Due to scarce building materials in those days, prickly pear cactus was often used to build fences. This worked well with livestock but not with the camels, who found the fencing quite tasty. On the way to Camp Verde the group made camp near Victoria. Major Wayne gave some camel hair to a woman who said she would knit a pair of socks for the president. Her daughter tells how "the odor was most terrible." The wool had to be washed and aired many times before it could be spun. Another stop was at San Pedro Creek's headwaters near San Antonio, where Major Wayne felt the proximity to town was good for neither his men nor the camels.

The group arrived at Camp Verde in 1856 accompanied by four native drivers with the nicknames of Greek George, Long Tom, Mico, and Hi-Jolly

(Hadji Ali). They built a *khan* or caravansary with 16-foot walls in the Arabian style from a diagram Wayne brought with him. Trainers entertained the soldiers with the sport of camel wrestling. As described by one observer, "The camels would fight much after the manner of human beings. They would stand on their hind legs and strike with their front feet." Another suggested that if camels failed as pack animals, they could be used for entertainment. Wayne advised Davis to use the first camels as breeding stock to establish the population. His advice was not taken. The War Department told him to first find out if they would be of use.

More camels arrived in 1857. In 1861 Camp Verde and its 53 camels were surrendered to the Confederacy, and then in 1865 went back to the Union. Although the camels proved their worth by traveling longer distances and carrying heavier loads than mules and horses, the War Department decided to end the experiment. Camels smelled bad, frightened horses, and were generally detested by handlers. The fort was deactivated in 1869 and the camels sold at auction or turned loose. In 1910 a fire destroyed all of the fort but one building.

The Williams Community Store opened in 1857 to supply the needs of the soldiers, mostly their need for intoxicants because these were prohibited for sale on the post. Williams sold out to Charles Schreiner in 1858. Schreiner and his partner, Caspar Real, opened a post office and contracted to sell beef and supplies to the camp. Originally the store opened only on army pay day. After the post closed, the store stayed on to serve ranchers as post office, meeting hall, and supply store. It opened and closed several times over the years until reestablished in 1899 by Walter Nowlin. The original building was lost during a flood around the turn of the century. The present store still serves as the local post office, and also operates as a gift shop and restaurant.

CAMP VERDE WALK

General Store, shady walk along creek to cemetery and Camp Verde marker. 2.0 miles short walk, 5.0 miles long walk. Along undulating road (nothing really steep), little traffic, ample grassy shoulder, okay for strollers and wheelchairs. Park in picnic area below store. No public restrooms.

❶ From the parking lot, cross 173 (carefully) and walk up Verde Creek Road.

At the beginning of the walk the road is only slightly above creek level, but it gradually rises.

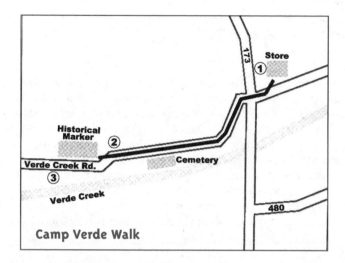

Camp Verde Walk

It is very quiet along here. You can hear the sounds of nature: birds singing, insects buzzing, water trickling over a small waterfall. You might spot cattle, deer, or rabbit along the way.

About one-half mile along the road, on the left, is the Camp Verde Cemetery, burial ground for many of the area's early settlers.

A half-mile past the cemetery is the Camp Verde historical marker on the right. From here you can see the barracks, the only building surviving the 1910 fire and now renovated as a private residence. Also to be seen is a cypress water tank and a windmill.

❷ For a 2.0-mile roundtrip walk, stop here and retrace your steps to the start.

❸ For a longer walk, another 3.0 miles roundtrip, continue along Verde Creek Road until it ends at a gate.

Along the way, across on the left, is a 300-foot limestone bluff named Camel's Leap after several camels fell from it. A legend says that soldiers disliked one particularly nasty camel and one day when they found it at the top of the bluff they pushed it off.

❹ Retrace your steps to the beginning.

The return walk offers different, even more beautiful vistas.

Center Point

Off I-10 west of Comfort on Hwy. 27. Population 566. No walk.

Center Point, perched above the Guadalupe River, got its name quite logically: It is halfway between Kerrville and Comfort in one direction and halfway between Fredericksburg and Bandera in the other. Originally it was Zanzenberg, named for the Austrian Tyrol home of Dr. Charles Ganahl, who opened the post office in 1859. Many early settlers were from Tennessee and owned slaves. Dr. Ganahl signed the Texas Articles of Secession. When the slaves were freed, many established homes on Elm Pass Road south of town.

The settlement got its new name in 1872 when the post office moved out of Dr. Ganahl's home and across the river and the town became a thriving trade center until the highway bypassed it. The town incorporated for school purposes in 1889. In February 1913 it fully incorporated, only to dissolve as a municipality that October.

Of particular historic interest is the Center Point cemetery, burial site of 32 Texas Rangers, believed by some to be the largest number in any one cemetery. The reason for the large number from this area may be due to the captain and leader of the group, Neal Coldwell, considered a forceful, dynamic leader and a respected and persuasive recruiter. A historical marker near the entrance of the cemetery commemorates this bit of history.

Comfort

West of I-10 southeast of Kerrville at Hwys. 27 and 87. Population 2,358. One walk.

Comfort has long been a favorite among Hill Country aficionados. It has one of the best-preserved nineteenth-century business districts in Texas, most of the buildings listed in the National Register of Historic Places. A particular favorite among these, with both locals and visitors, was the Ingenhuett General Store. Founded in 1867 by Peter Joseph Ingenhuett the store remained in continuous operation by five generations of the same family, and became the oldest such business in Texas. In March 2006, it was tragically destroyed by fire.

Freethinkers were among the Germans who emigrated to Texas to escape religious and political persecution. In 1852 some of this group settled along

Cypress Creek above the Guadalupe River in a cooperative community that eschewed both organized religion and formal local government. It would be 38 years before Comfort, the town that grew from that early settlement, had a church building. Although Comfort has remained unincorporated, there is a move toward incorporation.

In 1854 John Vles, a New Orleans cotton merchant, acquired a tract of land in the vicinity and sent an employee, Ernst Altgelt, to investigate its value. When Altgelt reported that it looked good as the site for a town, Vles told him to survey and lay out lots. Surveyors named the site on the creek where they camped while laying out the town Camp Comfort. Ferdinand Lohman in *Comfort of 1904* suggests it expressed wishes of settlers for relief from privations. Another suggests it came from the German word *Gemuetlichkeit,* its meaning akin to "comfort." Another says early settlers' relatives urged them to *komm fort* from the wilderness.

Comfort, however, in no way describes the early years of the settlement. Outlaws and bands of renegade Indians still roamed the area. The settlers were more intellectuals than farmers, but by 1860 Comfort had become a thriving town and also a center of Union sentiment. Having already pledged allegiance to a new country and being against slavery, settlers could not condone secession. In 1862 a group of area men decided to escape to Mexico and join Union forces rather than fight for the Confederacy. While camped on the banks of the Nueces River, they were attacked by a large Confederate force. Many were killed during the battle, their remains left unburied. After the war family members gathered the remains and buried them in Comfort. The monument *Treue der Union* (Loyal to the Union) honors these 36 dead.

Comfort's earliest industry was cypress shingles and lumber. Farming, particularly cotton, ranching, and limestone quarries, added to the economy. It took a week or more to haul freight to San Antonio by oxcart until the arrival of the San Antonio and Aransas Pass Railroad in 1887. With this increased marketing range, the town grew. New hotels went up, a larger variety of goods appeared in stores, and the excellent climate brought tourists.

There's a certain "spirit" in Comfort. Perhaps it's that of early settlers. Or is it the friendly natives who create a welcoming atmosphere? Browsing its antique shops in their well-preserved antique buildings, enjoying its good food, you feel, well, comfortable.

COMFORT WALK

Historic District, Treue Der Union Monument, residential neighborhoods. 2.3 miles. Mostly flat, one slight grade, few sidewalks but little traffic and ample shoulders. Start at High and Seventh Streets. Public restrooms at start in library if open. Several restaurants along walk. Note: Homes and buildings, it seems, were first numbered starting from the "wrong" end. Not only that, but the odd and even numbers were on the "wrong" side of the street.

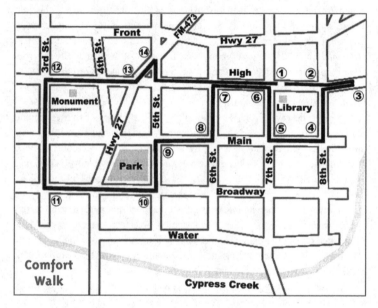

A few years ago the citizens of Comfort received notice through the mail that their homes and businesses had been given new numbers. This was done to satisfy a federal mandate for standardized numbering to facilitate emergency vehicles. Since this is a practical need, perhaps if the change had been discussed with the residents beforehand it would not have received so much opposition.

Whatever might have been, the result was that some people renumbered, others held out with the old numbers, and those whose homes had never had numbers continued not to. ("Everybody knows where everybody lives.") As a consequence, there is no rhyme nor reason to the current numbering system. You will find odd and even numbers on both sides of the street as well as different hundreds blocks.

To direct your gaze in the proper direction I have put "R" (right) or "L" (left) after each number. For buildings without numbers I revert to the local method of giving directions: "It's next to . . ." or "It's two doors north of . . ." or "It's across the street from . . ." If it's worked all these years for the citizens of Comfort, it should work for you, too.

❶ From the intersection of High and Seventh streets, facing High, with back to library, turn right.

The Comfort Public Library, organized in 1956, now occcupies the two-story Arno Schwethelm Building (marker), built in 1916 as a mercantile store. Schwethelm's son and grandson donated the building in 1981 for use as the library. It was renovated in 2000.

Next is Gael's Barber Shop, formerly the home Julius Holekamp built in 1876 for his bride, Suzanne Fricke. This is probably the oldest limestone structure in Comfort. It served a variety of businesses until becoming a barber shop in 1910. Gael Montana took over in the mid-1980s and ran it until ill health led to her retirement in 2008.

Next to Gael's, the Soda Shop occupies the store Dan Holekamp Sr. built in 1895 for druggist T. O. Codrington. The white marble soda fountain is original. When Codrington wasn't filling prescriptions he operated Comfort's first telephone switchboard, disconnecting it at closing time.

Across the street, the building City Cleaners occupies has been a cleaning establishment since 1954. Back in the 1870s Daniel Holekamp, Sr. built it as a pool hall and saloon. The Holekamps originally came overland with Prince Solms to New Braunfels, then on to Comfort in 1854.

Back on this side, set back from the soda shop is a Fachwerk cabin dating from around 1863. It was the first Ingenhuett home, then later a wash house and storage room.

Next to it, the house with the marker was the 1888 home of Peter Joseph Ingenhuett and his wife, Marie Karger. It remained in the family until about 1960.

The red brick building next to the house was designed by architect Alfred Giles in 1910. It served as post office until 1952. For many years, under different owners, it has been a cafe.

Giles designed six commercial buildings and one residence in Comfort. He so liked the Hill Country that, with his brother-in-law, John H. James (son of John James Sr. who laid out several Hill Country towns), he bought land north of Comfort, eventually accumulating 12,000 acres. Giles rode horseback, stagecoach, and then train into San Antonio each week, perhaps the first local commuter. He used carrier pigeons to let his wife know he had arrived safely.

No. 714L dates from 1918. It was built for Rabb Edwards as a meat market. His son, O. C. Edwards, ran it until the mid-1990s. It has become a 1960s-themed wine shop called, appropriately, the Meet Market.

No. 726R is the former Volunteer Fire Department building, constructed in 1962 and now the home of High's Cafe & Store.

Back on the right, Comfort Commons is the former Ingenhuett-Faust Hotel, another Alfred Giles design, dating from 1880. The original eight room hotel was built for Peter Joseph Ingenhuett. It was enlarged to 18 rooms in 1894 and sold to Louis and Mathilda Faust in 1909. After their deaths the building declined until it was restored in 1985.

Next is the tin-sided 1900 Karger Building. After an active life as pool hall, confectionery, cleaners, cafe, grocery, ice cream parlor, variety store, and shoe repair shop, it now stands idly by as a storage place.

The next limestone building is an Alfred Giles design built in 1891 as a saloon for the Ingenhuetts. Ehlers and Karger had a saloon and dance hall here some time in the 1900s. It saw further use as a Hermann Sons Lodge and a Kash and Karry Grocery. In the late 1940s Fred Koerlin opened a cabinet shop here, which he operated until the early 1970s. His son now owns it and continues to use it for woodworking and storage.

No. 813L, the corrugated metal building, is the "old salt house." Originally the Ingenhuett Livery Stable, the Ingenhuetts later used it for many years to store feed and salt.

No. 734R was the Letz Blacksmith Shop from 1925 to 1939. For a while it was used for wool and mohair storage, then it became an auto shop.

No. 830–834R at the time of this writing is the sad, fenced remains of the Ingenhuett General Store, its restoration undecided. The store was an 1880 design by noted architect Alfred Giles. The first Ingenhuett Store, built in 1867, was on the site of the hotel. The Ingenhuetts ran a bank here for many years and the post office from 1869 to 1894. Family enterprises included an opera house, a cotton gin, and a wool and mohair business. Paul and Ida Ingenhuett lived upstairs from the time they got married and he took over running the store in 1891 until their new limestone home, also designed by Alfred Giles, was ready in 1896. Before the fire, the store was as much museum as general mercantile store.

On the corner, at Eighth Street, is a former blacksmith shop designed in 1891 by Sisterdale architect Gottlieb Lobeer for Jacob Gass. Unique among blacksmith shops, it was built of limestone and had living quarters upstairs. Paul Ingenhuett bought the building in 1903 for additional storage. In 1933 his widow, Ida, and the members of the Literary Social Club converted it into a private museum for the upcoming state centennial. For many years Guido

Ransleben, author of *A Hundred Years of Comfort in Texas*, kept it open on Saturday. It is now run by the Comfort Historical Society and, regrettably, is only open on special occasions.

❷ Cross Eighth Street and continue down High Street.

No. 823R, the small limestone building, was built as a private cooperative filling station.

No. 845R (marker), the Meyer Bed and Breakfast on Cypress Creek, is a complex of buildings dating from the late 1800s. As you enter, the stone building in the center is the 1869 home of Frederick and Ernestine Meyer and their eight children. The Meyers took in overnight guests, so it is only appropriate that it is part of a bed-and-breakfast today. Behind it is the White House Hotel, built to accommodate passengers when the railroad came through in 1887.

Turning left from there, along the side of the lot, you'll see the two-story stucco fourplex, built in 1920 as the Meyer Hotel. Next to it is the 1872 cabin where Mrs. Meyer had her midwife clinic. At the end is the 1857 stage depot, the last stop on the Old Spanish Trail to San Antonio before it crossed the Guadalupe River.

❸ Retrace your steps to Eighth Street and turn left.

The small house on the right, behind the museum, was even smaller when Paul and Ida Flach Ingenhuett built it around 1900 as a playhouse for their three daughters. Later it doubled in size to become a "summer house." In more recent years it was moved forward to its present location.

Next on the right, behind the ornate iron fence is a tank house and the first swimming pool in the area, dating from the mid-1930s.

Farther back, behind and to the left of the tower, is the Ingenhuett Opera Halle that Alfred Giles designed for Peter Joseph Ingenhuett in 1882. This was the cultural center of the town at the turn of the century. Besides all-night dances, local and visiting talent performed here. For a while the building belonged to Hermann Sons Lodge. Eventually it came back into the Ingenhuett family and by 1936 was used for sorting and grading wool and mohair.

Next behind the fence, streetside, is the one residence Alfred Giles designed in Comfort. Construction on this house for Paul Ingenhuett began in 1895 and was completed in 1897. It is still in the family.

Across on the left is a house originally built in 1900 as a single-story wood frame for Christoph Flach. The second story and stone veneer were added in 1936 by the Peter C. Ingenhuetts, who purchased the property in 1920 at the time of their marriage. A three-story stone water tower and windmill are in back.

Cabinetmaker Otto Brinkmann built this home in 1894 on Main Street in Comfort.

Throughout the walk you will see several water tanks and windmills. The cypress cisterns were built on elevated enclosures to keep plumbing from freezing, to create storage space, and for gravity water pressure. The tanks have no nails or screws; metal bands on the outside hold them together. Expansion of the wet wood fuses the tanks into waterproof containers.

Submersible pumps and pressure tanks eventually replaced the windmills and wood tanks, but it was not until a water district was created in 1947 that the need for individual tanks ended.

No. 413R is the 1906 Ernst Ingenhuett residence. Ernst and his wife, Katy Brinkmann, operated the 1880s hotel on High Street from when they were married in 1894 until 1910 when both the house and the hotel were sold to the Faust family.

❹ Turn right on Main Street.

Halfway up the block on the right, the raised, one-story frame house was the 1894 home of cabinetmaker Otto Brinkmann Sr. and his wife, Marie Ochse. Two east-side extensions were added later. Brinkmann came to Comfort in 1858, the only member of his party to survive yellow fever after landing at Indianola. He later established a lumberyard and furniture store. This was at one time the home of Comfort historian Guido Ransleben, who married one of Brinkmann's granddaughters.

Across Seventh Street, on the left side of Main is a tin building dating from around 1912 that was the Comfort Volunteer Fire Department. To the right of the building is a tall wood frame that held the fire bell. Twin live oak trees where Ernst Altgelt, his survey team, and other pioneers celebrated the founding of Comfort in 1854 once stood here. The sale of the first lots was possibly transacted under those trees. The town's market square was planned for here, but frequent flooding of Cypress Creek made that impractical. Both trees succumbed to old age in recent years.

⑤ Turn right on Seventh Street.

On the left corner is the Faltin Store. Originally a log store built in 1854 for the Goldbeck brothers stood here. It was Comfort's first mercantile store. August Friedrich Faltin bought it two years later when he came to Comfort. In 1879 he commissioned Alfred Giles to build a two-story limestone store, Giles's first work outside San Antonio and the first commercial two-story limestone structure in Comfort. A general store occupied the first level, the family the second. The Faltin sons sold the business to their brother-in-law, Dan Holekamp, in 1907. Albert Faltin brought it back into the family in 1968. Note on the window the sign showing the business originated in Prussia in 1819. You can identify the original building from a 1907 addition by the stones. The rough-hewn stones were used after higher labor costs made it impractical to smooth out the stones.

On the right-hand corner is the 1883 Brinkmann and Sons building. At least a portion of the walls are of *Fachwerk* construction. A trip inside is worthwhile. In 1911 a brother, Herbert, had a furniture store here. Hooks on the walls where they hung chairs, and hooks from the ceiling that supported a rack for mattresses, are still there. The two-story limestone building covered with pressed tin dates from 1880. Brinkmann's wife and three daughters had a millinery shop here.

Next to it is the 1896 building that was Walter Brinkmann's tinsmith shop. The tin cornice around the previous building is probably his work.

On the left, behind the Faltin store, is the Faltin Homestead, one of the oldest dwellings still in its original location. The log portion is the original 1854 cabin built by Fritz and Theodore Goldbeck. Theodore was also Comfort's first postmaster. Fritz wrote poetry about early German pioneer life in Texas. The Faltins bought the cabin in 1856 and added the *Fachwerk* section on the right.

No. 413R was the Walter Brinkmann home, built in 1897.

No. 421R dates from about 1907. It was the home of Dan Holekamp, who operated Dan Holekamp and Sons Mercantile across the street in the Faltin Building.

The house next to it was built in 1915 by Ernst Doebbler and served as a funeral home during the 1930s, after which it was purchased by Peter Hohnstedt, a prominent artist who lived most of his life in Comfort.

The Faltin Store was built on Main Street in Comfort in 1879, before a flood caused the main business district to move up to High Street.

PHOTOS BY WILLIAM M. FISHER

Boots are left at the front door of Comfort's Faltin Building, designed by noted architect Alfred Giles.

⑥ Turn left on High Street.

On the corner at High is the former 1934 Fellbaum Drugstore. A dental office, medical office, and various businesses, including another drug store, occupied the sight until it became an antique store.

No. 635L is a new house built by the Potters, who restored the Ingenhuett Hotel and several other properties around Comfort.

No. 629L is the Conrad Strohacker house, circa 1890, moved in the 1920s from its original site on North Creek. Strohacker's wife, Anna Wiedenfeld, in 1853, was the first Anglo child born in the vicinity.

No. 625L is the 1916 Gottlieb Fellbaum Saddlery Shop, later operated by his son, Willie. Paul Flach joined his brother-in-law here in 1925. He did shoe repair. It was a dry goods store after 1942.

No. 712L was built around 1900 by Fellbaum, postmaster from 1898 to 1908.

❼ Turn left on Sixth Street.

No. 427L, the Ferdinand Pfeiffer home, dates from around 1910. Note the vintage lightning rods along the summit of the roof. There was a proliferation of these during the first three decades of this century due to the many salesmen traveling through the area.

Next on the left is the 1895 stone home of Richard Faltin, with its original windmill and outbuildings.

❽ Turn right on Main.

No. 519L, a 1910 wood frame house, was moved to this location from near the Catholic church where it served as the parsonage. Originally it had been the home of Hermann Kott.

No. 622L (the stone house) is the Methodist Parsonage, built in 1924. On the corner of Fifth Street is the 1924 Gaddis Memorial United Methodist Church, so named because Mrs. E. F. Gaddis donated most of the money for construction in honor of her husband.

Across at the northwest corner of Fifth Street is the 1888 Kott Hotel built by Richard Kott after the railroad came to Comfort in 1887. Later it became the Comfort Hotel, and, still later, apartments. After sustaining considerable damage in the 1978 flood, it sat boarded up for some twenty-five years before finally being restored.

Both the Guadalupe River and Cypress Creek are prone to flooding. Altgelt intended Main Street to be the business district, but after a major flood in 1870 most new businesses built on appropriately named High Street. In August 1978 a record 43 inches of rain fell on the area in 48 hours. Cypress and Verde Creeks and both forks of the Guadalupe flooded simultaneously. Water rose to 12 feet in some places and even reached High Street. Many homes were lost and many buildings severely damaged.

❾ Turn left on Fifth Street.

On the right is Comfort Park (originally called Union Park), where many of the town's activities take place, the biggest being Comfort's Fourth of July celebration. This has always been a major celebration. Before automobiles and super highways, because it took so long to travel even fairly short distances, the celebration lasted two or three days. The town goes all out with a grand parade ending here in the park, where there are craft and game booths and a barbecue dinner.

A bust of Comfort founder Ernst Hermann Altgelt backs on Hwy. 27. The original park gazebo, built in 1904 on the occasion of Comfort's 50th anniversary celebration, gave way to a tornado in 1976. Volunteer labor and funds rebuilt it.

On the northeast corner of Broadway is Sacred Heart Catholic Church, built in 1949 and restored after the 1978 flood.

On the southeast corner is St. Boniface Episcopal Church. This 1960 edifice of native rock replaced the 1907 frame church.

❿ Turn right on Broadway. Cross Highway 27—carefully.

Set back on the right corner after you cross Highway 27 is the beautiful yellow brick Victorian home Albert Beckmann, another San Antonio architect, built for August Faltin in 1894.

No. 304R, on the corner of Third Street, is the charming 1890 home Max Flach built for his bride, Tillie Schmelter. It later served as parsonage for the First Baptist Church across Third.

⓫ Turn right on Third Street.

The crosshatched line on the map shows where the railroad tracks ran at the base of the hill.

At High Street, across on the left is the 1893 limestone Comfort School, Comfort's third. The original bell tower at the entrance is over a time capsule to be opened in 2043, the 50th anniversary of the bell's dedication and the building's 150th anniversary. In 1922 the second story was added. The high school (now a middle school), was a WPA project built in 1939.

⓬ Turn right on High Street.

On the right is the *Treue der Union* monument, erected in 1866 at the burial site of the 36 victims of the Nueces River massacre on August 10, 1862. One name documented years ago never got carved into the stone and one man named on the monument is actually buried in the Cypress Creek Cemetery.

Except for national cemeteries, this is said to be the only Union memorial in former Confederate Territory. In 1991, by an act of Congress, it became one of six mass burial sites of American patriots allowed to fly the flag at half mast in perpetuity, and the only one to fly a period United States flag with 36 stars. The monument was officially rededicated on its 130th anniversary in 1996 after extensive restoration. A 500-year time capsule was entombed in its base during reconstruction.

No. 312L is the 1906 William Wiedenfeld home that later served as the Lutheran parsonage.

Behind it is the original Deutsche Evangelische Kirche, in 1892 Comfort's first church building, built 38 years after the town's founding. The tower was added in 1899. Cabinetmaker Christel Lindemann built the church, known then as the Community Church, the various denominations alternating their services. Prior to this religious services were held in local saloons. The building was completely restored for its 100th anniversary in 1992. Many of the interior furnishings are original.

Lindemann was also the town's first undertaker. He rode beside the driver of the horse-drawn hearse, sitting erect, arms folded across his chest, dressed in a cutaway coat and top hat. It is said that when Lindemann first saw a buzzard he wanted to know what kind of black chicken that was hopping around a dead cow.

⓭ Turn left on Highway 27.

This 1917 Comfort Railroad Depot replaced two earlier ones. When the San Antonio and Aransas Pass line arrived in 1887 the depot was located in a private residence. In 1889 the line extended to Kerrville and passenger service to that town began in 1890. The line was referred to as the "Hinky Dinky" or "Toonerville Trolley." Horse-drawn taxis from the local hotels met each train. The trains stopped running in 1972. Since then the depot was a delicatessen, saloon, church, and real estate office before becoming the Original Comfort Station selling antiques.

The two adjacent buildings are new.

⓮ Cross Highway 27 (carefully), walk down Fifth Street, then turn left on High Street back to start.

Along here High Street has some nicely restored homes dating from the late 1800s to early 1900s.

No. 602L, on the corner across Sixth Street, is the 1860 Otto Brinkmann cottage. When he first lived there with his twin brothers it was known as the "bachelor dude." Like most of the earlier structures it is built in the stone-filled *Fachwerk* style.

No. 606L is the 1907 Ferdinand Pfeiffer grocery. After World War II it served as a Handy Andy Grocery, various shops, and for a while as home of the *Comfort News*.

No. 612L was built in 1909 by Rudolph Allerkamp as a grocery store downstairs and a dance hall upstairs. The dancing caused the building to sway too much, and part of the second story was removed. For about 30 years the building was the Dan Holekamp auto agency and the Lone Star Beer agency. It was converted into apartments in 1980.

No. 622L, the gable roofed pre-1900 home of Ludwig Hein, was also the telephone office from 1923 to 1955. Hein's blacksmith shop was next door. After an extensive restoration in the late 1990s, it became a bed-and-breakfast and office.

The H-shaped complex was built as apartments in 1902 by Alex Brinkmann. Dr. C. C. Jones, one of the founders of the Comfort State Bank, used the east side as his office for 51 years. The building once was home to the *Comfort News*, the west wing the Justice of the Peace's office.

On the corner of Seventh Street is the picturesque former Comfort State Bank, built in 1907 by stonemason Richard Doebbler for Alex Brinkmann. Red granite for the columns came from the Fredericksburg area and was polished until it resembled dull marble, the only example of this use in town. It housed the bank until 1960, when Mr. and Mrs. Albert Faltin Sr. bought the building and deeded it to the Comfort School District for use by the community. The Comfort Public Library was here from 1982 until it moved across the street. The Comfort Heritage Foundation maintains the building as a museum and archive, open Tuesdays from 9 a.m. to noon.

Across Seventh Street from the bank is an 1870s building that has seen many lives. It once was a saloon first owned by Dan Holekamp Sr., and was later run by Henry Steves and Bob Stahmann. It is said that the first church services in Comfort were held here. (Church services were also held at the old Ingenhuett Saloon.) Most of the original building burned down in 1937, but this back part was spared and then moved to the front of the property. In recent years it has served as a restaurant, filling station, dance hall, studio, electric shop, and now as an antique store.

The frame building beyond originally stood directly across Seventh Street and served once as the town's second Bolstievik Halle, where oldsters gathered to play dominoes and card games while settling political and philosophical arguments. After two previous moves around town, in the 1980s the building settled here, immediately across from its original location.

Driftwood

West of I-10 between San Marcos and Austin, on FM 967 west of Buda.
Population 21. One walk (more of a stroll). The Salt Lick barbecue
restaurant is nearby at the intersection of FMs 1826 and 967.

A settlement along Onion Creek evolved into the Liberty Hill Community that eventually became Driftwood. In the early 1700s the creek was known as Garrapatas, which means sheep tick. It is said the name Onion Creek came about because the settlers found wild onions growing along its banks. In their 1970 book, *Driftwood Heritage*, the Driftwood Ladies Aid Society writes, "Neither name does justice to its beauty."

Methodist circuit rider Reverend James A. Garrison came here in 1878, liked what he saw, and decided to make it the center of his ministry. One stop on his circuit was the settlement of Purgatory, and he liked to joke about being a preacher in Purgatory. Garrison's father-in-law, James Thomas Martin, came to visit in 1881 and, impressed by the beauty of the land around Onion Creek, also decided to stay. He bought land, cleared it, and planted cotton, corn, and grain. When this enterprising man found there was nowhere nearby to process his harvest, he built a cotton gin and grain mill on Onion Creek. These conveniences drew others to the area. Martin then saw the need for a store and opened one next to his home.

By 1885 enough families lived at Liberty Hill to establish a post office, but another town already used that name. Legend says that while debating the name, settler Jim Howard, looking out the door and seeing a lot of driftwood lying around from a recent flood, suggested Driftwood. Martin, who had used driftwood in building his home where the post office would be located, agreed. The post office was established in January 1886 with Martin as the first postmaster, a post he kept until his death in 1901.

Driftwood grew as a supply center for the neighboring ranches and farms due to its proximity to the railroad terminals at Kyle and Buda. By 1890 it was a thriving town. Then trucking took over rail service and the town declined until by 1925 the population totaled 10 people. The Ladies Aid Society's *Driftwood Heritage* states that Driftwood is unique among other early small Hill Country communities because it remains a community while so many others are gone. By the end of the century, however, only the church and post office remained.

Nevertheless, the population around Driftwood is once again growing as new subdivisions sprout everywhere. Land the pioneers bought for $2.50 an acre is now selling for $10,000 to $15,000 an acre. Martin's great-grandson, who still lives on the family's remaining land, says subdivisions now abut his property. He accepts the possibility that his children may want to sell it after he is gone. Driftwood's old general store, which had not been used as a store for a long time, has been purchased by photographer Dan Winters as a home and studio.

A short distance east of Driftwood, at the junction of FM 1826 and FM 967, is Camp Ben McCulloch, on Onion Creek. In 1896 Confederate veterans began an annual reunion encampment here named in honor of a general who died in battle in 1862. Veterans and their families camped each July for eight days of remembering, fellowship, dancing, eating, and swimming. Their descendants continue to meet each year, on the last weekend of June.

Across the road from Camp McCulloch is the Salt Lick, with one of the few open pit barbecues remaining in Central Texas and serving probably the best barbecue you'll ever eat. Reunions, family ones in this case, led to the opening of the Salt Lick. The Roberts family began farming here after Civil War. They set out salt in the hollows of rocks for animals. Their barbecue pit was dug for their own use. Thurman Roberts, according to his son, made a hole with his boot, and holding a barbecue fork at arm's length, marked the perimeter. He dug the pit, lined it with rock and concrete, and welded on a grate. He often used pecan shells to fire the barbecue. This is where they held family barbecues. People driving by would stop and buy some to take home. Friends encouraged them to open a restaurant. This they did in 1969, choosing the name because "a salt lick is something where all the animals congregate. There is something good . . . something essential about it."

Eventually they put up a rock and hand-hewn board building. At first there were no facilities. If somebody asked for a restroom Roberts would wave his arm towards the back and say, "We've got 500 acres and 5,000 trees. Use whatever one you want." The restaurant grew as it gained popularity. There are restrooms today, but no air conditioning. Rock walls, open windows, and fans keep the interior comfortable on the hottest of days. The Robertses say their use of a vinegar-based sauce, allowing for cooking directly over hot coals, makes their barbecue so good. The usual tomato-based sauce would burn if you did this.

DRIFTWOOD WALK

Cemetery, church, and a few early buildings. Flat terrain. Park by church and cemetery. No public restrooms. (No map.)

A historical marker at the church describes its beginnings. The Methodist settlers organized a church in 1884. In 1911, the Baptists, who had their church farther out, decided to move it into town. They got the building in place but put off anchoring it until morning. That night a high wind came up; in the morning they found nothing but rubble. Methodists offered use of their church—and that's the way it's been ever since. A Methodist preaches on the first and third Sundays, a Baptist on the second and fourth, and they alternate on fifth Sundays. Members of both denominations attend weekly, no matter who is preaching. With the increase of population hereabouts, however, membership outgrew the little church and the Baptists, after 90 years of sharing the facility, bought land to build their own church.

Behind the church is the original two-room schoolhouse, remodeled into a one-room community center. Inside, a decorative plate in the middle of the back wall covers the hole from the old stovepipe. Each of the two rooms had its own stove that connected to this outlet. On the wall are photos of quilts auctioned each year as a fund-raiser. The community center has held a covered-dish dinner the first Saturday of each month (except July) since the mid-1940s. On the second Saturday in October the town holds "Heritage Days," popularly known as "Trade Days," that include a parade. Everybody is welcome to set up a table to sell their wares.

The historical marker at the cemetery notes that at least eight Confederate veterans are buried here. On a Veterans Day visit I counted 11 Confederate flags at gravesites. This cemetery replaced an earlier one known as the Old Community Cemetery. Some of the burials from there, including those of the earliest settlers, were reinterred here.

To the left of the church is a two-story stone building built in 1925 as the Masonic Lodge. After the lodge moved to Dripping Springs about 20 years ago this became a private residence.

Across FM 150 is the store Martin built, added onto over the years. Next to the store is the H. T. Dodson home, several sheds pulled together as one dwelling. H. T.'s wife, Ella, built the stone pillars in the late 1920s. Note how the base is round. She started them in five-gallon cans filled with cement and rocks and continued to build on this foundation.

Dripping Springs

US 290 and Hwy. 12 southeast of Johnson City and north of Wimberley,
midway between U.S. 281 and I-35. Population 1,548. One walk.

As Robert F. Shelton said when dedicating the historical marker, this is
where "the cool, clear waters of the Edwards Aquifer burst forth . . . and dripped
musically from the limestone overhead."

Willis Fawcett is the first known white settler. He arrived in 1853, followed
within the year by John L. Moss, Robert Lee Wallace, and Dr. Joseph M.
Pound. All came from southern American states, as did most of the settlers in
Hays County. A town was laid out in 1854, with streets bordered by flagstone
sidewalks. Robert L. Wallace established the first stage stop and post office
in 1857 as Wallace Mountain. Because he served in the Confederate Army,
after the war the reconstruction government did not allow him to resume
his postmaster job. Pound built a two-room log dogtrot home in 1853 on a
branch of Onion Creek at what is now Founders Memorial Park. An Indian
trail passed 100 yards away, but Indians were no problem as they saw Pound as
a medicine man. His home was hospital, school and Methodist church. After
four generations, the family donated it to the city. It was restored and opened
as a museum in 2003, the 150th anniversary of the town's founding (Tue., Thu.,
Sat., noon–3 p.m.).

Telephones came to Dripping Springs in 1890. Lines were strung along
fenceposts and trees, whichever was more convenient. Wind or rain meant
poor or no service. The first telephone office was at the Crenshaw Drug Store
with Dora Crenshaw as operator. Later it moved to Sam McClendon's home. Ila
Mae Harner was day operator and McClendon was night operator. When the
telephone company moved to its own building, Ila Mae stayed on as operator
until the dial system arrived in 1960. (Yes—1960!)

DRIPPING SPRINGS WALK

Historic buildings and homes. .75 mile, flat, no sidewalks but sufficient shoulder. Park in
the lot on Mercer. No public restrooms. Several restaurants, on College Street and along
Hwy. 290.

❶ Walk to the back of the parking lot.

William Jordan, a noted teacher and preacher from Alabama, came to
Dripping Springs to visit his uncle, Jesse McLendon. Jordan liked the town,
and the town's founders, wanting a good education for their children, needed a

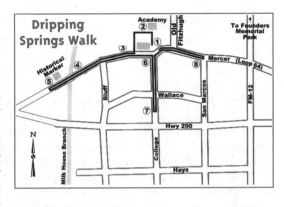

teacher, so Jordan decided to stay. In 1881 Pound, Chapman, and Davis founded the Dripping Springs Academy. Money was scarce, so Dr. Pound let citizens work their payment off by helping build the academy. Two years later the Pedernales Baptist Association bought the school. It changed hands several times until 1889 when the public school district took over. This was the first Dripping Springs High School. It was used until the Rambo Masonic Lodge bought the building in 1949.

❷ Turn left and walk along the driveway.

The vine-covered building is a 1901 drug store moved here for use as a storeroom for the grocery store in front. Set back to its left is the Rinkey Dink Domino Hall, originally on Mercer Street. But the women complained about gambling on the main street, so it was moved. It's as rustic inside as out, with one table and a half-dozen folding chairs. Two bare light bulbs provide light, a wood stove keeps players warm in winter, and a fan gives some relief in summer. On your right at the end of the driveway is the former J. L. Patterson grocery store. This 1906 building originally had 1 1/2 stories with a mezzanine around the interior. After a fire, only the first floor was restored.

❸ Turn right on Mercer Street.

No. 304 Mercer is one of two rock buildings F. W. Miller built in 1940. This one was a cafe and the next one a service station.

The next rock building is Garnett's Garage. In 1925 he added the rock front using karst limestone and fossils, the latter evident on the far side wall. With Highway 290, all service stations moved to the highway.

Garnett's house is next door. He used rock and fossils again on the house and its fence.

Another Garnett home, built of "patchwork" stone, is set back alongside Milk House Branch. (A "branch" is a stream that branches off a river or creek—in this case, Onion Creek.)

❹ Cross Milk House Branch.

In the winter, when the vegetation is bare, you can see the limestone cliffs above the stream. The springs that gave the town its name are on private property. If there's been enough rain they burst forth once again.

Across the bridge is a granite marker the Dripping Springs Lions Club erected in June 1980. The next house is one of the oldest in Dripping Springs. In 1871 Burrell J. Marshall moved his frame home from Moss Ranch to this bluff overlooking the springs. Later he made limestone additions. He was postmaster until his death the next year. His widow, Martha Ann, married William T. Chapman, who took over postmaster duties and held this position until 1889. Son Mercer followed in his father's footsteps, serving as postmaster from 1906 to 1919. Like many early homes, the interior doorways are short to conserve heat. This makes it difficult for the present 6' 2" owner.

❺ Retrace your steps back across Milk House Branch, then cross Mercer and turn left.

Again, in winter, you can see the cliffs and springs. A deep pool farther up gave this stream its name. Townfolk used it as a cooling place for milk and other foodstuffs. A big slab of rock under 30-foot cliffs by the pool made this a favorite picnic spot.

Back "downtown," the feed store was originally a hardware store. The shed across the back was the wool and mohair barn.

Next to it is a stone barber shop built in 1937. It served for 20 years as a post office, next as a beauty shop, and then a barber shop. The current owner services the whole family.

The building on the corner, built in 1890 of hand-hewn blocks, was the A. L. Davis Store. It originally had two stories, with the Masonic Lodge on the second floor. After a fire the second floor was not restored. The lodge then bought the old academy.

❻ Turn right on College Street.

Just before the highway on the right was the Lou Breed Boarding House, where academy students lived. Charles Christopher Haydon bought it in 1933. He and his wife, Beulah, married when he was 19 and she 17. After a stay in Driftwood they moved to Dripping Springs in the late 1800s. Haydon ran a cotton gin and grist mill down the way where the Texaco station is now. He also owned a threshing machine and well drill, making his services much in demand.

Charles and Beulah were known for their hospitality. Their son, Charlie, says, "Anyone who came along was never a stranger, everybody was welcome."

Beulah was known affectionately as "Short Mama." When the farmers brought their cotton in for ginning, they would stop by Short Mama's for dinner and dominoes. Once, when all the creeks flooded, their guests had to stay overnight.

Haydon died in 1938 during his term as county commissioner. Beulah finished out his term in office, becoming the first woman in Dripping Springs to hold a county office. She later married Wesley Malott and also outlived him, dying in 1989 at age 97.

❼ Retrace your steps to Mercer and turn right.

The "patchwork" rock building was the Central Garage, built in 1937 by one of the Wimberley masons who specialized in this style.

The next building was Crenshaw's Drug Store. Crenshaw was not a trained druggist, so the doctor came here and filled his own prescriptions.

The building past the drug store dates from 1925. The back portion was built first as a garage, then the front section was added in 1938 as a gas station.

The building at Mercer and San Marcos opened as a movie theater in 1937, closed in 1939, reopened under a new owner in 1946, and closed again shortly afterward. It was converted to a bank in 1981.

❽ Cross Mercer and turn left back to the start.

At the corner of Fitzhugh Road is the Crenshaw home.

Fredericksburg

Gillespie County seat, off I-10 north of Comfort at junctions of US 290, U.S. 87, and Hwy. 16. Population 8,911. Three walks.

In 1845, as the new head of the *Adelsverein,* John O. Meusebach sent a survey party from New Braunfels to select a site for the society's second settlement for German immigrants along the route to the Fisher-Miller grant. They located a tract of land 60 miles northwest where two streams met to form a narrow three-mile-long strip of land. This site and surroundings provided abundant water, lumber and limestone for building, and land for farming. Meusebach named the settlement Friedrichsburg to honor Prince Friedrich of Prussia (later anglicized to Fredericksburg). After a 16-day trek from New Braunfels, 120 settlers arrived on May 8, 1846. Each family or single man received a town lot and an outlot for farming.

Meusebach knew the settlement would not work unless there was peace with the nearby Comanches. In March 1847 he entered unarmed into the Comanche camp and negotiated a peace treaty. The Comanche chiefs agreed to come to Fredericksburg on the second full moon to officially sign the treaty. This is the only treaty with the Indians in Texas that was never broken, and one of the few unbroken in the United States. After the signing ceremony a procession marched up San Saba Street to lay the cornerstone of the Vereins Kirche (Community Church). A two-day celebration followed. Settlers in their German folk costumes and Comanches in their beaded buckskins and feathered headdresses took turns entertaining with their dances.

The Vereins Kirche, built as an octagon with a cupola in a style reminiscent of buildings in Europe, served as multi-denominational church, town hall, storehouse, school, and fort. Its shape led to the nickname of *Die Kaffee Muehle* (the Coffee Mill). As various denominations built their own churches the Vereins Kirche fell into disuse. The sides were removed in 1896 to create an open pavilion for the town's 50th anniversary celebration. The next year the entire building was razed. In 1934 the new Gillespie County Historical Society built a replica using the original cornerstone, which they rescued from being used as a water trough for chickens.

Main Street in most early towns was laid out wide enough for ox-drawn freight wagons to make a U-turn. In Fredericksburg though, we find many wide streets, probably an influence from such city plans as Paris, France, and Washington, D.C.

The first homes were of log or *Fachwerk* construction. Later, limestone block and wood frame houses replaced these. Those who settled on their outlot built a "Sunday House" on their town lot, usually one room with a sleeping loft reached by an outside stairway to conserve interior space. Families came into town on Friday or Saturday, sold their produce, did their shopping, and spent the evening visiting, playing card games, bowling, and attending dances. Then, after church on Sunday, they headed home. Fredericksburg has more Sunday Houses than other Hill Country towns because so many chose to live on their outlots. Fredericksburg's position as the last supply station for those heading west, its designation in 1848 as county seat of newly formed Gillespie County, and the safety provided by Fort Martin Scott led to further economic growth.

Like other German communities in the Hill Country, most citizens supported the Union in the Civil War. When the army left Fort Martin Scott, Charles H. Nimitz organized the Gillespie Rifles to protect local citizens. This put him on the "hit list" of J. B. Waldrip, head of the Haengerbande (Hanging Band), a gang of radical Confederates. When they raided the hotel, Nimitz escaped death by hiding in the brewery. Ironically, Waldrip was killed in 1867 under an oak tree next to the hotel.

After the war Fredericksburg continued to grow. The Gillespie County Fair, established in 1889, attracted large numbers. In 1913 rail passenger service from San Antonio brought more people. By 1928 Fredericksburg was the largest unincorporated town in the United States, but its continued growth did finally lead to incorporation. At one time the city was a principal manufacturing center with furniture, mattress, and sewing factories; cement, poultry, peanut oil plants; and quarries, metal works, and a tannery. By the 1930s it also had a growing reputation as a resort. Today its museums, abundant examples of early architecture, many now run as bed-and-breakfasts, a plethora of fine shops, German restaurants and bakeries, and the nearby peach orchards combine to make Fredericksburg one of the most popular of the Hill Country tourist towns. Unique among many special events is the Easter Fire Pageant. It combines the history of Fredericksburg, an old German Easter Eve tradition, a local Easter Bunny fable, and other historical legends into a delightful evening.

To illustrate Fredericksburg's hospitality, the first letters of streets running north and south from the *Marktplatz* read to the east "ALL WELCOME" (Adams, Llano, Lincoln, Washington, Elk, Lee, Columbus, Olive, Mesquite, Eagle). The streets to the west read "COME BACK" (Crockett, Orange, Milam, Edison, Bowie, Acorn, Cherry, Kay).

FREDERICKSBURG WALK I

Marktplatz, East Main Street, Nimitz Museum and National Museum of the Pacific War (open daily 9 a.m. to 5 p.m. except Thanksgiving, Christmas Eve and Christmas), *Der Stadt Friedhof* (City Cemetery). 1.6 miles includes walk through cemetery but not Nimitz Museum or National Museum of the Pacific War. Mostly flat, some grassy strips, streets without sidewalks have little traffic. Start at: *Marktplatz* at corner Main and Adams. Public restrooms at start. Visitor Center at 302 E. Austin St., east of Washington and across from the Museum of the Pacific War, open weekdays 8:30 a.m. to 5 p.m., Saturdays 9 a.m. to 5 p.m., Sundays 1 to 5 p.m. Many restaurants in vicinity, some along walk.

Note: Overhanging awnings on Main Street give welcome shade but block views of architectural features. Therefore, some buildings will be described from the opposite side of the street. "L" or "R" after an address denotes left or right side of street.

The *Marktplatz:* San Saba Street (now Main Street) ran east and west through two blocks designated as the *Marktplatz. The Vereins Kirche* was in the middle. The *Marktplatz* provided a gathering place for everything from markets to circuses to sports.

Today the *Marktplatz* is the center of city and county government. Over time the county courthouse, city hall, police and fire stations, and public library settled around the plaza. A replica of the *Vereins Kirche,* built on one side of the *Marktplatz* rather than in the middle of the street, is a museum. A *Maibaum* (May pole) depicts scenes from Fredericksburg history. Created by blacksmith Roy Bellows in 1991, it is typical of the storytelling structures erected in Bavarian villages. Behind the *Vereins Kirche* is the Pioneer Garden, which honors local dignitaries.

Across Main, the center building, now the public library, was the second county courthouse. This High Victorian Italianate design is the work of noted architect Alfred Giles. The yellow limestone is from a quarry northeast of town, while the quoins (corner stones), sills, lintels, arches, and paving are from quarries east of town. The locks, door latch plates, hinges, and doorknobs are etched in an intricate hummingbird design.

The "new" courthouse is to its left, and the former post office, now county offices, to its right.

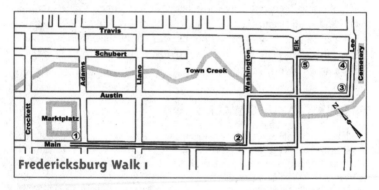

❶ **With your back to the *Marktplatz,* turn left on Main.**

No. 107R E. Main (across Main on the southeast corner of Adams) is the two-story stone mercantile store Edward Maier built in 1874. He also had a grist mill and a steam cotton gin on Town Creek. Maier was killed when the boiler in his cotton gin exploded.

A few years later Temple D. Smith opened a bank in this building. Fredericksburg's only bank robbery took place here on July 2, 1888. Robbers made a clean getaway in spite of being shot at as they ran across the *Marktplatz.* After Smith built the Bank of Fredericksburg up the street, this building had several owners before coming back to his son, Richard, who opened the Bank Saloon. When Prohibition came, he made it a grocery store.

This octagonal structure in Fredericksburg's Markt Platz replicates the original Vereins Kirche, or Community Church.

No. 109R, the two-story concrete block building, dates from 1913. It was Alex Maier's saddlery and leather work business. Jack Estes bought the building in 1975 and added the porches and fretwork (gingerbread) trim. He ran Jack's Emporium downstairs and lived upstairs.

No. 123R (marker), the two-story with the ornate iron pillars and trim, is the Frank Valentine Van der Stucken birthplace. His father joined the Confederacy. When he saw that the Confederates would lose the war, afraid of reprisals, he returned with his family to Belgium. Young Frank Valentine, who showed great promise as a musician, studied with the European masters, becoming part of the circle that included Liszt and Verdi. After he gained fame in Europe, the First Lady, Mrs. William Howard Taft, convinced him to become the founding director of the Cincinnati Symphony. Fredericksburg honors him with an annual concert.

No. 131–133R is Dooley's 5-10 & 25¢ Variety Store established in 1923 by Charles Dooley and now run by his son, John, and grandson, Tim. This is one of the few old-time variety stores remaining in the country and carries stuff you thought was no longer available. "We sell things big stores don't want to fool with," says John Dooley.

No. 141R, another two-story with iron trim, is the 1888 Priess Building, built by Louis Priess as a general store and home. In 1923 George R. Stucke bought it and opened a bakery, confectionery, and soda shop. Each evening at 6 p.m. he fired up the brick oven in back, and by 1 a.m. it was ready for baking. First in were French and rye breads, then pan breads, and, as the oven cooled, cakes, pies, and cookies. In 1945 he installed a new gas-fired revolving oven indoors. This location has remained a bakery through several subsequent owners.

No. 205R, across Llano, is the 1897 Schandua Building (marker). Johann Schandua inherited the lot from his father, Peter, a stonemason and respected builder. Johann, who already had a hardware business, wanted to build a new store and home at this location but did not have enough money. Along came the local Masonic Lodge, which offered him an interest-free loan in exchange for a lodge room on the second floor. Sadly, just months after Schandua finished paying the five-year loan, he died of a heart attack. His widow married his brother, Henry, who took over the business, sharing the downstairs with Otto Evers' saddlery while the family continued to share the upstairs with the Masonic Lodge.

No. 222L, the Richter Building (marker), was known for years as "Domino Hall." Originally, the front part was a house, probably built by John Schmidtzinsky, who acquired the property in 1850. After it changed hands several times, Henry R. Richter acquired it in 1901 and operated a jewelry and musical instrument store in the front room. Richter, who played several instruments and also composed, organized the *Philharmonische Gesellschaft* of mixed chorus and orchestra. They frequently gave concerts here. After the Richters moved out it was a cafe and then a domino parlor–pool hall that served cold drinks and short-order food. In more recent years it became a restaurant with a beer garden in back.

Next on the left is the White Elephant Saloon John W. Kleck built in 1888. A white elephant is a legendary symbol in Germany for hospitality and *gemuetlichkeit* (fun, fellowship, and pleasant times). Kleck held high stakes gambling games upstairs. The ornamental wrought iron along the roofline is an embellishment rarely seen in early Hill Country buildings. The White Elephant locked its front door the day the Sunday law was enacted, but its back door remained open for thirsty regulars. When Dr. Albert Keidel bought the building he leased out the saloon and used the back rooms for patients to stay after emergency surgery. The saloon closed with Prohibition.

A white elephant, German symbol for fun and hospitality, was designed on John Kleck's White Elephant Saloon, built on Main Street in 1888. •

Next on the left is Gillespie County's first medical building, built by Dr. Albert Keidel in 1908. Note the metal plate on each side of the columns that identifies them as the work of "Mersher Brothers, Front Builders." This appears on several buildings on Main Street and in other Hill Country towns. Albert's son Victor had medical offices upstairs. Sons Felix and Werner had dental offices there. Son Kurt ran a drug store on the ground floor. Kurt's daughter, Alberta, married Dr. Albert Bonnell, who also kept his office here, as did their daughter, Bonnie. The Keidels date back to the earliest days of Fredericksburg. Dr. William Keidel was Fredericksburg's first "real" medical doctor. Meusebach had appointed Dr. Friedrich Schubert as the town's first city director and physician. Schubert turned out to be an impostor using an assumed name and was fired. Dr. Keidel was elected as the first chief justice when Gillespie County was organized. He practiced medicine here from 1846 until his death in 1870.

Next on the left is the two-story home Dr. Albert Keidel renovated and added onto in the 1880s. His name is carved in the stone lentil over the door, and on the iron gate.

Next to it is the business and home Adolph Lungkwitz built about 1867. As a metalsmith he made fine jewelry and silver flatware. The bow-and-arrow design on the transom above the front door is unique. Dr. Felix Keidel bought the property for his dental office and home in 1920.

The corner building was built by Charles F. Priess as a home and store in 1883. As a Lone Star Beer distributor, he stored beer in the huge cellar, bringing ice from his ice factory uptown to keep the beer cool. After he closed his business in the late 1890s the building was a tailor shop and later a boarding house. Dr. Victor Keidel bought it in 1919 for his home and medical office but sold it in 1937. When the need arose for a new, larger hospital, his son Albert, a preservationist, convinced him to buy it back and remodel it into a hospital.

Albert was the only member of the Keidel family who did not go into medicine. He broke some preservation rules by making additions and changes to historic buildings. However, according to John Davidson in an article for *Preservation* magazine, "he was working in the tradition of his German forebears in the Hill Country, who kept recycling houses to make them work, who wasted nothing, and who used the materials at hand." Albert helped save many of the Main Street buildings.

Some townspeople thought it unrealistic that Fredericksburg could use its history to attract tourists. Then Lyndon Johnson became president. The national press corps discovered Fredericksburg on their way to the LBJ ranch and began writing articles about it. Then you could buy a small unrestored rock house for some $5,000. By the beginning of the new century it would have cost $100,000, and a decade later, if you could find one, it would cost around $400,000.

No. 310L is a two-story stone L-shaped home built in 1908 by Robert G. Striegler. Upon the birth of their son, Kermit, the Strieglers put in the fountain and pond.

No. 312L is the Wahrmund store (marker), renovated by First Federal Savings and Loan in 1975. It began life in 1852 as the homestead of Heinrich Wilke, a wheelwright. The outstanding feature of the building is the mansard roof, one of the few in Fredericksburg. George Wahrmund acquired the property in 1876. His wife had a millinery and dressmaking shop in part of the first floor. After serving as a boarding house for the James Clark family, it was purchased by Martin Schult in 1924. He modernized it, adding new glass show windows and opening a bakery. The bakery passed through several hands that included Moellendorf in 1929 and later his brother-in-law, Theodore Dietz. When the bank took over they reconstructed the front.

Looking over to the right again:

No. 327R, left of the Auslander Restaurant, began as the Heinrich Schaetter family home, later became the Schaetter Funeral Home, and later the Schaetter Furniture Store. Schaetter started as a cabinetmaker who also made coffins. By 1882 he found himself in the undertaking business and in 1885 brought the first hearse to Fredericksburg. He hitched his two black horses, Nick and Prince, to the hearse and donned a formal black coat to take the departed to the cemetery. The first funeral home was built in 1928 behind this building and later moved across San Antonio Street.

No. 329R, on the other side of Auslander, had many different owners in its early days. The little stone house probably dates from 1854, when it was owned by Christian Kraus. In 1892 Christian Mathisen came here from Denmark and bought the property. His parents and siblings arrived the next year. They lived in a house next to this. Christian was a blacksmith and his father a wheelwright. When Christian married in 1897 he converted the shop into a home, adding floors and ceilings to make it more livable. His family later moved to a farm in Rocky Hill and the Jens Hansen family bought this for a Sunday house.

No. 340L, the Nimitz Museum, was originally a hotel owned in 1860 by Captain Charles H. Nimitz, the grandfather of Fleet Admiral Chester Nimitz of World War II fame. Charles Nimitz added the steamboat superstructure some time after 1870s. The hotel offered the only hot bath along the six-day stage ride from Austin to El Paso. Before the 1870s it was the last real hotel until travelers reached San Diego, California. In the bathhouse water was heated in an iron kettle in the middle of the stone floor and carried to tin bathtubs in private stalls. The hotel had stables, an orchard, vegetable garden, and smokehouse, as well as a brewery, dance hall, theater, and casino. Nimitz was "a jolly innkeeper," and the dining room was reputed to be the best on the frontier.

The building underwent many changes through the years but is now restored to its original "steamboat" look. The museum opened in 1964, dedicated to "Admiral Nimitz and all the men and women who served under him in the Pacific in World War II, and to those who helped preserve our American Heritage." It now overlooks a six-acre campus, owned by the Texas Historical Commission and operated by the Admiral Nimitz Foundation, which has opened, behind it, the National Museum of the Pacific War.

❷ Turn left on Washington, left on Austin to the entrance of the National Museum of the Pacific War and then back down Austin to continue the walk.

The National Museum of the Pacific War is the nation's only institution dedicated solely to the story of the Pacific and Asiatic theaters of World War II. Its centerpiece is the 33,000 square foot George H. W. Bush Gallery, a world-class exhibition area opened on December 7, 2009. Some 900 artifacts are arranged in a progression of spaces in which three dozen media installations dramatically portray. the progress of the war in the Pacific and China/Burma/India theaters. A centerpiece is one of the five two-man Japanese submarines that took part in the attack on Pearl Harbor. World War II veterans are admitted at no charge. Allow several hours for your visit. Two blocks west on Austin Street is the three-acre Pacific Combat Zone, with a host of aircraft, boats and other large artifacts, seen on regular guided tours only.

Charles Nimitz, grandfather of World War II Admiral Chester Nimitz, added a steamboat superstructure to the front of his Main Street hotel about 1880.

As you retrace your steps back east down Austin Street and return to the corner of Washington Street, you pass the Japanese Garden of Peace, a gift from the military leaders of Japan in honor of the mutual respect between admirals Nimitz and Togo and with prayers for everlasting peace.

No. 107 N. Washington is the Julius Hollmig home, built after the Civil War. Hollmig's blacksmith shop was on the corner of Main, a particularly good location as he got the horse, wagon, and carriage trade from travelers stopping at the Nimitz Hotel. Austin Street follows alongside Town Creek.

On the left corner is the home of Johann Joseph Walch (marker), who arrived in Fredericksburg in 1847. He and his father first built a log cabin, then went to work for John Meusebach as stonemasons and later as farmhands. When his son Felix married, Walch deeded him part of the lot. Felix remodeled the stone barn into a home. The property was almost devoid of trees until Mary Louise Denman bought it in 1950. Now the trees are so dense it's hard to see the houses.

On the left at the corner of Elk is a Santa Fe–style home, unusual architecture for Fredericksburg. Owners remodeled it from an older home and barn after they fell in love with this style when living in Santa Fe.

Across Elk on the left is the two-story stone home of Peter Schmitz, dating from 1872. It remained in the family for 99 years.

❸ Turn left on Lee to Cemetery.

The entrance to *Der Stadt Friedhof* (the city cemetery), bears the date 1846. Newer burials are toward the front.

Walk down the main aisle to the stone marker commemorating early settlers of Fredericksburg, who are buried here in marked and unmarked graves. Many died during a plague.

A red granite stone near the fence line of the old section marks the interment of Charles and Sophia Nimitz. At the far back of the cemetery are the African American burials.

The small size of the burial plots in a large section, from behind the windmill and storage buildings over to the road, identifies these as the gravesites of children. This children's section began when more than 100 children died during a diphtheria epidemic.

❹ From the cemetery entrance walk straight ahead on Schubert.

On the right, although the Old Mill Settlement looks old, it isn't. Third-generation log cabin builder Steve Rice Jr. of Greeneville, Tennessee, had these mostly old cabins dismantled and moved here from their original locations. Build as a bed-and-breakfast development, it is now owned by San Antonio Shoes (SAS) and is used for company meetings.

No. 507L is a Sunday House built in *Fachwerk* style with a frame addition.

❺ Turn left on Elk. At Main cross to the other side and turn right.

No. 420R E. Main (across from the Kindle house) was built in the early 1850s by Carl Weyrich and remained in the family until 1955. Weyrich was a gunsmith and locksmith. He also bartered with the Indians for buffalo hides. His two sons, Gustav and William, are shown overlooking the valley of Fredericksburg as they watched over the family's sheep in the well-known sketch by Hermann Lungkwitz.

No. 414R was probably built after the Civil War by John Adam Alberthal. It was sold in 1878 to Christian Kloth and served as both home and business to several owners. Arman Hillman, an editor of Fredericksburg's German newspaper *Wochenblatt (Weekly Blade)*, had his print shop here.

No. 405L is the two-story stone building built by blacksmith Friedrich Kiehne in 1850. When the Indians brought their horses in to be shod, he communicated with them by hand signals. Many arrowheads have been found on the property.

No. 247L (marker), across Lincoln, dates from 1866. Heinrich Henke bought it in 1873. He had his butcher counter on the front porch. Each day after the shop closed the porch was scrubbed and the family sat there to relax and greet neighbors. His daughter, Anna Nimitz, bore her son, Chester William Nimitz, here in 1885.

The Fredericksburg Brewing company is located in the 1926 Louis Kott Building. Owners traveled to Europe to learn specialty beer brewing.

Across Llano on the right, the Palace Theater, with its tile-trimmed art deco facade, dates from the 1920s.

Also on the right, across from Dooley's, is the small red granite jewelry store that Alphons Walter, a jeweler and watchmaker from Switzerland, opened in 1908. It has been a jewelry store ever since.

The building to its left was the Central Drug Store, which Alphons Walter built in 1905. Part was his jewelry store and the rest a drug store, book store, and medical offices. When he retired his son took over. Originally the building did not have a porch. The Texas Telegraph and Telephone Company leased part of the second floor until 1954. In 1909 Walter sold the building to Robert Striegler. It was a drug store for 70 years.

No. 120R, the Bank of Fredericksburg Building, was designed by Alfred Giles. Temple D. Smith, popularly known as Banker Smith, came to Fredericksburg in 1887 from Virginia and opened a bank in the Maier Building. In 1913 he was instrumental in bringing the first railroad to the city. The Bankersmith Community, a railroad town south of Fredericksburg, was named for him. When Smith died in 1926, his funeral service was held in the bank.

No. 119R, the yellow brick Richardsonian Romanesque building was built by A. C. Bonn in 1913 as the National Bank of Fredericksburg. The red granite trim is another example of stone work by the Nagel Brothers. The cornerstone states that they produce "the best granite for building and monument work." The night deposit box is still in the wall.

FREDERICKSBURG WALK 2

Residential neighborhoods. 2.2 miles, mostly flat. Start at Marktplatz. Public restrooms at start. Many restaurants in vicinity.

❶ On Austin Street, with back to *Marktplatz,* turn right.

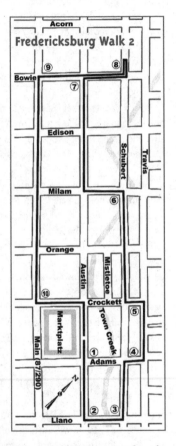

Across Austin Street, Bethany Lutheran Church (marker) was organized in 1887. The original building was moved. This dates from 1954.

No. 102L W. Austin is the two-story home that Alfred vander Stucken built. (Alfred "Americanized" the name by making "van der" one word.) It is possible that this part was built before the "1891" above the entrance.

No. 104L E. Austin, across Adams, is the two-story home of Friedrich Wilhelm Schumacher, a tailor and one of the earliest settlers; it was built onto the one-room *Fachwerk.* When his daughter Bertha and her husband, Carl Leyendecker, inherited it they planted a vineyard and made wine in the huge cellar.

No. 111R is the Schandua home (marker). Schmidt family members owned this property and probably built the house. John Schandua bought it in 1883 and lived here until 1903, when he built the two-story home and hardware store on Main Street. Bethany Lutheran Church used it as a Sunday school from the 1920s until 1947. Burt Joiner bought it and donated it to the Gillespie County Historical Society for restoration.

❷ Turn left on Llano.

Across Schubert on the right is a house built around Conrad Hahn's 1869 two-room log cabin. In 1879 August Burgdorf bought it, plastered the inside, and covered the outside with frame, but some of the log portion is still exposed.

❸ Turn left on Schubert.

No. 108 E. is the almost square two-story limestone house that stonemason Charles Jung built for his own family in 1871. In the basement a ladder leads into an old rainwater cistern that is now a wine cellar.

❹ Turn right on Adams, then left on Travis.

The gray building on the left at Schubert is where the Basse Brothers produced the cement blocks used in many local homes. Present-day owners of these homes enjoy much lower insurance rates.

Around the corner on Travis is the Fredericksburg *Turn Verein* (marker). Established in 1871 at a different location, it has a gymnastics school and ninepin bowling alley and is one of the city's oldest continuous organizations. It moved here in 1909 and is now called Turner Hall. Members still gather to bowl and play billiards and cards, particularly Skat, and for weekend dances.

❺ Turn left on Crockett, then right on Schubert.

The first stone house on Schubert (marker) is the 1893 home of Heinrich Cordes, an architect, stonemason, and carpenter who helped build the Nimitz Hotel and the old St. Mary's Catholic Church.

No. 307L (across Town Creek) is the Christian Crenwelge home (marker). It was first restored by Albert Keidel, then by the Philip O'Brien Montgomerys. Crenwelge, a cabinetmaker by trade, ran a molasses press across from the house and on the other side of the creek built a lime kiln.

Next is the stone barn from the Knopp house. When Martin and Maurine Bogisch bought the Knopp property in 1971 they did more restoration and made the barn into a garden house.

No. 309L (on the corner) is the 1871 Johann Joseph Knopp house (marker on side). He worked in town while his wife and children ran the farm about a mile away. The house later had several owners until Albert Keidel bought and renovated it in 1937. It has undergone several more restorations since then.

No. 312R is another home belonging to Christian Crenwelge. It dates from around 1903 and had many owners and renters over the years. The McAdoo Whites bought it sight unseen in 1974, moved here from Oregon, and did much restoration, adding a guest house of cedar siding and a log cabin moved in from a nearby farm.

❻ Turn left on Milam, then right on Austin.

No. 408R W. Austin is the John Walter homestead, which started as a tiny log cabin. The rock addition came later. Walter was the local sheriff from 1876 to 1888. He had to use his home for a jail after the county jail burned down in

1885, which explains the bars on two of the windows. After his term as sheriff, he delivered ice, which he brought from San Antonio in large blocks packed in hay and straw to discourage melting.

No. 414R is the home Christian Strackbein built some time after 1870. It is typical of homes that started as a log cabin, had *Fachwerk* additions, and finally stone additions. Its 35-foot well was dug by pick and shovel as described on Walk No. 3. The log cabin in back was built as a smokehouse.

No. 418R is the Christian Vogel home, built in the 1880s as a wood frame Sunday House. His son Amanchus added the portion on the right at the turn of the century, covering all with pressed tin.

No. 420R possibly dates back to the mid-1800s. H. H. Sagebiel bought it in 1920. During remodeling, they found timbers used in the rafters and the floor joists bearing marks of the Mormon mill at the Zodiac Community that existed on the Pedernales River from 1847 to 1853.

🕖 Turn right on Bowie, to Schubert.

No. 210L Bowie, at the corner as you turn onto Schubert is the 1856 Johann Peter Tatsch home. What makes this small house unique, a home tour favorite, and perhaps most photographed of Fredericksburg homes, is the extra-large second fireplace. Tatsch, a cabinetmaker and wood turner, was noted as the inventor of "useful and ingenious devices." He added the gallery kitchen with its outsized fireplace onto the original house. One end of the fireplace has a built-in oven so it can be used for baking while it is also used for cooking and heating. At about 13 feet wide and 5 1/2 feet high, it is big enough to roast an entire ox. The house stayed in the family until recent times. Then the Girl

The much-photographed 1856 Tatsch home on Bowie Street is noted for its extra-large fireplace.

Scouts used it as a meeting place. It is once again a private home. During the Texas Centennial, detailed floor plans of the house were placed in the Library of Congress.

❽ Retrace your steps back to Bowie and turn right.

No. 110R N. Bowie is the 1889 home architect Alfred Giles designed for William Bierschwale. Bierschwale followed in his father's footsteps as county clerk before serving as a state representative for 16 years.

On the corner at Main are a stone house, log barn, and other outbuildings, some original to the site, some brought in.

❾ Turn left on Main. (The first block of Main is a bit hazardous as you have to walk in the street around parked cars part of the way, but there is sufficient room. The rest of Main will have a sidewalk.)

No. 508L W. Main (marker) dates from 1846 when Gerhard Rorig built a one-room log house and loft. Cabinetmaker Johann Martin Leveler added the rock and half timber rooms and a cooking fireplace in 1867. It served as Sunday House and home to the Loeffler and Weber families for 90 years. George and Gloria Hill bought it from the Weber heirs in 1964 and did an authentic restoration.

No. 425R, across Edison on the right, is the Kraus Building, originally built as a home and store in the late 1860s or early 1870s. Jacob Kraus bought it in 1898 and put in a soda water bottling plant. The term "soda pop" came into being from the type of stopper used in those days. To open the bottle, you "popped" a metal loop attached to the stopper, which then fell into the bottle. When the bottle was returned it was cleaned and the same stopper pulled up to seal it. Kraus contracted to bottle and distribute Coca Cola, and then after Prohibition to be the distributor for Pearl Brewery. For a time a cigar factory operated from the second floor, then later the family used it as living quarters.

Across Edison on the left is Zion Lutheran Church (marker) built in 1853 by its members, the first congregation to leave the Vereins Kirsch.

No. 419R, the two-story stone next to the Crenwelge lot, built as a rent house by Wilhelm Crenwelge, dates from the 1860s or 1870s.

No. 415R, on the auto agency lot, is the Wilhelm Crenwelge home built in the 1860s. Originally it had a front porch where Crenwelge conducted his wheelwright business.

No. 410L was the 1870 home of Peter Behrens. He sold it to F. C. Rodeleff, the sheriff and county tax collector, on May 26, 1874. In December of that year a deficiency in Rodeleff's accounts was discovered. He sold this property to the Knopp family to make up the deficit of $1,400.

Fredericksburg is noted for its Sunday Houses, small structures built by area farmers wishing to spend weekends in town.

No. 402L was built in 1886 by William C. Henke, one of seven sons of butcher Heinrich Henke. At first William sold meat from his front porch, just as his father had done from his shop "downtown." Later he built a wooden structure over a large cellar at the rear of the house for the butcher shop. In 1925 he built a larger shop next door. One of Henke's sons, Alex, worked at the bank. All the rest went into the meat market or cattle-buying business. In the side yard is a memorial to the local stone masons.

Across Milam on the right, about midblock, is the Pioneer Museum housed in the 1846 Kammlah home and store, one of the first store-home buildings in Fredericksburg. Five generations of the family lived here. As the family grew so did the house, from four rooms to 11 rooms. The two back rooms have partitioned walls that can be unlatched and swung back to make one big room for family celebrations and dances. Its large cellar served as storage for wine and whiskey barrels and cured meats. The Gillespie County Historical Society restored the home.

Moved onto the property to complete the museum complex are the B. Fassell house, Weber Sunday House, Walton-Smith log cabin, and Firehouse Museum.

No. 320L was the Itz Saloon. Karl Itz was one of the few survivors of the Nueces River Massacre (see Comfort Walk). A hunting knife deflected the bullet that would have killed him. After his escape he returned to Fredericksburg, where he lived in the brush eating food friends left for him. The Confederates killed two of his brothers when they refused to reveal Karl's hideout.

No. 312L, the Krauskopf Building, dates from 1900. Enghelbert Krauskopf, a cabinetmaker and gunsmith, arrived in Texas in 1846. After first earning his living as a hunter, he later built a saw mill and a cotton gin. He did the most business, however, as a gunsmith. During the Civil War, when there was no ammunition available, Krauskopf worked with Adolph Lungkwitz to design two bullet-making machines and made improvements to the Winchester rifle.

No. 309R is a stone barn, its foundation and walls of limestone block. Interior rafters, floors, and stalls are of rough-hewn post oak timber.

No. 307R (marker), built in 1878 for Henry B. Meckel, originally had a two-story wraparound porch supported by wide white columns. In 1866 Henry's father, uncle, and another man herded some cattle to the Meckel ranch. They planned on taking 12-year-old Henry along but couldn't find a horse for him. That saved Henry's life, for on the way back the men were attacked and killed by renegade Indians. Henry grew to be one of Fredericksburg's most prosperous businessmen. In 1927 the home was sold to Dr. J. J. Hanus, who removed the porch and remodeled the home into a hospital. The hospital closed when he left to serve in the Medical Corps during World War II. Robert E. Lucey, archbishop of San Antonio, bought it as a convent for the sisters who taught at St. Mary's School.

No. 301R, the Altdorf Restaurant, began as the stone-filled *Fachwerk* home of early settler, Conrad Wisseman, a carpenter and freight hauler. Paul Hanisch bought it in 1879, operating a drug store at one end while Albert Lee Patton had his tin shop at the other end. Hanisch's daughter Lisbeth lived here until her death in 1976 at age 95. She left it to Zion Lutheran Church, which sold it to Thomas and Alethia Alt; they turned it into the restaurant.

No. 244L, on the corner across Orange, is the 1870s Hoester-Wieser Building. At one time it was named the Racket. A "racket" store was the predecessor to a "five and ten." The building has been home to a diversity of businesses including millinery, fish market, dentist office, insurance company, and city offices. It has also been known as the Gartrell Building and the Blum Building.

No. 232L is the A. L. Patton Building. Patton arrived with his parents in 1851. After learning the trade of tinner, he opened a tin shop in the Hanisch Building, later a mercantile and hardware store. In 1897 he built this as business and home. The palm tree he planted still stands in the side yard. Later Patton founded the Citizens Bank. Look back and up to see the elaborate carved embellishments.

No. 218L began as the Schmidt's Hotel in the 1860s. Louis Dietz leased it in 1892 and operated it as the Central Hotel and later the Dietz Hotel. After he built a larger hotel across the street, the property was sold in 1899 to Charles Schwarz who ran a store here until he built a new one next door in 1907. This building was then saloon, drug store, home, and office.

No. 214-216L is the two-story stone building Charles Schwarz built to replace a one-story dining room and kitchen for the hotel.

No. 206L (marker) is the 1856 store and home of William Wahrmund.

⑩ Turn left on Crockett, then right on Austin back to beginning.

No. 114 W. Austin, across from the *Marktplatz*, is the Felix van der Stucken house. The two-story section is an addition to the original one-story home built after the Civil War. Looking down the driveway on the right you can see in back the oldest building on the lot, a one-room *Fachwerk* built over a cellar.

FREDERICKSBURG WALK 3

Residential neighborhood. 2.9 miles, mostly flat. Park at the Marktplatz. Public restrooms at start. Many restaurants in vicinity.

❶ On Main Street, your back to *Marktplatz*, turn right to Crockett. Cross Crockett, turn left, cross Main Street. At San Antonio Street turn right.

Fredericksburg Walk 3

No. 209L W. San Antonio was the home of cabinetmaker and carpenter August Jordan. The first two rooms were connected by a *durchgang* (dogtrot, or breezeway) to a cabin built by an earlier owner.

No. 211L is a stone house built in 1868 by William Jordan, a cousin of August. The porch is a later addition. On the right at this point is St. Joseph's Halle, built by the St. Joseph's Verein, a men's organization of St. Mary's Catholic Church. Few people know, but there's a "recreation room" in a special cellar where the men go to enjoy a bit of "German soda water." Currently the hall is used by both the church and the community for meetings and theatrical performances.

Next on the right is St. Mary's School in the three-story red brick building dating from 1923. The school was established in 1856.

Across Orange are the two St. Mary's Catholic churches. The congregation formed in 1846. Parishioners began building the Marienkirche, the smaller of the two, in 1860 and completed it in 1863. Before this, services were held in a 40-by-18-foot log church. When Jesuit Father Wenninger, a popular missionary, came to visit, the parishioners pleaded with him to stay. "Build a new church," he told them.

The second church, completed in 1908, is the work of noted architect Leo M. J. Dielmann. Enter by the side door to see its magnificent interior of Gothic arches. The two Guardian Angel windows behind the altar are a memorial to the many children who died in the late 1800s from an outbreak of diphtheria. The windows were crafted in Germany using photographs of two of the deceased children, James Blum and Erna Wagner, as models. Three bells from the older church were installed in this one. The stenciling and artwork are a 1936 addition. For more history and description of the windows and other artwork, you will find a walking tour of the church interior in the white notebook on the table at the head of the center aisle.

No. 312R is the 1855 First Methodist Church (marker), the oldest Methodist church in the Hill Country, founded in 1849. The church's pro-Union German members pulled out and organized the Edison Street Methodist Church (or Methodist North). The members of this church, Methodist Episcopal Church South, were mostly pro-Confederate Anglos. It is now owned by the historical society and is available for weddings.

No. 406, 408, 410R were all built as Sunday Houses. No. 408 belonged to Heinrich Speier, who arrived in 1850 as a widower with two sons. He remarried in 1865. He and his new wife kept the neighbors amused by their mating ritual, during which Heinrich would chase his wife around the house. As the family grew, he added more rooms to the house.

No. 515L began as a two-room log dogtrot, possibly built by Peter Staudt who took deed to the lot in 1852. A new breezeway connects it to another log house. After Staudt died his widow married Anton Loth. They continued to live here and probably enlarged the house. His son, John Lott (originally Loth), lived on a ranch and used this as his Sunday House, selling it in 1908 to John Weidenfeller. In the mid-1920s the Weidenfellers built a new house east of this and the back part was torn down. The heavy, square-cut logs are meticulously dovetailed and numbered with Roman numerals. Logs were usually fitted together when they were felled and hewn, then numbered for later assembly.

No. 516R is the 1895 home of well digger Joseph Killett. In those days wells were dug by hand with pick and shovel. They were lined with rocks fitted together so well that no cement was needed. As the hole got deeper a helper lowered the digger on a box at the end of ropes by means of a large reel. Some wells had to be dug as deep as 100 feet, posing the danger of asphyxiation. To guard against this, Killett first lowered a candle and kept it burning as he worked. With all his precautions, though, Killett met his death when the ropes broke as he was being lowered into a well.

➋ Turn left on Acorn, then left on Creek Street along Baron's Creek.

No. 605R, the first St. Barnabas Episcopal Church (marker), is the 1846 stone-filled *Fachwerk* home of Peter Walter and one of the earliest buildings in Fredericksburg. Walter was a farmer and a wagoner. He planted a small grape arbor behind his home with root stock he brought from Germany. The pecan trees grew from nuts planted by his daughter-in-law. The church bought the house in 1954 for their first church. LBJ and Lady Bird attended worship services here, often bringing visiting dignitaries with them. Tall Mr. Johnson had to stoop to enter. Of interest to San Antonians: Terrell Maverick, widow of Maury Maverick Sr., married Texas historian Walter Prescott Webb here in December 1961.

Next is the stone and cedar shingle 1964 St. Barnabas Episcopal Church. In one wall is a stone from St. Barnabas monastery on Cyprus sent as a gift to Lady Bird Johnson by the bishop. The cornerstone was set while LBJ was vice president. The Johnsons were members of the parish.

No. 512L is the Adam Krieger home. The oldest part is the west end, built of rock-filled *Fachwerk*. The east end is stone.

No. 413R was built about 1847. Frederick Kuenemann arrived in Texas in 1845, lived first in New Braunfels and bought this house in 1866. In 1875 his son, Heinrich, inherited the complex, including the furniture shop, lumberyard, and hardware store on Main. He added the galleries and gingerbread trim. It was a nursing home before being a private home again.

No. 405R is a Sunday House built in 1850. It is larger than average and has an inside, rather than outside, stairway.

No. 314L is the Ahrens-Langehenning house. The pressed tin roof imitates shingles while the pressed tin siding imitates rock.

No. 301R, the red brick Victorian, has a polished granite plaque above the window attributing the home to Charles Hotopp, 1914.

No. 223R, on the corner across Orange, possibly dates from before 1856. It too is a home built in several stages. A log room was later covered inside and out by frame walls. As the family grew, stone and frame additions were added. The George Jenschkes had 18 children. George lived to be 100; his wife, Lina, died just short of their 60th wedding anniversary. To honor his 100 years, the town selected him as honorary marshal for its 125th anniversary parade.

No. 213R (marker) was the home Reverend Gottlieb Dangers, Fredericksburg's second Protestant minister, built in 1851 on a lot he bought from Friedrich "Fritz" Pape. Behind it is Pape's 1846 log cabin. The Papes lost three of their four children on the trip from Germany. When they arrived here the wife was in such poor health the townsfolk hurriedly built this log cabin for them. The surviving daughter, Dorothea, married Carl Hilmar Guenther, founder of San Antonio's Pioneer Flour Mills. Guenther built his first mill on Live Oak Creek south of town. He sold the mill to his father-in-law and moved to San Antonio in 1859.

No. 101R is the Jordan-Tatsch-Finkernagel home that is now dental offices. The original owner of the lot, Heinrich Jordon, built a log house around 1849. In 1853, he sold it to Nicolaus Gerhard, who made improvements. He in turn sold it in 1856 to Johann Tatsch. It stayed in that family until 1922. Andreas Finkernagel bought it next. His wife had a home laundry business that employed several women. The classic *Fachwerk* designs were added by the present owners.

At Adams, up the street to the left, is the Peach Tree Tea Room, so popular with both locals and tourists there is always a waiting line. This home was built by Peter Bonn's son, Adolph.

At Adams use the crosswalk button to get across this busy street.

❸ Turn left on Llano, then left on San Antonio.

The Holy Ghost Lutheran Church (marker) was dedicated in 1893. Carl Priess donated land for this church.

At Adams, to the left, No. 206, next to the Peach Tree, is the oldest of two Peter Bonn homes built after the Civil War. Because of his Union sympathies, he made the *Haengerbande's* wanted list. When the gang came looking for him, he hid under featherbeds in his wife's cedar chest and to work his fields he donned his wife's dress and sunbonnet. In the small strip mall, Pape's Barber Shop has a distinctive red granite plaque.

No. 105 W. San Antonio is the home that stonemason Johannes Ruegner built in 1854. Among his stone works is the two-story "college" that is now the middle building of the old public school and the stone wall on the lower side of the oldest part of the cemetery. Nagel Memorials, established in 1904, remains in the family. The local pink (also called red) granite is becoming scarce, and therefore very expensive. The Nagel name is in evidence on buildings and gravestones around the Hill Country.

No. 117L (marker), the second of Fredericksburg's four jails, dates from 1885 and has been used in several movies. Fredericksburg's first jail was destroyed by fire; the third, built in 1938, was on top of the courthouse; and the current jail is behind the county courthouse. This old jail is set up as a museum, open for tours by special arrangement with the county judge's office at (830) 997-7502. On the first floor is the sheriff's office, kitchen, and living quarters. The cells are upstairs. Graffiti scratched into the floors and walls of the cells is still intact.

No. 125L (marker) was built by Albert Meinhardt in 1850. His widow, Doris, sold it to their son-in-law G. Adolph Pfeil, who ran a cotton gin. He converted part of the house into a blacksmith shop and later ran a soda water factory here.

❹ Turn right on Crockett back to *Marktplatz*.

Grapetown

Southeast of Fredericksburg off U.S. 290 on Old Hwy. No. 9, also known as Old San Antonio Road. Population 71. One walk.

This area attracted early settlers because of its abundance of wildlife and suitability as cattle range. In 1860 Friedrich Doebbler opened a general merchandise store two miles south of Grapetown on the north bank of South Grape Creek that served also as post office, stagecoach stop, stable, inn, and local gathering place.

When the Fredericksburg and Northern Railway began its run parallel to the San Antonio Road in 1913, several railroad towns developed along the route. Of these, Cain City has completely disappeared. The Grapetown schoolhouse, teacher's home, and the Eintracht Schuetzenverein Halle—the sharpshooters' club—still exist, as does a bit of Bankersmith. The Schuetzenverein, in fact, is still active. On the second Sunday afternoon of each month, and on the first Sunday in May, you can watch members practice, some with vintage firearms. (Bring earplugs!) Among special events held there is the two-day *Bundes Schuetzenfest* each August, carrying on a tradition begun in the mid-1800s.

Grapetown prospered for 91 years until the railroad ceased to run and better highways replaced the old road.

GRAPETOWN WALK

Country road past early homesteads and a historic cemetery. 3.3 miles on lightly traveled blacktop road with ample shoulder. Some slight grades. Park at turnoff to the Schuetzenverein (Grapetown Eintracht Halle). No public restrooms except when Schuetzenverein is open, or at your own risk in the outhouse behind the school. Eat in Luckenbach on Saturdays and Sundays or in Fredericksburg.

At the beginning of the walk:

The school (marker) Grapetown's third, dates from 1882. Frederick Baag donated the land, and the community supplied materials and labor. All seven grades were taught by one teacher. In 1905 it became a county school known as

Grapetown Line School, District 14. In 1949 the school closed and the district consolidated with the surrounding community schools. The domino club meets here now.

Next to the school is the home provided for the teacher. The other rock building was probably for storage.

At the end of the road is the Rausch family home. (Please respect the privacy of the current owners by not going beyond their entrance gate.) The Eintracht, dates from 1887. The word eintracht pertains to unity or tradition.

❶ From the Schuetzenverein, turn left on the road. Walk on the left side facing traffic, being alert to oncoming traffic. There's ample shoulder to step onto. It's usually quiet enough to hear a car coming, but don't count on it.

At the curve of the incline, on the right, is the Grapetown Cemetery, founded in 1902. The burial plots are almost all concrete pads to prevent sinking. Most have lovely granite markers. Many gravestones have the German words *"Ruhet in frieden,"* which means "Rest in peace." Gravestones sometimes tell a story. In one family plot are buried three children born two years apart in 1916, 1918, and 1920. All three died within a few days of each other in August 1921.

Further, on the left, is the only remaining building from the Bankersmith community. Now a private home, this was once Casper's Grocery Store.

At the Kallenberg-Klinksiek Road, the stone wall on the right ends and is replaced by a stick fence around an early homestead. Shortly past this spot, on one of my walks a small herd of cattle resting in the sun watched as I went by. I surmised it was a rare sight for them to see somebody actually walking along the road. A short way beyond here, on the left, I spotted an emu strutting near some rundown sheds.

Farther along on the right is the Hohenberger homestead (marker). Besides a fine two-story limestone house in front are other stone and log buildings. Ferdinand Hohenberger and family first settled in Luckenbach, relocating to Grapetown in 1871. Besides farming, Ferdinand hauled freight between San Antonio and Indianola, and ran a store and post office. In 1882 he deeded 160 acres of land each to his sons, Wilhelm and Theodor. This is part of Wilhelm's land.

❷ Turn around and retrace steps to beginning.

Although returning by the same route, the view is different. Across from the old buildings where the emu sometimes wanders, cattle grazing on the rise above one of the creeks all came running (yes, literally running) over to the fence to greet me. I changed my earlier theory about it being rare to see anyone walking on the road. More likely, somebody approaching a fence means food.

At the Sikora Ranch is the foundation of a large house, including remnants of some stone uprights and the carved square pieces that sat on top.

After your walk, if you drive south on this road you will come to a tunnel of the old Fredericksburg and Northern Railroad. The 24-mile line connected Fredericksburg with the San Antonio and Aransas Pass Railroad near Waring. The line was used from 1913 until it closed in 1942. In 1926 the railroad owned two locomotives and one car. The tunnel is now home to a colony of Mexican Freetail Bats from March through October. There is a viewing site and restrooms.

16 Gruene

Gruene is not on the map. It is within New Braunfels city limits. From I-35 take the Hwy. 46 West exit. Turn right on Common (traffic light) at the brown Gruene Historic District sign. Turn left on Gruene Road. From downtown New Braunfels take San Antonio Street to Union. Turn left on Union, then right on Common to Gruene Road. One walk.

This early settlement on the Guadalupe River, once an active supply center for cotton farmers, slowly deteriorated into a ghost town. Saved in the early 1970s from a developer's bulldozer, it is now a tourist town known for its dance hall, restaurant, and crafts. Its name, pronounced GREEN, came late in its development. It first went by Thornhill because of the thorn bushes proliferating on the land. Settlers found that these made good temporary fences.

The Gruene family began acquiring land around here in 1847, eventually owning around 9,000 acres, mostly planted in cotton. In 1872 Ernst Gruene Jr. and his son, Henry (H.D.), built a steam powered cotton gin on the river, later adding a grist mill and saw mill. In 1873 Ernst Jr. bought the 52 acres where the town sits. Within six months he sold half to H.D., who developed much of what is here today. H.D. also set up a system of tenant farmers. In 1878 H.D. built a mercantile store for the convenience of the sharecroppers and to accommodate travelers along the stage route between Austin and San Antonio. That same year the Gruenes opened a dance hall.

In 1890, when the International and Great Northern Railroad arrived, a town named Goodwin was platted about a mile from Thornhill. Goodwin never developed but became the name of the post office located in the general store at Thornhill with H.D. as postmaster. Further growth came with the arrival two years later of the Missouri Kansas Texas Railroad.

By 1900 Gruene was the banking, ginning, and shipping center for the local growers. The dance hall and saloon were the center of its social activities. In 1916 a City of Gruene map was drawn up. The town never incorporated, but this is probably when it took on its present name. When the cotton gin burned in 1922, the Gruenes built an electrically powered gin. But in 1925 the boll weevil blight, followed by a drought, ruined the area's cotton crop. The Gruenes' chief overseer, Erhardt Neuse, hanged himself from the water tower in despair. This, followed by the Great Depression of 1929, started the town on a downward spiral. The Gruene family kept the mercantile store open by extending credit to their customers, but eventually they had to close. Through all this, Gruene Hall managed to stay open, a cold beer ready for anyone who happened by.

Chip Kaufman, an architect working for the Texas Historical Commission, first saw Gruene in 1972 while kayaking down the Guadalupe River. He recognized the historical significance of the little ghost town. Developers had bought the entire town from the Gruene estate and planned to raze most of it. Kaufman convinced them restoration was a better way to go and they agreed to sell the historic center of town. Kaufman interested Bill Gallagher and Pat Molak, who sold the Gruene home and some outbuildings to Bill and Sharon McCaskill who turned them into the Gruene Mansion Inn and Restaurant. Pat Molak was a real estate entrepreneur with the dream of running an old-time tavern. He bought the dance hall—its original bar still intact—and in 1975 fulfilled his dream by opening Gruene Hall. It was an immediate success as a venue for Hill Country musicians. He turned the ruins of the burned out boiler room into the Grist-Mill Restaurant. Molak and friend Mary Jane Nalley formed a partnership and bought and developed more of the town. Gruene is now listed on the National Register of Historic Places.

Gruene's homes and businesses are now mostly artisan shops and restaurants. Some have historical markers. A few private residences still exist. Gruene Market Days, a craft market, is held on the third weekend of each month, February through November, and the first weekend in December.

GRUENE WALK

The whole town of Gruene. About 1 mile, mostly flat. Ample free parking lots. No public restrooms. Greune Mansion Inn and Grist Mill restaurants are on walk.

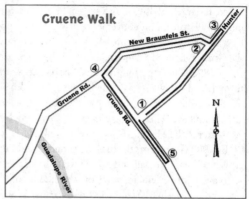

Gruene Walk

❶ The walk begins at the red brick H. D. Gruene Store, corner of Hunter and Gruene. With your back to the store, turn left along Hunter Road.

The two-story red brick H. D. Gruene Mercantile building was constructed in 1890. Gruene added the wings later, one for a bank and the other for a post office.

Across the street is the Gruene General Store, built in 1878, where the brick building stands now. Using logs and a mule team the old building was moved here, but couldn't be turned around. Therefore, what is now the front was once the back.

The brick building to the right of the Gruene General Store was originally an auto dealership and then a grocery store. The building to the store's left is a 1920s barn.

As you walk along Hunter Road, on the left is the 1875 home of Charlie Grosgebauer, the town butcher. In 1902 H.D. made some Victorian-style additions and presented it to his son Max and his wife, Olga.

Next left is the 1923 office (marker) Henry Jr. built for the cotton mill. The large corrugated metal building next to it was a garage used first to repair wagons and then for automobile repairs.

Across on the right is the 1897 home of Ella Gruene Ogletree; her father, H.D., gave it to her as a wedding present.

Next on the left was the storeroom, about 1882, for Max Jonas's blacksmith shop.

On the right is the house H.D. gave to his daughter, Paula Gruene Hampe, in 1896 as her wedding present.

❷ Cross New Braunfels Avenue, continue up Hunter Road a short way.

After you cross the street, on the left is the 1905 home of a Gruene foreman, Mr. Eichenrodt.

On the right is the 1914 home of one of the store's clerks, Mr. Mittman.

On the right, set way back from the road, is the old cotton warehouse. As Gruenewerks it serves as artisan studios and shops.

Next is the 1923 electric cotton gin completed after the first gin burned.

The open space between the road and the warehouse-gin complex is where 85–100 vendors set up to sell hand-crafted wares on Market Day.

The small house down on the end belonged to yet another employee, Fred Schneider, and dates from the 1920s.

Beyond are the new subdivisions.

❸ Retrace your steps to New Braunfels Avenue and turn right.

Cottage Court is a collection of shops in homes both original to the site and moved in from surrounding towns. This piece of land was the only one around here not owned by the Gruene family.

The first building, No. 1633, is new. The small house next to it was the old Luersen home. The houses behind it were moved in. The next little house was that of Max Jonas and the one next to that was built for one of the Gruene workers.

On the left at the corner is a former barn.

The road ahead leads to the Guadalupe River, where tubing outfitters will be happy to send you bobbing down the river.

❹ Turn left on Gruene Road.

The restored cottage on the right was the home of Gruene foreman Erhardt Neuse, who hung himself from the water tower. If you're thinking there were a lot of foremen, remember there were 9,000 acres of farmland.

Back at the town center, the water tower dates from 1923, replacing the cypress tank lost in the fire. In 1977, in a rash moment, its owner decided to tear it down. If you look at the left side of the roof, you'll see a dent where the crane was attached. Fortunately, his friends ran out, yelled "Stop!" and convinced him the tower was an integral part of Gruene.

The Grist Mill Restaurant (marker) is built around the remains of the 1878 brick boiler house of the old cotton gin that burned down in 1922.

Gruene Hall (marker), opened in 1878, is possibly the state's oldest German dance hall in continuous operation. During Prohibition it stayed open, whiskey buried in back when a raid was expected. The dance hall was Gruene's social center. On Saturday night the kids slept alongside while adults danced the night away. Since its revival, most country western entertainers have performed here. Autographed photos hang in an alcove. The stage's painted curtain backdrop has hung for a long time.

Gruene Mansion, a private residence, also serves as the office for Gruene Mansion Inn. H.D. built the house around 1872 as a two-room *Fachwerk*. He finished enlarging the first floor in 1877 and in 1886 added the second floor, Victorian galleries, and turret. The kitchen house in back was probably added at that time. A stone and brass marker alongside two of the original millstones honors those who settled here.

Behind the mansion, the original carriage house, corn crib, and barn are all remodeled as guest suites for the inn. The other buildings back there were either moved in or built from old barn wood. The Gruene Mansion Restaurant sits on a cliff overlooking the Guadalupe River.

Back along the road, the 1925 red brick house belonged to son Othmar.

The next two houses on the right were also Gruene family homes. One of them is half of the original O. A. Gruene home, cut off and moved here to make room for the brick house.

The house across the road on the left began as a two-room German *Fachwerk* home, built by Ernst Gruene Jr. in the 1850s. Later Ernst Sr. and his wife, Antoinette, moved in and added rooms, porches, and Victorian details.

Set back on the left is the 1854 C. J. Ludwig Furniture Store, moved in 1984 from New Braunfels. Note the pressed tin cornice. This is the only example in Gruene of this popular feature of early commercial buildings.

❺ Retrace your steps to the beginning.

Honey Creek

Hwy. 46 between Boerne and New Braunfels. One walk.

Honey Creek got its name quite logically, one story goes. In 1852 a group of German Catholic immigrants settled along a creek. When young Michael was sent to the creek for water he found a swarm of bees. He ran home and told his parents, "If there are bees there must be honey." Another story says the name came from the abundance of honeycomb rocks found around the creek. But then wouldn't the name have been Honeycomb Creek?

The first masses were celebrated in the homes of the settlers by a circuit-riding priest who stopped on his New Braunfels-to-Fredericksburg route. In 1876 the community built a log chapel they named for St. Joseph, but it burned before a year had passed. In 1878 Johann Adam Kneupper gave a portion of his land for a new stone chapel. This church and its cemetery still exist on private property but cannot be seen from the road. In 1892 a larger frame church was built high on a hill across the road (now Highway 46) from the original settlement. Father Virgilius Draessel, a Franciscan, arrived in 1898. He served St. Joseph's for 35 years until his death in 1933 and is buried in the church. A small stone chapel, built to commemorate a date important in Catholic history and dedicated to Father Draessel, sits higher on the hill. In 1909 parishioners, under the supervision of Father Draessel, built a new, larger church. Reflecting the growth today of the Honey Creek area, an even larger church building opened in 2006.

In 1985, parishioners built the Hill of the Cross Nature Trail on the crest of the hill behind the church. Not only is this a place of tranquility and worship, it affords a magnificent view across the Hill Country. The church welcomes all to enjoy the trail.

HONEY CREEK—ST. JOSEPH'S CATHOLIC CHURCH WALK

Church, cemetery, Hill of the Cross Nature Trail. 0.8 mile, uphill on paved road from church to cemetery and nature trail which is flat, mulch covered gravel. From the road to the chapel is uphill on a gravel walk. Handicapped and elderly may drive to the top. Park in church lot. Public restrooms. The closest restaurant is the Honey Creek Grocery, Saloon and Cafe east of the church on Hwy. 46.

❶ From the church, walk uphill past cemetery. At top turn left to Hill of the Cross Nature Trail.

NOTE: Please stay on the trail. At times there may be prayer groups here. Please be respectful and do not disturb them. On my first visit I met a group walking up the hill and was invited to join. I did for the first two stations, then excused myself and walked ahead. For those walking as a religious experience, at the trailhead is a leaflet with a dialogue for each station.

The trail winds through a cedar grove. The panorama is breathtaking. On a clear day you can see the Twin Sister Peaks to the north in Wimberley. Hanging from some branches are tiny birdhouses, more for decoration than occupancy.

Honey Creek Walk

Several have little crosses on their roof. Deer scat gives evidence of some of the wildlife that wanders through here.

❷ From the trail, walk over to the small chapel to the right of the main road up the hill.

Built in 1904, it is dedicated to the builder, the Rev. Virgilius Draessel, and is open on special occasions.

❸ Walk back down the road, entering cemetery at the first gate you reach.

The oldest marker I found here dates from 1890. Before then the Honey Creek settlers were interred in the cemetery by the original church. Descendants of many settlers still attend this church.

The perimeter of the older section is marked by graves facing inward. The long, narrow graveyard has two aisles. Stones marking burials on the inside of each are back-to-back. Orientation varies with cemeteries and customs. Terry Jordon covers this in *Texas Gravesites: A Cultural Heritage.*

Markers below in the newer section face the church, typical in church graveyards. Several unadorned, unmarked, cement crosses are along the side fence line. It is believed that these mark the graves of stillborn babies.

❹ Continue back down to the church. It is open.

Parishioners today come from Spring Branch, Bulverde, and other nearby towns. Stenciled designs border the vaulted ceiling. Quite often German tourists passing by on the road recognize the German influence of the church's architecture and stop to visit.

On Hwy. 46 east of the church is the Honey Creek Grocery, Saloon and Cafe, where neighbors drop by to pick up supplies, rent a video, or have a beer and catch up on neighborhood news. There's live music on weekends. This is a casual, friendly, family place to hang out awhile. There's a billiard room, too. The cafe is open every day except Monday. The food is good.

18
Ingram

West of Kerrville on Hwy. 39. Population 1,740. No walk.

Rev. John Charles Wesley Ingram bought six acres of land here along the Old Spanish Trail in 1879. He built a store, established a post office, and opened a church. Making shingles from cypress trees was an early industry. The town was founded in 1883 on the north bank of the Guadalupe River near Johnson Creek.

In a disastrous flood in 1932, 10 inches of rain fell in one hour, creating a wall of water 10 to 12 feet high. The highway department built a new road on higher ground and the town moved to the new road. Old Ingram is now a collection of studios, shops, and galleries strung along Old Ingram Loop, which is about a two-city-block walk. On first Saturdays of the month most of Ingram's shops and galleries stay open late, and an Art Walk is held from 6 to 8 p.m. Ingram's climate and the attractiveness of the countryside have made it a vacation spot since the 1920s. Sheep, goat, and cattle ranching remain important.

In 1958 the nonprofit Hill Country Arts Foundation was established across Indian Creek in the old town's rehabilitated commercial buildings, featuring a gallery, studios, gift shop, and both indoor and outdoor theaters. The Point Theater offers outdoor productions each weekend in the summer. In the "new" town, a series of 16 murals on the walls of the T. J. Moore Lumberyard at the junction of Hwys. 39 and 27 depicts the history of Kerr County. Artist Jack Feagan of Ingram painted the murals, funded by local donations as a centennial project.

Johnson City

Blanco County seat at junction of U.S. 281 and Hwy. 290. Population 1,191.
One walk. (See also Stonewall.)

Johnson City gained national recognition in 1963 when native son Lyndon
Baines Johnson took office as the thirty-sixth president of the United States.
Samuel Ealy Johnson Sr., LBJ's grandfather, owned land on the Pedernales River
(pronounced PERdenales). After the Civil War, when there was a demand for
cattle up north, Sam Sr. and his brother Jesse Thomas (known as Tom) began
running 2,500 to 3,000 head of cattle at a time up the Chisholm Trail. They
bought Spanish Longhorns on credit for $6 to $10 a head in Texas, sold them
for five times as much in Kansas, and made a lot of money, until a glutted market
brought the price down. After losing his money in the cattle business, Sam Sr.
sold his property to James Polk Johnson and moved to Buda where his son Sam
Jr., father of LBJ, was born.

The County of Blanco organized in 1858 with the town of Blanco, then the
geographic center, as county seat. Boundary changes later put Blanco at the
southern end of the county. With most of the population there this was not a
problem, but as settlers moved northward so did the need for a new, centralized
county seat. The first election to do this, held in 1876, failed by just 7 votes. A
second attempt lost by 15. In 1879 settlers around the Pedernales held a Fourth
of July barbecue to select a town site. James Polk Johnson was one of three who
offered to donate land. His was chosen and the new town given his name. The
town and its economy continued to grow. Finally, in 1890, Johnson City won
the election to become the county seat by a whopping 65 votes.

Sam Johnson Sr. returned in 1889, settling in Stonewall as a farmer. Sam Jr.
took over the farm, running it until elected a state legislator in 1904, a position
he held for twelve years. He married Rebekah Baines and their son, Lyndon
Baines Johnson, was born on the farm in 1908. Sam Jr. moved his family into
Johnson City in 1913 when LBJ was five years old. LBJ learned the "political
facts of life" as a boy of 10 when he went on the campaign trail with his father.
He later sat with his father during legislative sessions. Rebekah Johnson was
one of the few college-educated women in Johnson City. She taught elocution
and debating techniques from her home. Influenced by both his father and
mother, LBJ taught school before entering politics.

In 1937 he won a seat in Congress when Johnson City still had no
modern utilities. LBJ sponsored legislation to establish the Pedernales
Electric Cooperative, receiving power from the Lower Colorado River

Former President Lyndon B. Johnson's boyhood home in Johnson City is now part of LBJ National Historical Park.

Authority. As U. S. senator he saw that telephone service in Johnson City progressed from magnetic box phones to dial service and, eventually, to worldwide service. In 1960 he became vice president, and after the assassination of President John F. Kennedy in 1963 was sworn in as president. Throughout his career he promoted better education. During his administration Congress passed more than 60 education bills, including Head Start. He is also credited with 43 National Park bills. While in office he brought guests from around the world to Johnson City and Stonewall's Texas Summer White House. A federal building was built across from his boyhood home. He later donated Johnson properties in both Stonewall and Johnson City to the National Park System and gave money to buy the land and four remaining structures of the old Johnson settlement in Johnson City. Both are run by the park service. Since Lady Bird Johnson passed away in 2007, the ranch home has been turned over to the park service for regular tours.

Tourism brought new life to Johnson City. The visitor center offers two fine films: one on LBJ and one on Lady Bird, as well as informative exhibits. A walk through the old Johnson settlement gives the visitor insight into the lifestyle of earlier times.

JOHNSON CITY WALK

LBJ National Historical Park, LBJ's boyhood home, town square, Johnson Settlement. 1.6 miles, mostly flat. Park at the park visitor center. Public restrooms at visitor center, boyhood home, Johnson Settlement. Several restaurants in vicinity.

❶ From the Visitor Center walk down G Street to the boyhood home. (Tours on the half hour daily from 9 a.m. to 5 p.m.)

Sam Ealy Johnson Jr. bought this 1901 Victorian-style house and almost two acres in 1913 and moved his family from Stonewall. It is now restored to its 1920s appearance and part of LBJ National Historical Park.

❷ Continue down G Street to the courthouse square.

If only all post offices were as attractive as this, of native limestone! Across Main on the left is the Johnson City Park *Life Magazine* dedicated to Lady Bird in 1965 to honor her national beautification efforts.

At the corner of Pecan is the 1894 Blanco County jail (marker). The county's first courthouse was set up at the Johnson store, and its basement was used as a jail. Because it was damp and unhealthy, the Commissioner's Court ordered this new jail built. It is perhaps the oldest jail in Texas still in use, and one of the smallest, with a capacity of seven inmates. The interior has been modified to meet today's standards.

The building to the right of the jail was the hardware store Melvin Winters opened in 1948. His son, Nelson, ran the store, a wonderful step back into earlier times, until his retirement.

The courthouse itself (marker), designed in Classical Revival style by San Antonio architect Henry T. Phelps, dates from 1916.

❸ Continue down G Street.

The red brick Courthouse Annex was once a wool and mohair warehouse.

No. 202 G Street, the 1940s two-story building, was a doctor's office.

No. 204, Smith's Tin House, a bed-and-breakfast, was once the offices of the local newspaper, the *Record-Courier,* edited by Rebekah Johnson with Lyndon working as "printer's devil," a position below apprentice.

The large house at the end of the block belonged to Dr. Barnwell. The upstairs served as Johnson City's first hospital, and, for a time was the only hospital in the county.

❹ Turn left on Cypress, then left again on Nugent.

At the intersection with Nugent is a marker for Dr. Odiorne's office. The doctor used native herbs for medicines. He died from burns received when his lab exploded. Nugent was Johnson City's original Main Street.

The modern telephone building replaces the Byer home that served as the town's first telephone exchange.

The library is two older buildings joined together. The left was the law office of J. B. Goar. You can see it has the original facade. The right was Crider's Cafe. Its facade was added when the two were connected.

At the end of the block is the old Pearl Hotel built by James Polk Johnson.

Across Pecan Street, on the left, is the Johnson City Bank. Starting as the Johnsons' mercantile store, it has seen many changes and at various times was the Old Courthouse, Crider's Store, and the Opera House. James Polk Johnson designed and built several stone buildings around town. He died in 1885 during construction of this one. In 1890, when Johnson City won the election as county seat, this became the "temporary" courthouse. The new courthouse was ready in 1916.

In 1920 the Johnsons sold the store to W. E. Withers, who ran a store on the lower floor. On the upper floor he put an Opera House used also as community hall, meeting room, and dance hall. The town held graduation ceremonies, showed movies, and even conducted church services in the Opera House. Rebekah Baines Johnson held her plays and debates there. J. N. Crider and his son Rob owned the building from 1924 to 1928.

In 1929 the building was renovated with a bank on the south side, a hotel lobby in the center, a restaurant on the north side, and a private club in the basement. A doctor kept office hours in the hotel each Friday. Through the changes the hotel and restaurant remained. The Johnson City Electric Company operated from the basement prior to the establishment of the Pedernales Electric Coop. By 1964 the bank used all of the first floor.

In 1970 LBJ bought the buildings and maintained an office in the basement. He sold the bank the same year but kept his office.

Continuing up Nugent, on the right, the first building was formerly the Crider Garage where Model-T Fords were sold.

Next was the Casparis Cafe, said to be where LBJ developed his taste for chili, a pot of which always simmered on the stove at the White House.

The lot next door was a favorite gathering place for domino players. Here LBJ learned to play and often used the game to relieve stress.

The next building was a confectionery. Next to it, covered by pressed tin to resemble stone, was the barber shop. Both have pressed tin ceilings.

No. 106, on the left, is the Friendly Bar, opened as the King Casparis Palace Saloon in 1916 only to shut down two years later with Prohibition. At least the front doors closed. Favored customers could still get in through the back, where the locals enter today. In 1936 Guthrie Gibson reopened the place as the Friendly Bar. For $50 he bought the stained glass and mahogany soda fountain, built in 1883 by Ed Frederich of San Antonio, from the Davis Drug Store across the street. Clem Lindig took over the Friendly Bar in 1951, running it until at least 1978. In recent years it became the Friendly Bar Antiques and Ice Cream Parlor. Then in 1994 Linda (Lizzy) Wiles came in for a soda, liked the place, and decided it should be a friendly bar again. She talked the owner into selling. She had Austin artist Nathan Jensen paint a mural depicting Friendly Bar patrons "past, present and future," with Clem and herself behind the bar. She did such a good job of making it "friendly" that some customers have dubbed it "The Too Damn Friendly Bar."

Back, now, on the right side of Nugent is the 1949 yellow brick City Drug Store, which closed in 1997. The original two-story wooden building with a doctor's office and Masonic Lodge upstairs was destroyed by fire.

⑤ Cross Main and continue up Nugent.

The corner building on the left across Main was a general store and later a wool and mohair warehouse. The stone building to its left was the first bank in

Johnson City. The owner of the general store started the bank to protect his own money.

On the right across Main is the steam-powered cotton gin and grist mill James Polk Johnson opened in the 1880s. A 1901 addition used stones from a rock fence at the Johnson settlement. George Croft bought it in 1937 and converted the mill to produce agricultural feed. A mechanical genius, many of his innovative and unique pieces of equipment are still around. The mill remained in operation into the 1980s. In the early 1990s Austin architect and artist Charles Trois bought and renovated the property into restaurants and shops. Nathan Jensen painted the tower mural. At this writing there is still a restaurant but no shops at the mill.

❻ Turn right on Elm Street to the entrance gate of the Johnson Settlement.

In 1862 Tom Johnson moved onto the property as caretaker. His home was headquarters for the Johnson brothers' cattle drive business. As they prospered Sam bought more acreage. The Pedernales and Blanco river valleys provided ample water and pasture land for their cattle business.

When LBJ gave the National Park Service the money to purchase this land, four of the original buildings still stood. The park opened in 1970.

Walking ahead on the road, at the first fork bear right. Stay on the right at the next fork.

A small herd of Longhorn and other cattle graze in corrals that once stretched from here to the river. The windmill, water tank, and cooler house were added by James Polk Johnson.

Next is the barn he built in 1875. His two-story frame house was destroyed by fire in 1918.

Continuing along, the large stone barn is one John Bruckner built after he bought some of the property in 1884.

The log cabin dates from 1867. The left portion was built by the first owners, James and Martha Provost. Tom Johnson added the breezeway and right portion. Sam Sr. brought his bride to live here.

Stay on the path to the right, past the chuck wagon.

The exhibit center is next along the trail. It offers an excellent photographic display of cattle drives and frontier life.

❼ Exit the settlement, cross the bridge over Town Creek, and follow Lady Bird Lane back to the visitor center.

Kendalia

Between Boerne and Blanco at FM 473 and FM 3160. Population 76.
One walk.

In the 1840s a small community of Anglos, mostly from the south, settled along Curry Creek about four miles south of here. They worked as charcoal burners and cedar cutters. With the Civil War, many returned to fight with their families in the south.

In 1883 Carl Gustav Vogel, editor of Boerne's Union Land Register, bought land on Curry Creek and built a cotton gin and a gristmill. Other German immigrants followed. After a flood wiped out the mills, Vogel had a surveyor, D. W. Grady, lay out a town at a higher location that he named Kendalia. Whether he named it for George Wilkins Kendall or for the county that was named for Kendall is lost to history. The survey shows a square, college, park, garden, church, and school, plus many blocks for development. The post office at Curry Creek closed in 1895 and records were transferred to Kendalia. By the early 1900s the town was prospering with several stores, a hotel, garage, doctor, and churches. But it never grew to Vogel's expectations. The college, park and most streets never materialized and are now pasture land.

Today, some of the early stores and homes still stand. The population remains small but steady, big enough to support two small churches and a library. The Kendalia Store and Post Office is the local gathering place. A small café serves breakfast tacos, hamburgers and a daily lunch special. Homemade brownies are usually available, too. Besides being the local gathering place, the Kendalia Store is a designated stop on a major cross-country bicycle trail. It's a rare day that several bicyclists don't stop by to take a break.

KENDALIA WALK

Historic buildings and homes. Almost one mile, flat. Park at Kendalia Store. No public restrooms. Limited menu at store cafe.

❶ With back to the store, turn right on Hwy. 473.

The first store at this location was an octagon-shape, traditional to Europe. The left portion of the present store was originally a home.

❷ Turn right on Arthur Street.

Across Martin on the left was a blacksmith shop built in 1905 by Joe Woods and later owned by Ben Jonas. In a 1954 interview, Jonas stated, "These days I

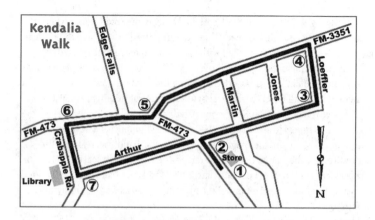

do every kind of blacksmithing except shoe horses." He claimed he'd probably shod more horses than any other man in the county and had had too many broken bones from it. His timed record for putting on a round of shoes was 14 minutes.

The rock building on the right was the Lawhon store, where you could buy anything from a pin to farm equipment. A two-story boarding house behind it was torn down and materials used to build two houses in Blanco.

A small herd of goats graze and gambol in the lot just past the old Lawhon Store.

The Community Church (marker) was originally the Methodist Church. All denominations meet there now. In the back to the right are two charming Sunday school rooms built in more recent years. To the right of those, the small building is a well house.

❸ Turn left on Loeffler Street.

As you approach the road ahead, the large flat area across the road was a favorite grazing spot for the town's free-roaming livestock. This sometimes caused problems, of course. It was the early 1950s before fences kept livestock at home.

❹ Turn left on FM 3351.

Before the railroad came out to the Hill Country, lumber, predominantly cypress, was milled at plants along the river. The buildings have stood so well because cypress does not rot. Some of the buildings here are a combination of factory-milled lumber brought in by train and locally milled cypress.

On the right, just before the Kendalia Halle, is the small home where the Valdez family of 13 children lived. They couldn't afford to go inside the Halle to attend the dances, so they danced with each other outside in their yard.

Kendalia Halle dates back well over 100 years. In earlier days, dance halls were a family affair. The kids curled up along the sidelines to sleep while Mom and Pop danced all night to the local band, stopping at midnight to eat.

A few years ago Tom McKenney, a retired oil field welder, sometimes played at the dances here. He and his wife, Glenda, were looking for a new enterprise. One night, sitting on the stage playing with the band, he realized that he wanted to run the dance hall, so he talked the owner into leasing it to him. The McKenneys ran the Halle until late 1999. The dance hall has been updated with new floor and ceiling fans. Dances are held the second Saturday of each month.

As the red granite marker on the next building indicates, this is the 1911 George Elbel store. At one time it was the town's meeting place. Traditionally, on Wednesday night the farmers and ranchers brought in their cream and eggs and caught up on the local news. Elbel also ran a garage, cotton gin, dance hall, and the first telephone exchange. Besides using factory-milled lumber, Elbel imported iron and tin work to decorate the front of his store, the most elegant in town.

Next to the Elbel store is the Elbel home.

Across on the left, the Feed Store was originally Conrad Bechtold's Kendalia Garage and Hardware. In the early 1900s Bechtold had a cotton gin behind the garage. This enterprising man bought the dance hall in 1927, opened a general store in 1929 and a hardware store next to his garage in 1931, and later bought the Elbel store.

❺ Turn right on FM 473.

Edge Falls Road leads to Edge Falls, on the 1869 homestead of G. W. Edge and described as "a green, cool place even during a hot dry summer." A spring bubbles out of an opening over tall rock cliffs, falling to form a pool in a large sinkhole. This was a popular place to swim until it was closed to the public in the 1970s after an accident.

Where the volunteer fire department is located, to the right between Edge Falls Road and Crabapple Road, is the area platted for Vogel Square. It never materialized.

Across Crabapple Road on the left is the library. A frame schoolhouse, moved here from Mountain Gap, stood where the little merry-go-round is now. After it burned, the town built a new school of limestone block, now the library.

Florence Richcreek Walker, who moved to Kendalia in 1949, was instrumental in starting the library. She also collected a history of Kendalia for the library archives.

A historical marker telling about George Wilkins Kendall was placed here in 1965, though Kendall never lived here.

❻ **Turn left on Crabapple Street, then left on Arthur Street to the start.**

Kerrville

Kerr County seat, 2 miles west of I-10 at Hwys. 16 and 27. Population 20,425. One walk, plus parks.

In 1848 Joshua Brown and 10 other settlers established a shingle-making camp here. Discouraged by Indian raids, they left. In 1852, accompanied this time by soldiers, Brown returned with a small colony of settlers from Tennessee and Mississippi. As more families arrived, Brown donated four acres of land to establish a town named in honor of his friend James Kerr, a Republic of Texas soldier, statesman, surveyor, doctor, and the first American to settle on the Guadalupe River. Kerr, who made his home in Gonzales, never visited his namesake town.

The reestablished shingle industry grew. Mercantile and freighting enterprises followed. Kerr County organized in 1856 with Kerrville as county seat. In 1852 Charles Schreiner, 14, came with his parents from France. After serving with the Texas Rangers and the Confederate Army, he returned and opened a general mercantile store. This began a business enterprise that grew to include retail, wholesale, banking, ranching, marketing, and brokering operations, the catalyst of Kerrville's early prosperity.

The Civil War slowed progress here as elsewhere in the Hill Country. During Reconstruction, San Antonio's need for lumber, produce, and craftsmen, plus the expansion of ranching, led to a new economic boom for Kerrville. Captain Schreiner, with his brother-in-law Casper Real, brought sheep and goats to the area, eventually making it the mohair capital of the world. The Schreiner family contributed heavily to get a railroad to the town so they could ship their wool and mohair. Arrival of the San Antonio and Aransas Pass Railroad in 1887 further accelerated the town's growth. Kerrville soon evolved into a supply and shipping center for the middle and upper parts of the Hill Country, leading it to become the medical, recreational, cultural, and educational hub of a multi-county area. In 1918 Schreiner contributed again when he founded Schreiner Institute, now Schreiner University.

Kerrville continues to grow. In the 1990s the Wall Street Journal described it as one of the wealthiest small towns in America. Outstanding among things to see is the Cowboy Artists of America Museum on Hwy. 173 south of town (closed Monday). A major event is the Texas State Arts and Crafts Fair the last weekend in May on the Schreiner University campus. Beginning the same weekend is the Kerrville Folk Festival, the largest and longest-running celebration of original songwriters, which draws performers and fans from around the world. Many of its early, then-unknown performers are now known nationally.

KERRVILLE WALK

Historic downtown Kerrville, Hill Country Museum (Monday through Saturday, 10 a.m to 4:30 p.m., admission). 1.7 miles, flat. Park on Jefferson near Earl Garrett Street. Public restrooms at start in courthouse, visitor center at 715 Water Street, library on Water Street, all if open. Several restaurants along walk.

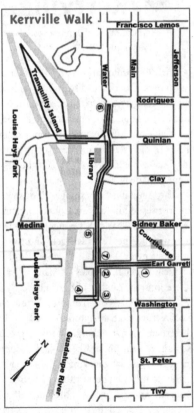

❶ **From courthouse square walk down Earl Garrett Street toward river.**

Although the county organized in 1856, it was 1876 before a courthouse was built. The present courthouse is the fourth built on the square and dates from 1926.

No. 241L Earl Garrett, on the corner of Main, is the 1887 Guthrie Building, originally home to Robert Guthrie's newspaper the *Kerrville Eye*, still later, the *Kerrville Mountain Sun* published by J. E. Grinstead, and from 1900 to 1921 the Guthrie Hotel.

No. 211L, designed by San Antonio architect Alfred Giles in 1890, housed the post office until 1916. Mrs. C. C. Butt, a widow, and her son Howard E. Butt (H.E.B.), ran a grocery here from then until 1926. The Masonic Lodge No. 697 met upstairs.

No. 201L, at the corner of Water Street, was the 1890s Barlemann Saloon. Through several owners, a saloon remained to 1922, when R. H. Chaney bought it for a confectionery store. Remodeled as a restaurant in 1995, its upstairs tenants have included city and medical offices.

In the middle of the intersection at Earl Garrett and Water streets is the Heritage Star. A plaque on the corner gives the history of this spot, head of the Chisolm Trail. It has always been the town's gathering spot for special events.

❷ Turn left on Water Street.

No. 820 Water Street, the two-story Fawcett Building, dates from around the turn of the century. Willis A. Fawcett Sr. bought half interest in a furniture business. Two years later he owned all of it. By 1907, due to his reputation for "square deals," the business had grown big enough to buy this building. At first the store occupied the first floor, with the second floor leased to fraternal organizations. By 1914 the furniture store had expanded into the whole building, and closed in the mid-1970s.

No. 824 was once a bakery owned by Mr. Ahnard. C. H. Wolfmueller expanded the business in 1922.

There's a legend about a small frame store the Jackson brothers owned at Water and Washington but closed when they joined the Confederate Army. Planks in the corner saturated by salt stored there were discovered by a herd of Longhorn cattle. In their eagerness to lick it from the planks they loosened the walls from the foundation and the store collapsed.

❸ Cross Water Street.

At the back of the One Schreiner Center parking lot a marker describes the saw and grist mill Christian Dietert and Balthasar Lich built on this 30-foot bluff over the river. A dam provided power to a waterwheel placed inside the edge of the cliff for protection. Dietert also opened mills in Comfort and Fredericksburg. Captain Schreiner later bought the mill and enlarged it.

❹ Retrace steps to Water Street and turn left.

In the 700 block of Water is the Arcadia Theater that Bart Moore and Edward Patton built for silent movies and stage productions in 1926. Big names in vaudeville and theater played here. It operated as a movie theater until 1988

Charles Schreiner had Alfred Giles design his 1879 Romanesque Revival home, now Kerrville's Hill Country Museum.

and reopened in 1996 as a theater for live performances.

Among various "happenings," there is one seat in the front row that is always clean when the other seats are dusty. Some think the ghost might be that of Norman Hines, who managed the theater for over twenty years and took his own life there.

No. 715 is a branch of the Kerrville Visitor Center. Note the carved pineapple detail on the cornice. (Restrooms available here.)

No. 709 is an Alfred Giles building dating from the 1870s. It served as the first wool warehouse owned by Captain Schreiner.

No. 707, the Davis building, still has its original pressed tin ceiling and Mexican terrazzo floor. The roof overhang is also pressed tin.

No. 701, at Sidney Baker Street, was originally the St. Gregory Hotel. J. L. Pampell bought it in 1901 for his drug store, ice cream parlor, and candy store. He operated a 450-seat opera house on the second floor. The drug store eventually closed, but under various owners the old-fashioned soda fountain, with its beautiful wood furnishings, continued to serve refreshing ice cream cones and sodas to locals and tourists through 1999. Pampell's is now a restaurant and bar, but at lunchtime an old-fashioned soda fountain menu prevails.

❺ Cross Sidney Baker and continue ahead.

No. 529 is the home San Antonio architect Atlee B. Ayres designed for A. C. Schreiner in 1906.

From the parking lot behind the Butt-Holdsworth Memorial Library steps descend steeply to a bridge across the river to Louise Hays Park. Midway across is Tranquility Island, a pleasant 0.8 mile roundtrip walk. Turtles are often spotted basking on outcroppings of rock and logs.

No. 433 was Kerrville's first bowling alley, built by Louis Schreiner for his daughter May Louise. The alley and equipment are now part of Schreiner Institute at Schreiner University.

No. 425 is the 1914 Whitfield Scott Schreiner home, also designed by Ayres. Schreiner specified that each of the 10 rooms have four windows.

No. 405 is the 1897 home Alfred Giles designed for Charles Sr. to give to his son Charles Jr. as a wedding gift. Originally one story, the second floor, arched porch, and tile roof were added in 1927.

❻ Turn around and retrace your steps to Earl Garrett. Turn left to cross Water Street and walk up the left side of Earl Garrett.

Across Water Street at Sydney Baker is the Sid Peterson Memorial Hospital. When it opened in 1948 a service station on the corner helped support the hospital.

At the corner of Water and Earl Garrett is where the Schreiner Department Store did business for 138 years, from 1869 until it closed in 2007. The present building dates from 1969.

No. 226L Earl Garrett is the Hill Country Museum in the 1879 Romanesque Revival home Alfred Giles designed for Captain Charles Schreiner. Schreiner brought masons and stone carvers from Italy to work on the intricate exterior designs. Even the brackets on the drainpipe carry out the theme. The home was built in three phases; the last, completed in 1897, added the porches and archways. The home's parquet floor is made from eight different hardwoods. Downstairs the museum offers examples of furnishings typical of this period, while upstairs is an eclectic collection of Hill Country memorabilia.

Next to the Schreiner home is the Kerr Arts and Cultural Center in a former post office. (At Main, to the right, is the Hill Country Cafe, a local favorite for downhome-cooking.)

Back at the courthouse square, cater-corner across Jefferson is the First Presbyterian Church. Kerrville's first church was the 1885 Union Church on Junction Highway, shared by several congregations. In 1925 sole ownership was granted to First Christian Church. Presbyterians organized their own congregation in 1888. Their first church, built the same year, was replaced in 1923 by this Beaux Arts style sanctuary that is listed as a Texas Historic Landmark. The captain's eldest son, Aimé Charles Schreiner, and his wife, Myrta Scott, had the church built as a gift to the congregation.

Three blocks east at Jefferson and Tivy is the 1890 D. H. Comparette home, now a favorite restaurant known as the Jefferson Street Café.

ADDITIONAL WALKS

Riverside Nature Center at 150 Francisco Lemos St. presents a self guided tour of native trees, flowers, and grasses on three-fifths acre overlooking the river. Open daily from dawn to dusk. Handicap accessible.

The Chervil-Schreiner State Park on Hwy. 173 and Loop 534 has hiking and hike/bike trails. Entrance fee.

Kyle

I-35 between San Marcos and Austin. Population 5,314. One walk.

In 1880 Jay Gould extended his International and Great Northern Railroad south toward San Antonio. Bypassing Mountain City, he laid track to the east along the border of the blackland prairie farmland and the higher ranchland of the Balcones Escarpment. Two new towns sprung up along the route: Buda and Kyle. Not to be left behind, Mountain City folk loaded their homes and businesses on wagons and moved them to the new towns.

Fergus Kyle and his father-in-law, Judge David E. Moore, deeded 200 acres to the railroad for the new town. Fergus was the son of early settler Claiborne Kyle and his wife, Lucy Bugg, who moved to Texas from Mississippi in 1844. Kyle Field at Texas A&M University is named for Fergus's son, Edwin, who served as dean of the School of Agriculture and also as ambassador to Guatemala. Martin Groos surveyed and laid out the town. On Oct. 14, 1880, lots went on sale from under a shady live oak tree, known ever since as the Auction Oak. The railroad offered prospective buyers free rides into town. Families donned their best clothes, packed picnic baskets, and turned out for a big celebration. Most of the lots were sold that day. Within a year Kyle was a self-sufficient town and an important trade center. The first business to open was Tom Martin's saloon and meat market. After four more saloons had opened, Kyle gained the reputation as a wild frontier town. The good citizens of Kyle solved this problem by voting out saloons in 1899.

Nicholas C. Schlemmer, a New Braunfels station agent, was appointed postmaster for the new town. He arrived on a dreary day in November and was not impressed with his new post. When he heard the Mountain City postmaster, William E. Roach, wanted the job, Schlemmer caught the next train out and let Roach have the post. In 1884 Schlemmer came through Kyle again, found things more to his liking, and opened a mercantile business on Center Street. Before long he became postmaster. In 1887 some of the townspeople decided they should have a waterworks. They pumped water for two miles from the Blanco River to a large wooden tank. Each customer paid a flat rate plus extra for each head of livestock and a bathtub, if they had one.

Just as the railroad had pulled folks away from Mountain City, so did trucking bring an end to the railroad boom and the railroad towns. Kyle faded into a quiet, self-sufficient little town. Today it is experiencing new growth as subdivisions developing along its outskirts attract commuters from Austin.

The 1850 Clairborne Kyle log house and the Kyle Cemetery are on Old Stagecoach Road (to the left at the end of Center Street). You will pass the St. Vicente Cemetery on the right and the Skyview Cemetery on the left, then come to a red street sign on the right for the Claiborne Kyle Log House; the cemetery is on the left a bit farther up. The house is the only known linear four-pen log home surviving in Texas, according to Terry Jordan in *Texas Log Buildings: A Folk Architecture*. It cannot be seen from the road, but it is open on the first Sunday of the month, May through August, from 2 to 5 p.m. On the first weekend in April the Kyle Log House Commission holds the "Blooms above the Blanco" open house there. On the fourth Saturday in September, they hold Kyle Log House Fried Chicken Day as a fund-raiser for its upkeep. In the late 1840s cowboys working for the Kyles found an unidentified man hanging from a tree on the property. They cut him down and buried him under the tree. When Colonel Kyle donated 15 acres for a cemetery it included this spot. Willie Parks, an orphan adopted by the Kyles, was the first recorded burial.

The depot built at Center and Front streets for the International and Great Northern Railroad in 1882 is now the home of the Kyle Area Chamber of Commerce and Visitors Bureau.

KYLE WALK

Historic buildings and homes. 1.4 miles, flat. Park at City Hall/ Community Building on Burleson. Public restrooms in building (when open). Several restaurants in town.

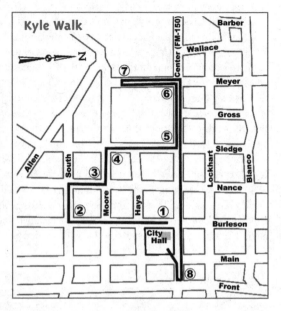

❶ With your back to building, turn left on Burleson.

This building, dating from 1912, was originally the town's community building. In 1976 the Bicentennial Committee restored it. Later City Hall moved here from across the street at the Young store. It has returned to its original use as a community center.

To the right at the first corner (Miller Street) is the former Young Mercantile Store (marker), Kyle's first permanent building. David Alexander Young moved his business from Mountain City and built this stone store. Young, a civic leader, land developer, and church school teacher, as well as store keeper, was described by the local paper's editor as "clever, genial, and a fair dealer." As a civic building it has been a fire station and city hall, and now houses offices for the Texas Game Warden Association.

Up Miller Street on the right is a stone building that was the store's milk storage shed. Farther up, and across from it, stood another stone building that was the town's first livery stable.

❷ Turn right on South Street, then right again on Nance.

No. 302 Nance is the two-story frame house of Otto Groos, son of Martin Groos, who laid out the town. Otto moved here from New Braunfels and opened a store. Later he went into real estate, helped form the Kyle Bank, and organized the Kyle Water Works and the Kyle Oil Company.

❸ Turn left on Moore.

No. 408 More, at the corner of Sledge, dates from 1908. Its last owner, P. J. Allen, was known throughout Texas for his parade floats and holiday displays. His grandfather, P. Hansbraugh Allen, known locally as P, was the first Anglo child born in Hays County. He died in 1938. P.J. had a short career as a dancer on the Broadway stage before establishing a commercial design business in San Antonio. In 1958 he moved his operations to this house, bought by his father in 1943. He did his prefabricating work here and hauled it to the required site for assembly. His work received many awards, including eight out of nine at one parade. Remnants of his floats still existed in the long shed on Moore until P.J.'s death in recent years.

❹ Turn right on Sledge Street.

On the left is the Auction Oak (marker just beyond). Behind it is the 1925 William Groos home on the site of a Kyle Seminary dormitory. In its early days Kyle did not have a reliable public school. Two Baptist ministers established Kyle Seminary on land donated by the railroad. Two years later the San Marcos Baptist Association made it a denominational school. The campus started with one two-story building with an observatory. Two more buildings were added later, one as a dormitory and the other for classrooms. In 1889 the main building burned and in 1890 fire destroyed the classroom building, leaving only the dormitory.

The Seminary closed in 1890, the property was sold, and the money was donated to the public school system. The A. O. Duty family used the old dorm as their home for 20 years. The Groos family tore that down to build this imposing brick home.

❺ Turn left on Center.

No. 501 W. Center, at the corner of Sledge, is the 1895 Wallace home. Rockdale resident Hiram Craig Wallace, searching for a new site for his lumberyard, arrived on the first train to cross the Colorado River. Deciding to settle in Kyle, he loaded the contents of his lumberyard into five boxcars and shipped them here. His wife, Julia, a nurse, served as midwife before the town acquired a doctor. Every Tuesday Julia got up at 4 a.m. and baked bread to distribute to the needy.

No. 601 W. Center was the home of Fergus Kyle's daughter Mary Kyle Hartson. At age 76 she was elected mayor of Kyle by write-in vote and remained in office from 1937 to 1946. During her tenure, Hartson claimed, "We balanced the budget and cleaned up the town." When she felt she had everything under

Noted author Katherine Anne Porter lived between the ages of two and eleven in her grandfather's home at 508 Center St., now restored as the Katherine Anne Porter Literary Center.

control she retired. From 1944 to 1946 women held all but one city office, that of city marshal. When the man holding that office wouldn't resign, they chose to ignore him so they could declare themselves an "all women government."

⑥ Turn left on Meyer.

No. 106R S. Meyer, a 1912 yellow brick, is the Richmond home. Thomas Rollin Richmond's father and grandfather were cotton farmers. During his time at the USDA and as a Texas A & M researcher he solved many problems for cotton farmers and helped upgrade the quality of cotton.

No. 200 is the 1912 Robert John Sledge Jr. home. It combines Queen Anne Victorian architecture with a Classical Revival entryway. Sledge Sr. raised cotton and grain, as well as cattle that commanded top prices at market. In 1880, Sledge Sr. invited some German immigrants, whom he considered "hard working, home-loving, and law abiding," to move to Kyle and work for him. Being thrifty, they soon owned their own farms. Sledge Jr. ran a mercantile store at Center and Main Streets. His son, William Terrell, was a Rhodes Scholar who returned to Kyle in 1929 after his father's death. As of this writing, Terrell's widow still lived here.

⑦ Retrace yours steps to Center Street, cross carefully, and turn right on Center.

No. 508 Center St. (at Groos) is the childhood home of the Pulitzer Prize and National Book Award winning writer Katherine Anne Porter. It was built by Katherine Anne Porter's grandfather, Asbury Porter, not long after Kyle was founded in 1880, is listed on the National Register of Historic Places and was dedicated as a National Literary Landmark by Laura Bush in 2002. The home is leased as the Katherine Anne Porter Literary Center by Texas State University in cooperation with the Hays County Preservation Associates.

Callie Russell Porter was born in 1890. After her mother died when she was two, her father and his four children moved here to live with his widowed mother. When his mother died in 1901 they moved to San Antonio. Callie married at 16 and was divorced after nine years. She adopted her grandmother's name and became Katherine Anne Porter, left Texas at 28, traveled widely and married often. Her first book of short stories, *Flowering Judas and Other Stories,* was published in 1930. In 1965 *Collected Stories,* including "Pale Horse, Pale Rider," won a Pulitzer Prize. In 1962, at 71, she wrote *Ship of Fools,* a widely acclaimed novel that became a movie. She was among the first female writers to enjoy wide success, according to Texas State University's Thomas Grimes, who considers her one of the classic American short story writers of the 20th century. She died in 1980.

At Sledge Street is the First Baptist Church (marker) founded at Mountain City in 1872. The congregation moved here after the advent of the railroad. When the 1880s church burned, this one replaced it in 1948.

Downtown Kyle begins at Burleson. Although many of the early buildings still exist, most have been altered, including new "modern" fronts. If you look closely you can see portions of the original architecture, particularly on the corner buildings.

The growth of subdivisions around Kyle has led to a revitalization of the downtown area along Center Street, with most of its historic buildings preserved. One major achievement has been restoration of the historic 1882 train depot at the northwest corner of Center and Front streets as the home of the Kyle Area Chamber of Commerce and Visitors Bureau.

❽ Cross Center Street and turn right back to the start.

A marker in the square gives a brief history of Kyle. The bell tower was donated by the family of John Wheeler Bunton, a signer of the Texas Declaration of Independence and one of seven who captured Santa Anna. As an adult, he decided to be baptized, and it is said the creek was dammed to get enough water to immerse this exceptionally tall man.

Leakey

Real County seat at US 83 and FM 337, 50 miles west of Bandera.
Population 387. One walk.

When I first visited Leakey (pronounced LAKE-ee) when scouting walks for the first edition of this book, it didn't appear to be a likely place. So I drove on. Some time later I read that the approach to Leakey on FM337 from Bandera and Vanderpool was one of the most scenic drives in all of Texas. So I took it, and found it to indeed be spectacular, and the hills deserving, as I'd read, to be called the Swiss Alps of Texas. Streams flowing from springs of the Edwards and Glen Rose limestone formations have carved a terrain of sharply dissected canyon lands. Both the Nueces and Frio rivers, from their respective headwaters in Real County, have cut deep canyons through the area, with elevations ranging from 1,500 feet in the valleys to 2,400 at the edge of the plateau. There was no direct route between the two canyons until FM 337 was completed to Camp Wood in 1948.

On reaching Leakey the second time, I took a closer look and discovered the Real County Museum, a treasure of a small museum; the friendly Frio Canyon Lodge Café, serving up great down-home food; an interesting cemetery; and a good thrift shop. Exploring further, one mile east on FM 337 I found the Frio Pecan Farm where, each October through December, you can observe different phases of the harvesting of eight varieties of pecans; interesting displays on pecan growing and harvesting can be seen any time of the year in the gift shop. Then, a few miles south down FM 1120 in Rio Frio, I located the impressive Landmark Oak, the second-largest live oak tree in Texas (historical marker). After that, the trip from Bandera to Leakey became one of my favorite outings.

Real (REE-al) County was formed in 1913 from parts of Edwards, Bandera and Kerr counties and named for Julius Real, the only Republican in the Texas Senate at that time. It lies on the southern edge of the Edwards Plateau. Evidence exists of human habitation around the Frio River sine prehistoric times. In recorded history, Lipan Apaches, Comanches and Tonkawas lived here. A number of legends about lost and abandoned silver mines in the area and tales of buried treasure still entice a few treasure hunters to the area.

When John Leakey and five other families settled near the site of some springs, it became known as Leakey Springs. Cypress shingles and water-powered lumber mills were early industries, as were raising cotton and corn. Ranching, especially raising Angora goats for mohair, later took over as the chief industry. By the early 1910s the area supported more Angora goats than any other area in Texas. In 1883 A. G. Vogel established a general store with the post office.

Economic changes through the years led to great fluctuations in Leakey's population, which fell from 218 in 1904 to 150 in 1926 and jumped to 700 in 1931 only to drop back to 150 just two years later. After a peak of 762 in 1956 it dropped again, to 387. Except that it may not have dropped. It's said that the Census Bureau sent someone from New York who didn't know the area and missed almost half the people. Recreational pastimes and ever-increasing tourism plus informed census takers should take the population back up with the next census.

LEAKEY WALK

Cafe, museum, churches, library, courthouse, cemetery. 1.2 miles flat, part without sidewalks, but little traffic. Ample street parking.

❶ Begin at the Frio Canyon Lodge Cafe. With your back to the cafe, turn right and walk along Hwy. 83 to the corner of Fourth Street.

The Frio Canyon Lodge, built with native limestone and cedar, dates from 1994. Its cafe is open 11 a.m.–9 p.m. daily except Monday in summer, Wednesday–Sunday 11 a.m.–3 p.m. in winter, 830-232-6800.

At the start of the walk, across the highway at 5th Street is the Frio Canyon Chamber of Commerce. Its design reflects its beginnings in the 1920s as a Sinclair filling station. It continued servicing automobiles into the 1980s.

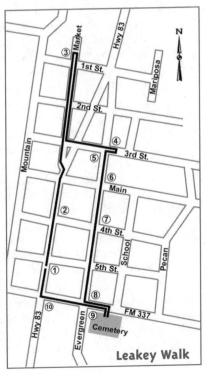

Leakey Walk

At Fourth Street is the classical revival Real County Courthouse, designed by H. A. Reuter and built of local limestone in 1917. There are three markers around the courthouse: a plaque commemorating establishment of the county seat, a marker noting 1918 as the date the county seat was made permanent and a granite memorial to county residents who lost their lives while serving in the military.

Continuing along Hwy. 83, at the corner of Main Street is a red granite marker commemorating John and Nancy Leakey as the "First White Settlers in Frio County" in 1853.

② Continue on Hwy. 83. At Main Street, Hwy. 83 bears to the right. Cross Hwy. 83 carefully. Cross Market Street, then turn right on Market Street to First Street. Cross First Street to the church.

Several early commercial buildings including the former movie theater run along this block of Main.

Across First Street at the end of Market is the Leakey United Methodist Church. As early as 1859 Andrew Jackson Potter, known as "The Fighting Parson," was holding Methodist services under a live oak tree at the home of the M. M. C. Pattersons in Rio Frio. By 1871 he had established a school nearby. Traveling preachers later arrived by horseback to conduct services in the Leakey home. Besides offering hospitality, their hostess often had to do their laundry.

Services moved into the Leakey schoolhouse after it was built in 1883. Brother Orceneth Fisher, the preacher, but died a few months later. His son Sterling took over at the age of 19 and served for four years. After that a steady stream of preachers arrived and left. In 1891, parishioners hauled wood and stone to build a church that remained in use until it was condemned about 1921. Services were held in the courthouse until the present church was dedicated the next year. The steeple was added in 1986. We were intrigued by the "windows," colored glass set in concrete to imitate stained glass.

③ Cross First Street to the other side of Market Street and walk back on Market to Third Street. Turn left on Third. The next street is Evergreen (no sign).

On the corner of Evergreen is a limestone rubble house that dates from 1934 and served as the Methodist parsonage into the 1960s. The first waterworks in Leakey was at this location, where Jesse Bell drilled a well and hauled water throughout the neighborhood.

Further down Third is an Apostolic church of rock and wood construction. A close examination of the walls reveals a fascinating collection of different kinds of rock. We discovered pieces of petrified wood and rocks imbedded with fossils. Deed records for the property state it can never be used for any purpose other than an Apostolic church. In trying to establish from what year the building dates, I asked a neighbor who was out watering his garden. "Well," he said, "it was here when I was born and I'm over 60." He referred me to an old-timer down the street, who told me, "It's been here since I was born, and I'm 74 years old." Next I turned to a 95-year-old member of the local historical society. At first she said, "It's been there as long as I can remember." But, after thinking about it, she remembered it was built when she was a teenager. Doing some math, I came up with the late 1920s.

❹ Retrace your steps to Evergreen and turn left to the Real County Historical Museum, open 10 a.m.–2 p.m. Fridays and Saturdays, closed January and February.

The museum was formed in 1986 to preserve the history and heritage of Real County. A volunteer docent will answer questions and show you around. On my first visit it was Darlene Buchanan Sharp, a descendant of early settlers. She knew the origin of every item in the museum and had a story to tell about most of them. The back wall of the museum is a reconstruction of the fireplace wall from her great-grandfather's cabin. The cedar logs are from the original cabin William and Frances Buchanan built in 1882 on Patterson Creek. The museum wanted to reconstruct the whole cabin, but it was too long for the lot. The limestone rocks used for the fireplace came from abandoned pioneer homes. Displays of typical rooms from early homes give a feel of living conditions in those days. A metal shed annex houses ranch equipment, and in the yard at the back is farm equipment and a log corncrib. On my next visit I met Susan Knight, whose mother, Rosetta Casey Nance, was one of the founders of the museum. The stone and cedar post fence around the museum is dedicated in her memory.

❺ Exit the museum, cross Evergreen and turn right.

On your left is the parking lot for the Leakey Public Library. On private property behind the lot you can see an old rock cistern.

In front of the library is a lovely spot to sit awhile under a beautiful live oak tree.

❻ Continue on Evergreen. Cross Main Street.

On the left across Main Street is a series of buildings that once housed a garage, barber shop, mercantile store and hotel.

No. 122 in 1913 was the Woodmen of the World building, and later the Real County State Bank. It is now the Big Springs Thrift Store, open Thursday, Friday and Saturday from 1 a.m. to 4 p.m. with two floors of fun shopping. Proceeds provide funds for the 7,000-acre Big Springs Ranch for Children, donated by Oma Bell Perry, whose mother always bid her to "keep the land just as the Indians left it." Parts now serve as a wilderness adventure park, sculpture part and working ranch, but a major purpose is being an intergenerational home providing long-term care and substitute parenting for abused and abandoned children. The ranch was named Big Springs because it is home to the largest single headwaters of the Frio River. It is also known by the nickname "Country of 1,100 Springs," a term made famous in the 1970s when its falls and river were featured in a TV advertising campaign.

❼ Continue on Evergreen.

Across on the right after Fourth Street, is the Bank of Frio Canyon. The next street (no sign) is Fifth Street. Across Fifth on your left is the Leakey Garden Club, not open to the public. On a mid-September day we enjoyed watching a variety of butterflies, including swallowtails, fluttering around, sipping nectar from the many flowering plants along the fence.

❽ At Hwy 337, cross carefully, turn left on 337, then right into the Leakey Cemetery.

On the left, just inside the cemetery, is the burial place of the town founders. Continue down the entrance road, curving left, and on around until the road returns to Hwy. 337.

❾ Exit the cemetery, turn left on Hwy. 337.

Immediately on your left is a historical marker relating the story of the first interments in the cemetery, Catherine R. McLauren and Allen Lease, the last white inhabitants of Real County to be killed by Indians.

❿ Continue up Hwy. 337 to the light, then turn right and cross Hwy. 337 back to the beginning.

Side trip: After refreshing yourself with the daily special at the Frio Canyon Lodge Café, consider a side trip to the Landmark Oak. To get there, head south on Hwy. 83. At the Texaco station, turn left on FM 1120 and drive about 5.7 miles to Rio Frio. Just past the post office, look on your right for the tree, just inside the fence of a white frame house. You can't mistake it, it's huge. There's a historical marker beside the road.

Luckenbach

Between Fredericksburg and Sisterdale on FM 1376. Population 3.
One walk.

Three Luckenbach brothers, Jacob, William, and August, moved to this area from Fredericksburg in 1852. William ran the South Grape Creek post office from 1854 to 1865. In 1886 August Engel, a Methodist circuit rider and teacher, opened a general store and post office on his homestead with his son August Jr. as postmaster. His sister Minna, who had just married Carl Albert Luckenbach, got to name it. She chose her husband's family name. Engel later moved the store and post office down the street and added a blacksmith shop, saloon, dance hall, and cotton gin. Although officially the post office was Luckenbach, people referred to it by the store's name and spoke of picking up mail "at Engel's." The saloon was torn down in 1954. Since then the back room of the store has served as a saloon. The dance hall was rebuilt in 1932. Luckenbach remained a neighborhood gathering place.

In 1972 folk humorist John Russell "Hondo" Crouch, with friends Kathy Morgan, and Guich Koock, bought 10 acres of land from the Engel family that included most of the town. In 1977 Willie Nelson and Waylon Jennings recorded the song "Luckenbach, Texas." That did it. Luckenbach was back on the map—and onto many a tourist itinerary. Crouch died in 1976. He left his share of the town to his daughter and her husband, Becky and Chris Graham. When Koock left he sold his share to the remaining partners.

The Luckenbach Store has some old stuff gathering dust on the shelves as well as new merchandise: souvenirs and Texas-made salsas and jellies. It's open every day except Thanksgiving and Christmas. There's a hat and boot shop open Friday, Saturday and Sunday in the former Sunday House out back. Dances are held about twice a month in the old dance hall, also rented for parties and weddings.

Luckenbach is still a gathering place, especially on weekends. There are bound to be musicians pickin' on the outdoor stage. So grab a cold one in the store, and—if it's Wednesday through Sunday—a pulled pork sandwich, some curly fries and a cherry limeade at the Feed Lot next to the dance hall. Then set yourself down under the 500-year-old live oak trees and enjoy the music. (In the winter months, Feed Lot is open only weekends.) The quiet weekends change when the crowds gather for Luckenbach's special events like its annual Fourth of July Picnic, Laborfest in September, the Ladies State Chili Bust in October, and the Valentine Day's "Hug In" on the Saturday closest to the 14th.

LUCKENBACH WALK

Engel house, store, and Sunday House. Flat. Park anywhere that makes sense. Public restrooms behind the store. (No map.)

There's not enough of Luckenbach for an extended walk. I'll just describe what's there.

❶ At one end of town is the Engel home (marker).

❷ A footbridge leads over almost always dry Snail Creek to a series of memorial fire pits dedicated to various entertainers. Here you can sit and chat, meditate, jam, whatever.

❸ Behind the pits, along South Grape Creek, the 1870s cotton gin stood until it was wiped out by the flood of 2002.

❹ Back across Snail Creek are the store and Sunday House Gift Shop.

❺ Across the road from the store is the dance hall.

And that, folks, is Luckenbach. If you feel the need for a real walk, try Grapetown down the road.

25 Marble Falls

On Hwy. 281, 50 miles east of Austin, 80 miles north of San Antonio. Population 6,000. Two walks.

For many Texans today, the name Marble Falls brings to mind not waterfalls but the Blue Bonnet Cafe; since 1929 people have driven from miles around to this citadel of down-home comfort food and great pies. Old-timers, however, remember the lovely falls, just upriver from Highway 281, which gave the town its name. As early as 1817 travelers made reference to the "marble falls" on the Colorado River that cascaded over a series of rock ledges from a height of twenty-two feet. Starting in the mid 1930s, a series of six dams was built upstream from Austin to produce electricity, control devastating floods and store water. With completion in 1951 of the last dams, the Max Starcke and Alvin Wirtz, the rising waters of Lake Marble Falls stilled the roar of these fabled falls. They can now only be seen during the infrequent times the lake is lowered for repairs and removal of debris, but even then they are partially filled by the buildup of silt.

Adam Rankin Johnson, a young Kentuckian, came to Burnet County (pronounced BURN-it) in 1854, then on the untamed Texas frontier, and took up surveying. When he viewed the falls, he realized their potential for powering a great industrial center. As the Burnet County Surveyor he surveyed vast areas of public land for the state. Johnson also provided supplies and mules for the Butterfield Overland Mail route and managed some of the stations most at risk from Indian attacks. When the election of Abraham Lincoln as president in November 1860 made it apparent that war would come, on New Year's Day 1861, thirty-one days before Texas seceded from the Union, Adam married 16-year-old Josephine Eastland. He made provisions for her during his coming absence and set his affairs in order. He returned to his native state, joined the Confederacy's Kentucky Cavalry as a scout and rose to the rank of general.

In 1865 Johnson was blinded by a rifle ball, captured by the Union army and held prisoner for six months. During his confinement he fell into a cellar and injured his leg. After the war he returned to Burnet, blind, broke and lame but not disheartened. He fathered nine children, six of whom lived to adulthood. Although blind, his incredible recall of land in the area enabled him to carry on a thriving land office business, but he never gave up his idea of a city by the falls. Along with a group of investors he finally acquired the land needed. With his eldest son, Robert, serving as his eyes, Johnson began laying out his dream town from memory.

Unlike so many cities, Marble Falls did not grow up around a trading post or at a crossroads. It was platted as a town and simply sprang into being on July 12, 1887, when lots went on sale. Soon the town was the busy hub of local commerce. Adam Johnson's gracious family home at 119 Avenue G, with its stately columns and view over the falls, dates from the early 1890s. Later it was owned by Dr. George Harwood and his wife, Ophelia "Birdie" Crosby Harwood.

In 1917, Birdie Harwood was elected mayor of Marble Falls. Today that doesn't sound like anything unusual, but this was three years before the Nineteenth Amendment to the U.S. Constitution granted voting rights to women. Birdie was not only the first woman mayor in Texas, an all-male voting population elected her. She ran on a platform for "A bigger town, a better town a cleaner town and a more progressive town." Defending her reason for running she said, "A woman's duty is to her home and children. When she has raised them to take their place in the world, it is her duty to turn to her state and there help make it a fit, abiding place for them." From a financial standpoint, "Another reason I am running for office is because our wealthier citizens don't want the job, and a poor man cannot afford it." She later served as a municipal judge.

The Johnson/Harwood home has been at various times a cafe, offices, apartments and antique shops until, as a bed-and-breakfast, it became known as Liberty Hall. At this writing it once again houses offices.

Another natural phenomenon that led to the growth of Marble Falls is Granite Mountain, an 866-foot batholith of solid pink granite, a pocket of granite just west of town formed in prehistoric times when magma surged into pockets below the earth's surface and slowly cooled, forming granite. As the Llano Escarpment rose the earth over the granite washed away, exposing a granite dome with few fractures or seams. When the latter-day owners of Granite Mountain offered free stone to built the state capitol in Austin, Adam Johnson and others cinched the deal by donating land for a railroad spur to reach the mountain from the existing rail line. Convict labor laid the tracks and cut the 15,700 carloads of granite blocks shipped to Austin. Since then granite blocks have built the Galveston seawall and other projects throughout the nation and the world. Extension of the railroad spur to Marble Falls itself in 1889 brought further business and growth to the city.

Marble Falls in recent years has gained a reputation as a venue for live music. Music in this area, however, predates the city's founding, as pioneer settlers brought with them their musical instruments and fostered family bands and musical societies. Adolph Fuchs, a German immigrant and Lutheran minister who settled nearby in 1853, was a noted composer as was his grandson, Oscar J. Fox, whose nationally known compositions of Western music include *Oh Bury Me Not on the Lone Prairie* and *The Hills of Home*. A granite monument honors him at the hillside stop on Hwy. 281 south of the Colorado River bridge. Although the hills that inspired Fox are more developed now, the view as you crest the hill northbound is still awesome.

MARBLE FALLS WALK I

Historic buildings and The Falls on the Colorado Museum (open Thur., Fri. Sat., 10 a.m.–5 p.m.). Appx. 1 mile, mostly flat with sidewalks. Second and third streets are slightly downhill, Third Street has a short flight of steps or one can detour in the street. Ample free street parking, free public lot at Main and Third streets. Restrooms at Old Oak Plaza by tree and in museum. Several restaurants along route, including Blue Bonnet Cafe on Hwy. 281 between Second and Third streets (open Mon.–Thur. 6 a.m.–8 p.m., Fri.–Sat. 6 a.m.–9 p.m., Sun. 6 a.m.–1:45 p.m., Pie Happy Hour Mon.–Fri. 3–5 p.m.).

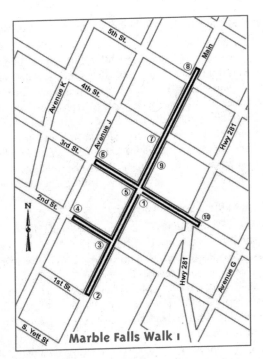

Marble Falls Walk ı

❶ With back to parking lot at Man and third streets, turn left, walk toward Second Street.

Along Main Street you'll find a variety of retail shops and art galleries interspersed with everyday businesses. Buildings date from as early as 1903.

The first building after crossing Second Street was for many years Hallman's Garage, which started by servicing carriages.

Next is the 1910 Post Office building, constructed of poured concrete and used until 1950 (historical marker).

Next is the new public library. Ask the librarian for books with photos of Main Street's earlier days, when there was no dividing strip and the street was wide enough for freight wagons to turn around.

❷ At First Street, cross Main and turn right back toward Second.

On this block are four small houses now businesses, built in 1904 by Malcolm Hiram Reed (known as M. H.), who arrived in marble Falls in 1893 as a young businessman. He ran a store, organized a bank, and dabbled in real estate before moving to Austin in 1908.

❸ At Second Street turn left and walk to the end of the block.

On the right, at the end of the block, is a small concrete building. This is a two-room jail used mostly as an overnight holding cell for drunks. In one of those moments that historians love, Fran McSpadden, secretary of the Falls on the Colorado Museum, was coming out of the former museum building on Second Street when she saw a man taking a photograph of a woman standing in front of the jail. Naturally, she had to go over and ask if they knew any history of the jail. They certainly did. Her father had built the jail. Later, in a conversation with her brother, the woman learned that the concrete was mixed by hand in troughs by their father and another man. Their father told them there was a weakness in the wall so that in case he was ever in the jail he could get out.

❹ Walk back to Main Street. Turn left.

On the corner of Second and Main, the two-story granite block building was the 1891 First National Bank. In a 1915 bank robbery the bookkeeper, Robert Heinatz, was killed. The robbers, who had taken $2,875, were apprehended, and the case received national coverage.

No. 214 Main is where the E. G. Michel family opened a drug store in 1893. A fire in 1905 destroyed the store and they rebuilt it as a grand three-story building with the drug store and soda fountain on the first floor an opera house seating 300 on the second floor and family living quarters on the third. In 1927 a burglar broke into the store and, to cover his tracks, set a fire that destroyed the building and most of the others on the block. It was replaced with the present building. (Historical marker.)

The drug store remained a family business for 108 years. A home and garden business now occupies the building but the soda fountain is still there, although sadly, no longer in operation. "But people still like to come in to see it and tell their stories about it." Near the back on the left wall is an exposed remnant of the original building, and in the right rear corner is the original vault.

The Michels owned four buildings on this block. An early ad boasts "a Theatre; Headquarters Chamber of Commerce; Justice Peace—here you can get married, too; Refreshments, Music and Many Things to Make Many Hearts Happy." The ad goes on to list Drs. Yett & Yett; 5c, 10c and 25c Department selling china, brassware, books and stationery, toys and novelties, wall paper and paints, heavy drugs, watches, clocks and jewelry; dentist upstairs; confectioner; entrance to theater; Miss Ida Houck millinery; fine toilet goods; drug sundries; prescriptions; Dr. Harwood's office.

At the corner of Third Street is the Uptown Marble Theater, built by Mayor R. O. Smith in 1942 on the site of a building that burned in the 1927 fire. It operated as a movie theater until 2003, and reopened a year later as a live entertainment venue. Mayor Smith also owned the Roper Hotel.

❺ Cross Third Street and turn left down Third.

No. 905 is the second and "larger" location for The Falls of the Colorado Museum since it opened in 2003. In spite of its small size, the museum holds a wealth of information about the settling of Marble Falls, a collection of photographs and displays of home life in earlier times. It was here that we browsed through the *Burnet County History*. On page 91 of volume 1 we found this delightful story:

One bright starry night in 1924 or 1925, Mrs. G. L. Jones sat on her second-floor porch in her rocking chair meditating and wondering at the splendor of God's universe. Suddenly she heard a deep, loud voice cry out from the heavens, "What town is this?" She looked up and saw "a sky ship as big as the factory building!" Other citizens, she learned later, saw "that thing" hovering above the town. E. G. Michel climbed onto the roof of his three-story building with a megaphone and shouted back, "Marble Falls." "Thank you," replied the deep voice, and the airship drifted off.

As the story has been handed down, the airship was the Hindenburg and it was lost on a flight between Dallas and San Antonio. However, the dates don't work, as the Hindenburg didn't fly until 1936. But the fact of a lost sky ship stands as there were other dirigibles flying around at the time of the Marble Falls incident; Brooks Field in San Antonio was used for dirigible training and Dallas had a Naval air station.

Across Third Street from the museum, at 910, is the two-story, galleried Wallace Guest House. Opened in 1907 as the Bredt Hotel it offered lodging and meals for 25 cents. In 1914 the Wallaces bought it, offering rooms for $1.50 and all-you-can-eat meals for 25 cents. They raised chickens for both meat and eggs, and had a vegetable garden. Meals ended with Mrs. Wallace's fabulous desserts. After the death of her parents in the 1940s, Margaret Wallace gave up the business and the house became her private residence. In 1976 she sold the house and contents to Judge Ed Yturri and his wife, Dottie. After considering several uses for the grand old house, they opened it again as a guesthouse. The next several owners used it for apartments, until Phil and Rebecca Gatton in 2002 did another major restoration and opened it as a suites hotel. The property was sold once more, but the current owner continues to run it as a hotel.

If you're a thrift store buff, don't miss Liberty Thrift Store further down Third at the corner of Avenue J. Great bargain and treasure hunting in a bright, well appointed store that looks more like a boutique than a thrift store

❻ Walk back to Main Street and turn left towards Fourth Street.

On the corner at Main, the two-story sandstone block building opened in 1909 as Ellison Mercantile. A doctor's office, now an apartment, occupied the second floor. One couple recently occupying the apartment reported numerous sightings of two different ghosts, one a nurse and the other a small boy of four to six years. The couple moved after six months.

Across Main on this block is a magnificent live oak tree in a small plaza. We'll come rest in its shade later.

❼ Continue up Main Street, cross Fourth and continue toward Fifth.

At No. 416 Main, if the "Open" sign in the window is on, don't let the jumble of stuff in the front yard deter you from a trip inside. Betty O'Conner will welcome you to her home and shop. She lives on one side of the house. The rooms on the other side are filled with antique jewelry, china, knickknacks and furniture, most of it for sale. The house has never been sold. M. H. Reed built it for his sister-in-law, J. C. "Mammy" Reed, around the turn of the century. She gave it to her daughter Elizabeth Alexander. Elizabeth had no family, so she bequeathed it to her good friend Betty.

No. 508 Main on the left across Fifth Street is the Galloway/Odiorne house, built in 1911 by Stephen Galloway. The next owner, Ernest Lee Odiorne, is described as "a very colorful character," said to be an experience unto himself. The last bit of humor he left for the town is on his tombstone. "I've led a wild life boys,/but I've earned all I spent./I paid all I borrowed/and I lost all I lent./I once loved a woman/and that came to an end./So get a good dog boys,/It will be your best friend."

The house served as a bed and breakfast—Harlyn House—in the 1970s, and was an antique store after that. From the third floor window facing west you can see Granite Mountain. When asked if there are any resident ghosts, the current owner replied "Sorry, it's a very pleasant-natured house. In fact, the woman who owned the antique store and lived upstairs felt the house was a very healing place to live."

For those who like to browse cemeteries, visit the Marble Falls Cemetery by going down Second Street to Avenue S, turn left on Avenue S until it dead ends at Johnson Drive, then right on Johnson Drive to the cemetery entrance.

❽ Cross to the other side of Main Street and head back to the start.

No. 501 Main, on the former at Fifth, is the Darragh/Liggett home, built of granite rubble for Rosa Darragh in 1936. Work was slow at that time due to the Depression, so to keep his workers on the payroll Mr. Darragh, who owned Granite Mountain, had them build the house.

At Old Oak Square, in the welcoming shade of the old oak tree, you'll find a bench on which to sit and rest awhile, although it is a bit eerie to be sitting under the branches of what may have been the local Hanging Tree. There used to be another large oak nearby in the middle of Main Street, but most old-timers, I'm told, think this one was the Hanging Tree. The limestone block building to the right of the tree is said to harbor a ghost or two, perhaps of those who met their final fate at the tree? Owners of the various businesses that have occupied the building have reported hearing mysterious footsteps and seeing mysterious footprints.

The double row of shops to the left of the oak tree was a lumberyard and hardware store under various owners for many years. Also in the square at one time was the Evans–Ebeling Banking Company, one of the first banks in Marble Falls. On the second floor of the bank building was a funeral parlor that had a ramp for moving the horse-drawn hearse and the coffins up and down from street level.

There are public restrooms in the plaza.

⑨ Continue along Main back to Third Street, turn left and walk one block up to Hwy. 281. Cross at the traffic light.

On the left, at No. 707 Third St., is the former Roper Hotel, built by George C. and Elizabeth Roper about 1888 (historical marker). Later known as the Central House and the Francis Hotel, it was renovated back to nearly its original use in the early 1980s and used as a restaurant. It is currently an office building.

If you're ready to refuel, across Third on the right is the parking lot for the Blue Bonnet Cafe.

⑩ Retrace your steps to Main Street.

MARBLE FALLS WALK 2

Historic residential neighborhood. 1.8 miles, gradual hills, no sidewalks but little street traffic. Park at Visitor Center off Hwy. 281 at Broadway and Avenue H or on street, Restrooms in Visitor Center (open Mon.–Fri. 8 a.m.–5 p.m., Sat. 10 a.m.–2 p.m.) Public restrooms in Old Oak Square on Main Street between Third and Fourth streets.

When planning this walk I wondered why the alphabetically numbered streets started at the highway with H and worked uphill to A. Usually they would go the other way. Everyone I asked replied, "No one's ever asked that before!"

One person humorously suggested that Johnson was blind when he laid out the city. I did get an answer, though: The avenues began not at the highway, which didn't exist at that time, but at the river. In fact, what is now Hwy. 281 was at one time, Avenue H; Main Street was Avenue I.

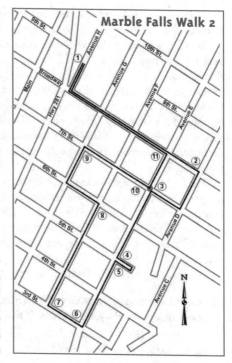

Marble Falls Walk 2

❶ From the Visitor Center walk out Broadway and turn left.

The Visitor Center is in the city's first train depot, moved here in 1976 from its original location at Avenue N and south First Street. The railroad's arrival in 1889 was so important to Marble Falls that when the last spike was driven at close to midnight a large crowd was on hand to celebrate. The depot, built in 1893, became the social gathering spot for the town. Everybody met the 10:30 a.m. train to Austin and were back for its return at 1:30. From the station they headed to the post office to wait for the mail to be put up. The tracks are still in use, but the depot was closed in 1968 and later purchased by local newspaper publisher William D. Bray and given to the city as a bicentennial gift in 1976.

No. 617 Broadway, at Avenue G, built in 1910 for A. C. Lacy, was later the home of sisters Sofronia and Wilhamena Hale. This is one of several area homes restored and remodeled by Ollie Ann Baker. In recent years it has been a tearoom and restaurant, but was vacant at the time of this writing.

No. 902 Avenue F, on the left as you approach Avenue F, is the Hoag–Faubion–Fuch house, built in 1910 (historical marker). It has been owned for the past fifty years by Max Copeland, pastor Emeritus of First Baptist Church. "Retired" is only the official standing for Brother Max, as he's referred to locally.

He's often seen sitting on the porch chatting with people who drop by to visit and seek his counsel, and he still gets asked to officiate at weddings and funerals. I asked his wife why, as longtime residents, the Copeland name had not been added to the marker, and learned that a name cannot be put on a historical marker until the owner has been deceased for twenty years.

No. 501 Broadway, at Avenue E, is the 1927 house built for G. L. and Jeanette Dorbrandt. He served a term as mayor and she was a much beloved high school teacher. Later Ray and Millie Dorbrandt Galyean, who owned the graphite mine near Lake Buchanan, bought it, and it is still owned by a family member. The columns are hand carved.

Many homes in the area are built of stone "rubble," the smaller pieces left in the process of quarrying the larger blocks. A popular treatment of rubble masonry is called grapevining, the outlining of mortar joints or courses with a raised bead of white lime mortar. Some fieldstone rubble houses built with different colors of stone are called patchwork.

Across Avenue E, the two corner houses offer an opportunity to compare the two kinds of local stone popular as building materials. No. 419 on the left is built with fieldstone, also referred to as limestone. No. 418 on the right is built with granite.

❷ Turn right on Avenue D, then right again at Seventh Street. (The street sign reads "Villa Vista" to the left and "Seventh Street" to the right.)

No 412 Seventh St., the Marrs/Hearn home, with its granite foundation and low granite wall, dates from 1908 and received a major renovation in 2008. Inside are two mirrored white wooden fireplace mantels, back-to-back to share one chimney. The fireplace in the first room faces straight into the room, while the one in the second room is placed at an angle. C. M. Marrs owned the Hudley–Marrs Company, a mercantile store, and was elected mayor in 1931. John Granville "Granny" Hearn was postmaster.

On one walk, as we approached the live oak tree in the center of the intersection of Seventh Street and Avenue E a roadrunner darted across the street. It was originally not unusual for trees to be left in the middle of the road but they were later usually removed due to "progress." This tree remains because the neighborhood fought "tooth and nail" to save it. It was a favorite place for neighborhood children to gather and sit on a branch to read call to friends passing by and to drop water balloons on unsuspecting passersby.

Seventh Street has some of the oldest homes in the neighborhood, dating back to 1905–07.

❸ Turn left on Avenue E.

No. 609 dates from 1906. It has two chimneys, of different colored brick as the one now of yellow brick was rebuilt after having been destroyed by a fire.

No. 601, a 1947 stone house with a low wall, is notable for its two huge clumps of spineless prickly pear cactus, a plant that generally does not grow around here.

No. 510 Avenue E has been added onto. It was built in 1933 for Richard and Marie Giesecke as a two-bedroom granite rubble cottage with a detached granite garage. About 1957 the garage was incorporated into the house, with an addition on the right side. The left side of the house got a breezeway addition and carport. Later the carport itself was enclosed one stall at a time.

❹ Turn left on Fifth Street. Walk to the end, then turn around and retrace your steps to Avenue E.

No. 401 Fifth Street, at the top of Fifth, was built in 1941 for W. K. Shipman. Stucco now covers the original granite walls. At one time it was owned by A. L. and Gabriella Bradford. Gabriella was from New Orleans, where her father worked in the French consulate. I was told that at the time they moved here there were no foreign language classes in the local schools, so Gabriella taught private French lessons in their home. Note the whimsical tree trunk sculpture in the side yard.

As you turn to walk back to Avenue E, you are treated to a view of Granite Mountain.

❺ Turn left on Avenue E.

No. 416 Avenue E, built in 1908, has an unusual clipped gable roof topped with decorative metal cresting typical of the northern Germany roots of the owner, Walter Giesecke. Mr. Giesecke never had a chance to go to school, so he traded his ranch for this property and moved into town so his children could attend school. It stayed in the Giesecke family until 1981.

No. 408 is a granite bungalow built in 1934 for Robert Jay and his wife. The house needed extensive repairs after a fire during remodeling.

No. 402 is a 1909 Craftsman style bungalow with a foundation of river stone and a magnificent live oak tree in front.

No. 311, on the left across Fourth Street, built in 1893, originally had two stories. Note the interesting fan design on the front gable.

❻ Turn right on Third Street.

No 503 Third Street, at the corner as you turn, is the 1894 E. G. Michel home. It's said that Mrs. Michel got tired of waiting for her husband to come home from his drug store on Main Street, so when he rebuilt the store after a fire (see Walk 1) he included living quarters on the third floor and they moved there. The house is an interesting study in angles. It is built in the shape of a cross and positioned to have river views from any angle. The upper room served as a vent. Note in particular the awning over the window on the left side with its peaked metal roof and gingerbread trim. The house has 1,409 square feet with 11.5-foot ceilings.

❼ Turn right on Avenue F.

No. 307 Avenue F was built as a frame house in 1909. The pink granite rubble veneer was added in the 1930s.

No. 512, on the corner of Sixth, is the patchwork house of Frank Byers. Patchwork homes were popular throughout the Hill Country in the 1920s and 30s. A mixture of limestone and sandstone create the patchwork effect. The reddish stones are sandstone with granite in it.

No. 601, on the right corner at Sixth Street, is the 1891 Eastlake Victorian home of Otto Ebeling (historical marker). Otto was a rancher until his marriage to Emilie Giesecke, who did not take to rural life. They moved to Marble Falls, where Otto opened the city's first bank (see Walk 1). When the Ebelings decided to move to Austin in 1913 the house was sold, and over the years passed through several owners until Edna Mae Smith bought it about 1947 for use as a nursing home. When she retired the house again went through a series of owners and uses until 1980 when, after 67 years, it came back into the ownership of the Ebeling family with its purchase by Robert Ebeling, Otto's great-nephew, and his wife Jean.

The grand old house had suffered badly during those 67 years, and the new owners were determined to return it to its original grandeur. They ripped off the additions, had it leveled and the foundation rebuilt, replaced the porch columns and reshingled the roof. Inside, amazingly the stained glass windows had mostly survived, as had glass transoms over the doors. Plaster was removed from the walls and insulation installed, wiring and plumbing renewed and central heating, air conditioning, closets and bathrooms added. The neglected grounds were cleared and replanted. What had become a neighborhood eyesore was turned into something wonderful to behold.

When first restored the house was painted white with blue trim. Its current colorful paint job has engendered mixed reactions. I was told some of the neighbors objected, but on my first walk-by the neighbor I met described it as "fun." My walking companion and I agreed. The house is now occupied by Robert and Jean's daughter Nancy, an artist, whose influence is apparent in the yard. The more we looked, the more delightful details we found. A gazebo, playhouse, guesthouse and birdhouse designed to match the house; sculptural pieces made of glass nuggets hanging here and there; angel, flamingo and rooster sculptures; the scatter-painted driveway sign signed Paige Ebeling. Perhaps you can find even more.

No. 610, across from the Ebeling house, is the Fowler–Lechow home, the latest house, at this writing, restored by Ollie Ann Baker. She opened it as a bed-and-breakfast. My friend and I stayed there while working on these walks. Ollie did much of the work herself, retaining as much of the original wood, glass and fixtures as she could. She found parts of the porch balusters under the house and had them restored and copied. Where she had to remove cedar and long-leaf pine from the walls, she used it for cabinets and floors.

Built in 1907 by newlyweds Mamie and Emmett Fowler, the house passed on to their daughter Beryl Mae and her husband, Gerhard Lechow. They owned the whole block, and kept a herd of cattle and sheep. There was once an old milking shed. What is now the guesthouse was once garages. Note also the brick chimney on the far side of the house. The round part accommodated two flues from adjacent rooms. Family members lived in the house until 2005, just short of one hundred years. There are many interesting stories about the house: Mrs. Fowler enclosed the back porch for raising parakeets, the large hook in the ceiling near the bathroom wall is where the family hung their deer to chill. My favorite is the basement poolroom where Mr. Fowler and his friends gathered. Mr. Fowler kept his beer there, as Mrs. Fowler would not let him keep it in the house. Later Gerhardt Lechow was known to brew his own beer in the basement.

8 Turn left on Sixth Street, then right on Avenue G.

No. 700 Sixth St., across on the left before turning onto Avenue G, was the Methodist parsonage. Its veneer is dolomite, an unusual and extremely hard stone that is a transition between limestone and marble. The stone was reused from the Rockvale Methodist Church when that was torn down in 1904.

No. 601 Avenue G belonged to Nell Jay and her sister, who lived in this house from birth to death. Every day Nell Jay walked to and from her job as a cashier at the theater on Main Street. This is another house renovated by Ollie Ann Baker. When she added the second story, due to a spiral stairway she had to remove part of the ceiling to get a four-foot cast iron tub to the upstairs bathroom.

9 Turn right on Seventh Street.

No. 603 Seventh St. is the Christian–Matern home (historic marker). George Christian, an owner of the Texas Mining and Improvement Company that developed Marble Falls, married Juliet Johnson, daughter of the town's founder. They built this home in 1892. Ivo B. Matern, a rancher and mayor of the city in 1937, and his wife, Mina, bought the house in 1908 and lived here fifty-one years. The current owner restored the house and hosts a Victorian Christmas Open House here each year for the museum. A twelve-foot tree decorated with Victorian-era ornaments stands in the bay window.

No. 518, across Avenue F, is another patchwork limestone, and dates from 1945. The gingerbread porch trim and two-story addition were added in 1985.

No. 511 dates from around 1895. Walter Cox, a barber, and his wife Viola, bought the house at a sheriff's sale in 1938. It is said her ghost still wanders around upstairs. Note the charming wagon wheel spandrel across the porch.

No. 503, an 1899 gray wood-frame Victorian, has decorative metal cresting on its roofline.

⑩ Turn left on Avenue E by the tree.

As you start down Avenue E you get a view of the First Baptist Church of Marble Falls, established in 1888. The small steeple is from the original church built on this site, after a fire in 1962 destroyed the earlier location on Main Street.

⑪ Turn left on Broadway and walk back to the start.

26 New Braunfels

Comal County seat, I-35 north of San Antonio. Population 36,494.
Five walks.

As agent of the *Adelsverein* (Immigration Society), Prince Carl of Solms-Braunfels purchased land some 200 miles inland from the port of Carlshafen (later Indianola), too far for a single trek. He settled New Braunfels as the first way station between the port and the land grant. The site had rich soil, abundant timber, water power from the Guadalupe and Comal rivers, and it was near San Antonio for supplies. The first wagons set up camp on a bluff overlooking Comal Creek. Saints Peter and Paul Catholic Church occupies that site. New Braunfels was officially founded on Good Friday, March 21, 1845. The newcomers set to work building homes of log or *Fachwerk*. They opened businesses. Reverend Louis Ervendberg held the first religious services under a grove of elm trees and Hermann Seele started a school under the same trees. Ervendberg and his wife opened an orphanage, the first in Texas, for children of immigrants who had not survived the journey to their new home.

This was a land of plenty but also of dangers. While the woods abounded with rabbit, duck, turkey, and deer for food, they also were home to jaguar, panther, bear, and wolf. The rivers that provided fish, crab, and turtle also harbored water moccasins and alligators. Rattlesnakes, centipedes, and scorpions crawled upon the land. Although their Indian neighbors were mostly friendly and came to the settlement to barter, there were occasional attacks from renegade Indians in the more isolated areas. But the settlers persevered. Comal County organized in March 1846 with New Braunfels as its county seat. Businesses prospered, permanent buildings replaced tents and huts, churches and schools were built. A tax-supported public school system existed here 18 years before being mandated in 1876 by the Texas Constitution. By 1850 New Braunfels ranked as the fourth-largest town in Texas.

Social and cultural organizations, much a part of the German lifestyle, formed. The *Saengerverein,* or singing club, organized in 1850. Hermann Seele held the first Saengerfest in 1853. The Shepherd's Society initiated a weekly market in 1853. The first *Turnverein,* or athletic club, opened in 1855. By the 1880s New Braunfels was linked by telegraph and rail with Austin and San Antonio. Textile and other industries grew. Like elsewhere in the Hill Country, drought, the boll weevil, and the Depression halted growth. Not until after World War II did New Braunfels again prosper. Its proximity to San Antonio attracts commuters and retirees. The German heritage and attractions such as Natural Bridge Caverns, Schlitterbahn, and Canyon Lake make tourism a major industry.

There are many interesting neighborhoods in New Braunfels, so I divided the town into four short walks. Each begins from the plaza and can be combined into longer walks; a fifth is in Landa Park. You will see markers on some homes and buildings with names and dates, part of the walking tour compiled by the Chamber of Commerce and the New Braunfels Main Street Department.

In addition to the museums along the walks, trips to the Museum of Texas Handmade Furniture and the adjacent Conservation Plaza are a must. Bill and Nan Dillen arrived in New Braunfels in 1945. They restored the 1858 Breustedt home and were instrumental in founding the New Braunfels Conservation Society. They donated land adjacent to their home to the Society for Conservation Plaza, a refuge for vintage structures and antique roses, and then donated their home and its furnishings to the Heritage Society for the Museum of Texas Handmade Furniture. Enthusiastic, informed guides make both of these well worth the price of admission.

NEW BRAUNFELS WALK I

Historic Downtown District, Fire Station Museum, Railroad Museum, art museum, side trips to Buckhorn Museum, Sophienburg Museum. 1.5 miles plus side trip of 0.7 miles, flat except side trip slightly uphill. Park around central plaza. Public restrooms in courthouse, if open. Several restaurants along walk.

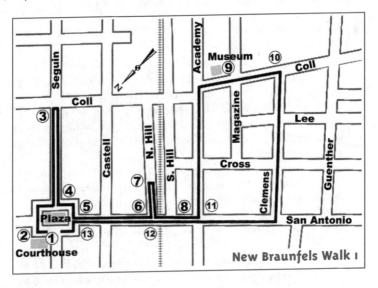

❶ At Main Plaza.

Nicholas Zink laid out New Braunfels in 1845 around a central plaza. The plaza has been restored several times. The fountain dates from 1896 and the bandstand from 1905. Two markers commemorate the Civil War and World War I.

On the northeast corner of the plaza is the 1898 Romanesque-style Comal County Courthouse. Architect J. Riely Gordon designed the courthouse with four entrances for the center of the plaza. It lost some of its grandeur when built instead on a corner lot. Later additions placed two of its graceful arched entrances inside the building.

The courthouse bells are a gift from Walter Faust Jr., local music teacher and noted organist. When growing up in his family's home next to the First Protestant Church he always thrilled to the sound of the church's bells. On a visit to Victoria, Texas, he heard the bells on that town's courthouse and decided the Comal County Courthouse should also have bells. He donated them in time for the U.S. Bicentennial celebration. The courthouse bells pealed out for the first time at midnight on Jan. 1, 1976, ringing for exactly 76 seconds. The local church bells followed for another 76 seconds. The four bells are tuned to tones C, D, E, and G. Besides ringing the Westminster Chime on the quarter-hour automatically, on special occasions the bells are played manually.

❷ With your back to the courthouse, walk left around the plaza and turn left on S. Seguin.

No. 129 S. Seguin is Naeglin's Bakery, reputed to be the oldest bakery in existence in Texas. Established in 1868 at a different location, it moved here in 1882. The original *Fachwerk* construction of this building dates from the 1850s. It is said that 22-year-old Eduard Naeglin and his wife, Fransica, started the bakery with less than one dollar and one sack of flour. Besides bread and pastries, Naeglin's still sells slabs of dark, rich gingerbread. Although no longer five cents, it's still worth the price.

No. 161, built in 1846 by carpenter Stephen Klein, is a fine example of rock-filled *Fachwerk* and one of the oldest structures in New Braunfels. Klein was 59 when he arrived here, one of the oldest in the first group of settlers.

No. 165, the Hoffman Building, is an 1890 Victorian Italianate commercial building. Originally Hoffman Jewelry, it was later the office of the *New Braunfels Herald*.

No. 173 (marker), built in the 1860s by master carpenter Friedrich Krause, has been the Hoffman Opera House, the Weber and Deutch General Store, and a drill hall for Clemen's Rifles of the Texas Militia.

Nos. 219–225, the Klappenbach Building, is an 1890s Victorian commercial/residential structure added to an older building and used as a general store downstairs with private residence upstairs. Olga Krause ran the store until son Felix took over in 1899. His son, Ernest, continued to live upstairs until 1990. A humanitarian and linguist, Ernest gave books to children using the trunk of his car as a bookmobile.

No. 251, set back on the lot (marker), is the 1850 adobe brick and cedar beam home of Heinrich Bevenroth, one of the original settlers. His wife drowned in March 1850 in the Comal River, and Heinrich died in October of the same year.

No. 275 was first the property of Friedrich von Wrede Jr., secretary to Prince Solms. Von Wrede's father, Friedrich Sr., came to Texas in 1836, then moved back to Germany. Later, when he came to visit his son, he decided to stay. He wrote *Sketches of Life in the United States of North America and Texas* about his experiences. On a trip back from Austin he and two other men were ambushed by renegade Indians. One escaped, but von Wrede and Oscar von Claren became the first settlers in the area to be killed by Indians. The governor ordered more protection, although it is conceded the men chose a bad place to camp. Von Wrede's book was little known until translated and published in 1970 by Chester W. Geue.

No. 283, the C. M. Ludwig Building, dates from 1929. It still has its original pressed tin ceiling and has always been a furniture store.

❸ At Coll turn right, crossing Seguin, and then turn right on Seguin.

Across Coll is the lovely Gothic Revival First Protestant Church, built in 1875 to replace an earlier 1846 log church, the first house of worship in New Braunfels.

No. 260 (Heritage House) is the 1904 Queen Anne home of Walter Faust Sr. Its octagon onion dome tower was a popular feature of Queen Anne Victorian architecture. It was from his bedroom facing the church that Walter Jr. learned to love bells, he says. I love bells too, but with that close a proximity, I'm not so sure I would have.

No. 240 (marker) is the 1928 Spanish Colonial Revival Faust Hotel (originally Travelers Hotel), in continual operation since its opening. Some of its earlier, friendly inhabitants are said to still roam the corridors. In 1936 it was renamed for the family on whose home site it is built. Its lobby and dining room are virtually unaltered. A bright yellow 1929 Ford coupe decorates the lobby. The once open courtyard is now a brew pub. The hotel's room decor is still 1920s. Tiny private baths, built into former closets, replace the central bath down the hall.

No. 228 is the c. 1870 Greek Revival home built by Johann George Kirchner. It has also been home to the Dittlingers and to Carl W. Groos, a Texas land commissioner in the 1870s. Among other businesses, he and his brothers ran freight from Indianola to El Paso before going into banking. He later moved to San Antonio and founded the Groos Bank there. The original house of adobe brick has been altered.

No. 190 is the 1854 Greek Revival Moureau house. In 1857 Franz Moureau was appointed German Counsel of the Western Region of Texas. He made his fortune in cotton after the Civil War. His daughter, Hulda, married Carl Groos.

❹ At Main Plaza, turn left.

No. 337 Main Plaza is the 1927 Wiedermann Building. The next building, Capital Plaza, opened in 1925 as the Capital Theater. It operated as a theater until 1957.

No. 367 (marker) is a brick building that replaced the original wood building after a fire in 1924. It was the Black Whale, a saloon owned by Charles Schumann Schwarzen Wallfisch, then a church. Inmates of the jail next door could be heard singing along with parishioners. Next it was home to the *Herald,* the first English language newspaper in New Braunfels that later merged with the *Zeitung* German-language paper.

5 Continue around the plaza to West San Antonio Street. Turn left.

Note: Building overhangs provide welcome shade on hot summer days but make it difficult to enjoy the architecture. Therefore, while on this side of the street I describe the buildings on the other side; then on the return walk, I describe the buildings on this side.

No. 148 (marker) is the 1910 R. B. Richter Building. In 1901 three members of the Richter family—Rudolph B., Emilie, and Lena—opened a pharmacy on this side. At that time No. 148 was a saloon. The Richters bought it in 1909, added a second-floor apartment for the family, and opened the new pharmacy a year later. The interior cabinets of cherry with marble and glass counters were manufactured by the San Antonio Drug Company and included a modern soda fountain. During the pharmacy's 70 years at this location it gained a reputation for both its pharmaceutical innovations and its homemade ice cream. Clerk Max G. Hartmann went to pharmacy school and later joined the firm. Rudolph retired as a pharmacist in 1936 and took up banking, cofounding Guaranty State Bank. Later, Louis C. Vollbrecht joined the firm and eventually became sole owner. In 1971 he moved the pharmacy to a plaza location.

No. 193 (on this side at the corner) was constructed as a two-story building in the mid-1800s. The Phoenix Saloon occupied the first floor, and the second was living quarters. Willie Gebhardt ran a lunch counter at the back of the saloon. He was an artist, musician, and mechanical genius who loved to invent and repair things. Gebhardt produced the first commercially available chili powder in 1894, devising a machine that seeded, cleaned, and dried the peppers before grinding and bottling them. In 1908 he canned the first chili con carne and tamales at a factory in San Antonio. Altogether, Gebhardt patented 37 machines. Proper ladies did not enter saloons. They and the children ate in the beer garden out back. Push buttons on the trees summoned the waiter.

Next to the beer garden, along Castell Street, was Heinrich Ludwig's hotel. It supplied meals for the prisoners in the county jail behind it. The 1868 two-story limestone Heinrich Hinman house sits on that site now. Hinman was both veterinarian and blacksmith. His son, Charles, a stonemason, built the house.

In 1922 A. R. Ludwig bought the corner building and added the third floor, where the Masonic Lodge met. Jacob Schmidt bought it in 1925 and opened a clothing store whose quality of merchandise and service earned it the nickname Neiman-Schmidt. It remained in business until 1995.

No. 214 (looking back to the other side of San Antonio) was originally the local Woolworth's, as evident by the architecture. Woolworth stores all (at least all I've seen), had similar fronts.

No. 246 is the Henne Hardware and Electric Store. Established in 1857, it is the oldest hardware store in Texas still in operation. This building dates from 1893. On the return walk take a moment to go inside this delightful old store, with its original wood floor and pressed tin ceiling. The cornice, as was common in earlier days, is actually tin made to look like carved stone. The Gothic arches and half-onion dome are more elaborate than usual for this type of building.

No. 264 is the 1857 Louis Henne Building. Louis took over the family's wagon shop at age 17 after his father's death.

No. 270 was the Henne Tin and Sheet Iron Shop, established in 1846.

No. 278, the 1872–1894 brick Victorian Italianate Clemens and Faust Building, was originally home to the First National Bank. Later uses included a savings and loan company, school district offices, and the newspaper office of the English-language *New Braunfels Herald*, competitor to the German-language *New Braunfels Zeitung*.

Next to it is the Brauntex Movie Theater. Opened in 1942, it ran continuously until 1999. It is now a performing arts theater.

⬤ At Hill (railroad tracks) turn left to the Fire Museum.

The old Central Fire Station dates from 1918. For a tour inquire at the new station next door. Usually someone is around to take you through the museum. Better yet, call (830) 608-2120, and make an appointment. Inside are 1886 man-drawn hose reels, a horse-drawn steam engine, 1912 pumper, 1923 Reo pumper, and 1950 Ford pumper. The pride and joy is the 1931 ladder truck used until 1982. After retiring it, the firemen worked in their spare time for a year refinishing its wooden parts. It's a beauty. In 1880 the International and Great Northern railroad laid its track down the middle of Hill Street.

Across the tracks, the Huisache Grill is in the former Hugo Bruno Wetzel home. This location has been a restaurant, an antique store, feed store, and even a haunted house. Don and Lynn Forres opened the current restaurant in the mid-1990s. In the front, facing on San Antonio Street, is the former Adolph Holz Building. Holz and his son sold carriages.

❼ Retrace steps to San Antonio Street. Turn left.

No. 361 San Antonio is the 1905 John Faust home. This imposing Queen Anne Victorian, set in its lovely garden, is still a private residence. Elaborate leaded glass windows enhance its entrance. When a former owner painted this beauty an "awful" color, it triggered the formation of the Conservation Society.

❽ Turn left on Academy to visit the Sophienburg Museum. (Three blocks, slightly uphill.) Turn right on Coll to museum entrance.

Academy Street led to the New Braunfels Academy, built in 1856 at Mill Street and in use until 1913. The museum is on the site Prince Carl of Solms-Braunfels chose to build a castle for his bride-to-be, Lady Sophia, princess of Salm-Salm. His princess let it be known, though, that she would not relocate to Texas. Henceforth, Prince Carl returned to Germany and married the Lady Sophia, and, so we are told, lived happily ever after. Historical markers honor Hermann Seele, who, among other positions, was New Braunfels' first teacher. In the museum is a model of Braunfels Castle in Germany. Displays trace the journey of the German immigrants to their new home and exhibits depict their way of life here. Members of various local needlework guilds demonstrate the needle arts of early times.

❾ On Coll, your back to the museum, turn left.

At the corner of Coll and Magazine Streets is the home of mill owner Hippolyt Dittlinger.

The charming frame Victorian next door is the home Dittlinger built for daughter Fanny when she married. A patron of the arts and a beloved member of the community, she died in 1994 at the age of 104.

❿ Turn right on Clemens, then right on San Antonio Street.

No. 521 W. San Antonio is the Buckhorn Barber Shop Museum (open Saturday and Sunday from 2 to 5 p.m.). Oscar Wagenfuehr opened his barber shop in a hotel across from the depot, and moved here in the 1940s. His son, Fred, kept the shop open until ill health forced him to retire in 1992. He died a few months later. The museum has much of the eclectic "stuff" they collected. Fred was the more avid collector and also a fine wood carver and lapidarist, making outstanding miniature circus pieces.

No. 505, the small frame Victorian, is the Wagenfuehr home, now a bed-and-breakfast. Both are owned by the Conservation Society. Its guides are on hand to give you a tour.

⑪ Cross San Antonio Street at the light. Turn right to the railroad tracks and the Railway Museum.

The 1891 International and Great Northern Railroad depot closed in 1982. The Historic Railroad and Modelers Society restored it in 1984. It is open Thursday to Monday from noon to 4 p.m. Two rooms hold elaborate model train layouts. On the far side are a steam engine and caboose that children of all ages can climb aboard and pretend to be engineer.

⑫ Continue down San Antonio.

The 100 and 200 blocks across San Antonio Street are commercial buildings dating mostly from the early 1900s.

At No. 246 be sure to step back in time with a trip inside Henne's Hardware.

⑬ Back at Main Plaza walk around to beginning.

No. 142 Main Plaza (marker) was the Halm Saloon back in 1891. In 1910 the second floor was added. There was a pharmacy and cafe downstairs and a residence upstairs.

The Two Brothers Saloon sat on the site of the bank at the corner of Main Plaza and San Antonio Street back in the 1880s. Originally there had been a store and barroom here. The brothers, Henry and William Streuer, relocated next to the Schmitz Hotel, adding a restaurant and a two-lane, ninepin bowling alley. They had the first telephone in town, connecting the saloon to their home. A friend put together some equipment and strung the line three years before formal service came to New Braunfels.

Between the bank and the Schmitz Hotel is the facade from the Guaranty State Bank that once stood here.

No. 471 Main Plaza, the Schmitz Hotel, started as the one-story Guadalupe Hotel built in 1850–52 by Jacques Coll and Rudolph Nauendorf. They offered it to the county for the courthouse but were turned down. In 1858 they sold it to Jacob Schmitz, who added a second story and galleries across the front. In 1873 he added the third floor and changed the name to Schmitz Hotel, a major stage stop back when eight stages a week ran through here. The hotel drew notable entertainers, statesmen, and military leaders. Mr. Eggeling bought it in 1920s or 1930s and altered the facade, and, removing columns and porches, renamed it the Plaza Hotel. In 1979 the Conservation Society restored the facade to its 1873 appearance.

NEW BRAUNFELS WALK 2

Lindheimer House and surrounding neighborhoods. Two miles, flat. Park around plaza. Public restrooms in courthouse when open.

❶ From the Plaza, walk east on San Antonio on the right side of street.

No. 170 East San Antonio is the 1910 Neo-Classical Revival home Sommers Valentin Pfeuffer built with lumber salvaged from the home of his father, George J. Pfeuffer, a judge, state senator, and mercantile store founder with his son. When Sommers's grandson, Walter Faust Jr., lived here he set up a music studio in the carriage house.

❷ Cross Comal and turn right, then left on Tolle, and walk around Market Plaza.

Tolle Street runs around the old market square where farmers gathered to sell produce.

No. 195 (at Market) is the first of many small Victorian era homes built around the market area.

No. 393 is the home Herman Tolle built in 1893. Three generations of his family lived here.

❸ Turn left on Comal.

This is a neighborhood of small and medium- size homes mostly from the Victorian era.

No. 166R is the 1875 P. Mergele house, originally brick with a Victorian front added in 1890.

Next on the right are three small houses. The first two have additions in the back, but the third one is the original size.

❹ Turn right on Coll, then left on Seguin.

No. 305 S. Seguin (corner of Coll) is the stately 1880 home of Joseph Faust, moved on skids from where the Faust Hotel (Walk 1) stands. He came in 1851 at age seven. After Confederate Army service, he clerked in a retail store and with two partners opened Tips Clemens Faust General Mercantile in 1871. He and Clemens opened the Clemens and Faust Bank, later First National Bank. He served as mayor for 10 years and as a state senator.

The Elk Lodge building dates from the 1920s. Originally the New Braunfels Social Club, it had both a nine- and a 10-pin bowling alley.

Across Seguin is the Chamber of Commerce and Tourist Office, open Monday–Friday. Next door is the New Braunfels Civic Center. A display on the patio wall depicts the first 150 years of New Braunfels history.

No. 405L, the 1915 Blumberg house, is noted for its gingerbread trim.

No. 421L (marker) is the 1860 home of doctor, pharmacist, and baker Theodore Koester. The house had a dumbwaiter from the basement kitchen to the dining room and speaking tubes connecting all three floors. Dr. Koester was one of the most controversial of the first settlers. He arrived in 1844 at age 27 and was hired by the Verein as the official physician for the colonists. Dr. Ferdinand Roemer, on a trip to New Braunfels, is quoted as saying, "I did not make use of his medical services nor his pharmaceutical. However, I learned to know through daily use the product of his bakery oven as very good wheat bread." There were many complaints about Koester's abilities as a doctor. About an epidemic, Alvin H. Sorgel in *A Sojourn in Texas, 1846–1847* says, "In New Braunfels people were dying of fever, dysentery, and from the Society's physician, Dr. Koester."

No. 447L, a 1917 Victorian home restored as offices in the late 1980s.

No. 447L, the Hoffmann Financial Center, the 1913 home of A. Eiband.

No. 453L is another earlier Eiband home dating from 1880.

No. 480R, a Victorian commercial building, dates from around 1900. It used to be a sales office for wagons and carriages.

No. 494R is the 1866–1910 Jahn Building. Johann M. Jahn was left crippled when hit by a tool while serving his apprenticeship with a cabinetmaker in Germany. He came to New Braunfels in 1845 and established a reputation as the maker of fine hand-crafted furniture. He also cultivated mustang grapes and made wine in the cellar.

⑤ Turn left on Jahn, then left on Comal.

The triangular park is dedicated to Texas Germans in the Civil War.

No. 575R Comal, hidden away behind overgrown vegetation and waiting to be restored, is the 1857 home of Joseph Hoffmann.

No. 564L (marker) was the 1847 *Fachwerk* home of Heinrich Scholl Jr. The Victorian trim and siding were later additions. Heinrich arrived in New Braunfels with his parents in 1846. After his father died his mother took in boarders. Heinrich and his brother, Adam, learned carpentry and gained a reputation as excellent builders.

No. 550L (marker) was built by Scholl as the schoolhouse.

No. 491R is the home of Ferdinand Jacob Lindheimer, considered the Father of Texas Botany. After serving in the Republic of Texas army, he came to New Braunfels, where, because of his knowledge of German, English, and Spanish, and his ability to communicate with the Indians, Prince Carl enlisted his services. In gratitude, in 1846 Meusebach granted him land for a botanical garden. Lindheimer had 38 plants named for him. He also edited the *Neu Braunfelser Zeitung* from 1852 to 1872. In the Civil War he used the newspaper to promote the vote for secession. This made him less than popular with his

Ferdinand Jacob Lindheimer, the Father of Texas Botany, lived in this home in New Braunfels.

fellow German settlers, who were mostly against secession. Protesters once dumped the newspaper's type and presses into the Comal River. Lindheimer's carefully restored property now belongs to the Conservation Society. Open by appointment. Call 830/629-2943.

No. 480L, the 1859 adobe brick and cedar *Fachwerk* home of Carl Gramm, is built on a portion of the Lindheimer property.

At the corner of Garden, on the right, is an old barn and stone ruins of a woolen mill. Cloth for the first Texas A&M uniforms was woven here.

The house on the left corner at Garden is where Emma and Louise Andrea ran a *Stickstunde* (sewing class) every Saturday afternoon from 2 to 5 p.m. for girls 6 to 12 years of age who paid 25 cents a month to learn needlework arts. Traditionally girls made 12 quilts before they married. When a girl became engaged her mother held a quilting bee to complete a 13th and fanciest quilt for her trousseau.

❻ Turn right on Coll.

The lovely two-story Giesieck house on the right was empty for many years, but has now been restored.

❼ Turn left on Market.

No. 353R, the charming stone "castle," has a 1932 marker.

❽ Turn right on Napoleon, then left on Gilbert.

No. 418R, at the corner of Gilbert, with its elaborate scrollwork and door, can best be described as a "doll house."

❾ At San Antonio turn left back to the plaza.

Around the corner on the left the offices of the Dittlinger Mills are now part of Archer Daniels Midland. Hippolyt Dittlinger came to New Braunfels as a teenager in 1876 to visit the grave of his father and decided to stay. He started by clerking in a mercantile store. An astute businessman, he eventually owned mills, quarries, and kilns.

No. 308L (at Market) began in 1845 as a *Fachwerk* home built by schoolmaster Hermann Seele. In 1870 Dr. John Lehde built this two-story home around the original with one of the first mansard roofs in Texas. The Frank Voights bought it later, and Bonnie Gaye Haight and her husband beautifully restored it, opening Voight Antiques in a former outbuilding. The mountain laurel in the side yard is certified as the largest in the nation.

NEW BRAUNFELS WALK 3

Prince Solms Inn, Sophienburg Archives, old mill, historic neighborhoods. 1.3 miles, mostly flat. Park around plaza. Public restrooms in courthouse, when open.

❶ **From the plaza walk up the left side of East San Antonio.**

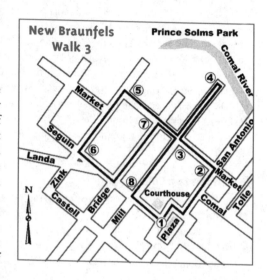

Beyond the courthouse is the New Braunfels Museum of Art in the former First Federal Savings and Loan Building. The Hummel Museum opened here in 1992, but that collection has been disbanded. The city opened it as the Museum of Art in 2000. The museum is on the site of Joseph Landa's imposing two-story brick Victorian with wraparound porches and octagonal turrets. The Landas lived here until 1926, when son Harry moved to San Antonio. His lovely home in the Monte Vista neighborhood there is now a branch library. During the Civil War, Joseph Landa fled to Mexico after being prosecuted for freeing his slaves. While gone, his wife, Helena, ran the store and mills. Landa Park is a portion of the estate they developed as a public park. (See Walk 5.)

No. 265 is an 1860 feed store, now renovated as a private home by the owners of the Prince Solms Inn. The bench in front is original. The wagon parked alongside is typical of those used to haul feed and manure. Set back to the left of the store are the 1840s stables.

At the entrance to Wolfgang's Keller are stones from the old Comal County prison. The two stamped "COMAL" and "COUNTY" are clearly visible. Another, with just "PRIS," is upside-down right at the gate.

A visit inside the Victorian-style Prince Solms Inn (markers) is a step back in time. It has been in continuous operation since Theodor and Emilie Kuse Eggling opened it in 1898 as the Eggling Hotel. Emilie was the daughter of shoemaker William Kuse, whose house stood on this site until moved back to make room for the hotel. Down the hall is an open atrium. Although today's guests enjoy air conditioning, in earlier days this skylight would be opened for summer cooling.

❷ Turn left on Market.

No. 135 North Market was the 1852 home of Joseph Klein before Kuse bought it. Klein arrived with his parents and siblings in 1845 at age 32. The home's doors and windows are original, as is the cypress floor inside. A standing-seam tin roof hides the original cypress shingle roof. Originally two rooms, a kitchen and bath were added later. When the dentist came to town the Kleins let him set up in a front room. The family grew mushrooms in the cellar. The house is now part of the inn.

❸ Turn right on Mill.

No. 343 E. Mill is an 1865 brick-filled *Fachwerk* with mud daub ceilings, once in a sad state of disrepair but lovingly restored by its new owner.

On the river, at the end of Mill Street, is the Dittlinger Roller Mill's 1870s dam. The stone ruin was a tower from which a 1,500-foot steel cable ran to the mill. Hippolyt Dittlinger worked at the Faust Store until, with partners John and Peter Faust, he bought an existing mill, which they named the Peter Faust Flour Mill. Dittlinger became sole owner in 1901. When the Landa Mills closed in 1930 Dittlinger bought those, too. He retired in 1931, turning control of the mills over to his son-in-law. They have been owned since 1979 by Archer Daniels Midland.

Between the mill and the river is a city park. Beside the three chutes that powered the mill the city put a long chute so tubers can go between the river's two levels. Earlier generations dove off the tower into the pits.

❹ Retrace your steps to Market Street and turn right.

Nos. 363–365L is a newer complex with bits of German and Victorian architecture.

❺ Turn left on Zink.

Several fine early homes exist along Zink Street, but unfortunately I did not find information on any of them.

❻ Turn left on Seguin, then left on Bridge.

No. 161L Bridge is a Victorian frame home dating from 1890.
No. 257L is the Neoclassical frame home of Theodore Heiber.
No. 264R was the home of Albert Ludwig and is still in the family.

❼ Turn right on Market, then right on Mill.

No. 295R E. Mill, the stone house on the corner, is the 1870s home of Anselm Eiband, who ran the newspaper after Lindheimer retired in 1872.

No. 273R is the Heinrich Hohmann home, also the first Western Union office. Built in 1853 of plastered stone and brick, the wood siding, porch, and gingerbread were probably added by Wilhelm Fischer in the 1880s.

No. 197R (marker) is the 1866 home of August Dietz, who arrived in Texas in 1849. Like many of the early homes, it was originally two rooms. The ceilings, window glass, and door are original.

❽ Turn left on Seguin back to the plaza.

At the right corner of Mill and Seguin is the Sophienburg Archives in the old Art Deco city hall, designed in 1929 by Jeremiah Schmidt. Inside are original colorful tile floors, light fixtures, and woodwork. In the gift shop, items related to the region include typical German costumes. The staff and volunteers are helpful in tracing genealogical and historical data.

NEW BRAUNFELS WALK 4

Residential neighborhoods, Saints Peter and Paul Catholic Church. 2.0 miles, no sidewalks on much of walk. Park around plaza. Public restrooms in courthouse.

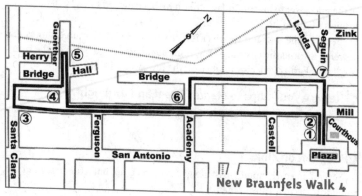

❶ From plaza walk up left side of North Seguin.

At the Mill Street corner is the Doeppenschmidt Funeral Home. B. Preiss had a livery and feed store here. He also made and sold caskets. In 1923 O. A. Doeppenschmidt bought the business. It's still in his family.

❷ Turn left on Mill.

The red brick building at the Castell corner still has Post Office sign. Starting at Castell you'll see a neighborhood of mostly small, frame Victorian homes with spindle work and jigsaw-cut trim known as Folk Victorian. When I first walked Mill and Bridge Streets I realized the homes are lookalikes, and though I do not admire lookalike homes in modern suburbs I can't imagine being bored by Victorian architecture.

No. 230R is the 1846 Johann George Pfeuffer house. As a state senator Pfeuffer was responsible for convincing the state to use Texas granite instead of Georgia marble in building the capitol building in Austin.

No. 292R is the 1880 Wagenfuehr home. The beautiful scrollwork on the porch is typical of Eastlake Victorian.

Across the tracks:

No. 387L was built around 1900 in the Victorian Vernacular style using beveled stone blocks.

No. 407L (marker), built in 1900, houses the offices of the New Braunfels Independent School District and Tax Office. This was the site of the shop building for the New Braunfels Academy located across the street. The school district's Education Center, the former New Braunfels High School, was built in 1913 on the site of the academy. This is the second-oldest tax-supported public school system still in existence. The freestanding marker in front of the school has an interesting history of public education in New Braunfels. I think it's worth a trip across the street to read.

No. 477L is a brick Eastlake Victorian built in the early 1900s for the Henne family.

No. 502R, in a garden setting, started as a small *Fachwerk* home.

No. 528R was a two-room *Fachwerk*. Victorian touches came later.

No. 543L is the 1862 home of shoemaker Julius Habermann. The cut limestone blocks in its Fachwerk walls are a rare material for filler.

No. 540R, hiding behind a huge Texas red oak, has a delightful porch rail. The tree is a magnificent sight when dressed in its fall colors.

No. 554R (marker) is the 1855 home of George Ullrich. Prince Solms hired him as *Wagonmeister*. According to the marker, Ullrich and his wife drove the first wagon of the German Emigration Company across the Guadalupe River in 1845. One historian told me, though, that this honor has been claimed by a dozen or so families. This is the first New Braunfels home to have a state historic marker.

No. 595L holds a surprise. Around the inside of the wraparound porch is lettered a quote from T. S. Eliot, "Time present and time past, both perhaps present in the future, and time future contained in time past." You can see a portion of it from the street. Please respect the privacy of the owners and do not go onto the property.

In the 600 block, to the right, is a stone "castle" Edward Schleyer Sr. built on the site of the Jeremiah Schmidt home. Though the home appears small, it is actually quite roomy. There are 25 pecan trees on the property.

❸ Turn right on Santa Clara, then right again on Bridge.

Before turning onto Bridge, ahead left on Santa Clara is a house with a wraparound porch on three sides. Judging by the roofline, the side facing the yard is the old front entry and the side with no porch is the back.

❹ Turn left on Guenther.

No. 307L Guenther (at corner) is another Victorian beauty, but I could find no information on its history.

No. 351L has a lovely fan design on leaded windows over the door. At the end of the street is the New Braunfels Smokehouse processing plant, once the New Braunfels Brewing Company, one of the town's four breweries. During Prohibition it produced a nonalcoholic near beer called "Bristo" or "Bistro."

❺ Retrace steps, continuing on Guenther to Mill. Turn left.

Because Bridge does not cut through we have to repeat part of Mill Street. You will see different details coming from a different direction.

❻ Turn left on Academy, then right on Bridge.

No. 354L, the one-and-a-half-story *Fachwerk* home built in 1850 of adobe and hand-hewn cedar, pine, and oak, with its steeply pitched roof and outdoor staircase, was the Leonardo (or Leonhard) Schmidt home.

At the railroad tracks, if you look to the left you'll see the red brick Comal Power Plant with its LCRA (Lower Colorado River Authority) sign. The plant closed in 1972. It is now the Landmark Lofts; see Walk 5 for details.

At Castell, on the left, is the Saints Peter and Paul Catholic Church (marker). This outstanding building is on a cliff high above Comal Creek on the spot where the settlers first set up camp. They built a stockade with guards patrolling against Indian attack. One never came. The first Catholic church, described as "a crude wooden hut," was replaced in 1849 by a new church known as the Walnut Church, having been built of black walnut. Through all this time, though, they did not have a resident priest until Father Gottfried Menzel arrived in December 1849. Recent findings indicate that the Walnut Church was dismantled and auctioned off in 1874. In 1871 they laid the cornerstone for the original stone church with its beautiful steeple. The church has recently been enlarged for the second time. (New research refutes some information on the historical marker.)

Across on the right is a fun thrift shop supporting the church school.

❼ Turn right on Seguin back to plaza.

No. 259R North Seguin is the 1850s home built by Joseph Peters.

NEW BRAUNFELS WALK 5 (LANDA PARK)

Panther Canyon Nature Trail, Arboretum Trail. Variable length, mostly flat. Park in lot at park office. Public restrooms. The Park Office is off Landa Park Drive at Golf Course Road. It is open Monday through Friday from 8 a.m. to 5 p.m., and between Easter and Labor Day also on Saturday and Sunday from 9 a.m. to 5 p.m. During these months park rangers give guided tours of Comal Springs and Panther Canyon. Call (830) 608-2160 for schedule of tours. Stop in the office for tour information, maps, and an Arboretum Guide.

Joseph Landa arrived in New Braunfels in 1847. After starting business in a tent he opened a store on Main Plaza. He did so well that in 1859 he bought the Comal Springs and surrounding land from William Meriwether. It came with a grist mill, saw mill, and cotton gin. Landa expanded the business, adding an electric plant, grain elevator, cotton oil mill, and ice manufacturing plant. His son, Harry, took over in 1890.

In 1897 Harry entertained Helen Gould, daughter of International and Great Northern Railroad tycoon Jay Gould. She was so impressed with the natural beauty of the Landa estate that she suggested the part along the railroad be opened to the public as a recreational spot. When the KATY railroad laid track in 1900 it also made a run to the park. The Landa family sold the park operation to investors in 1927. It closed as a commercial park during the Depression and was enclosed by a 12- foot barbed-wire fence. In 1936 the city purchased the land for a municipal park. About 1,000 people turned out to help with the cleanup.

In 1956, during a seven-year drought, the Comal Springs went dry for the first time when pumping excess recharge in the Edwards Aquifer. This led to the formation of the Edwards Underground Water District. Paul W. Jahn had warned that this would happen without conservation measures. The battle to conserve water from the aquifer still rages.

In a pulloff at the entrance to the park off North Seguin Street is a *Maibaum* (Maypole) that depicts the early history of New Braunfels. The three-story stone building to the right was the Landa Mill.

The red brick building on the left is the former Comal Power Plant, built by the City of San Antonio in 1925 and at the time the largest power plant in the world. The Lower Colorado River Authority (LCRA) took over the plant in 1947, making it the first non-hydroelectric plant operated by LCRA. After the plant closed in 1972, local residents saved it from demolition and saw that it received recognition as a Texas Historic Landmark and on the National Register of Historic Places. It is now the Landmark Loft apartments.

There are three walks in Landa Park:

1. A one mile gravel trail basically follows the miniature railroad tracks and river.

2. The Arboretum Trail walks past all the major trees in the park. You can buy an inexpensive book at the park office that identifies the trees.

3. The Panther Canyon Nature Trail is 1.6 miles roundtrip. A self guiding pamphlet is available free at the office.

San Marcos

Hays County seat, I-35 midway between San Antonio and Austin. Population 34,733. Three walks.

San Marcos sits along the Balcones Escarpment which divides Texas into uplands and lowlands. Aquarena Springs, the second-largest spring in Texas and the headwater of the San Marcos River, bubbles up from a subterranean lake along the fault zone. The Clovis Indians lived around the springs and river at least 13,000 years ago. This area is reputed to be the longest continuously occupied site in the United States. In 1755 the Spanish opened a mission on the San Marcos River, presumably where the Camino Real crossed the river four miles below the present city of San Marcos. The Spanish established Villa San Marcos de Neve in 1808, the last town settled in the name of the King of Spain, but abandoned it due to lack of government support. Comanche raids then increased until, by 1840, it is thought that no Anglos were left in the area.

After Texas independence, Anglo-Americans, mostly from southern states, began arriving. Edward Burleson was awarded land including San Marcos Springs, for his leadership in the Texas Revolution. He built a home on the hill overlooking the springs and a dam on the river to power a saw and grist mill. Burleson served in the Republic of Texas House of Representatives and the first Senate, and as vice-president during Sam Houston's term as president. In 1848 Burleson petitioned for and won legislation to establish a new county with San Marcos as its seat. He named the county for Texas Ranger Col. John (Jack) Coffee Hays. Hays sent a gold medal to the first child born in the new settlement. This went to William McGehee, born on December 23, 1846, to Thomas and Minerva Hunt McGehee, early settlers on the San Marcos River. In 1886 William's uncle, Charles McGehee, had the contract to do the stonework on the new capitol building in Austin, but he died before its completion. Perhaps this is what led William to impulsively add his medal to the items in the cornerstone—a move, it is said, he later regretted.

General Burleson, jointly with William Lindsey and Dr. Eli Merriman, obtained a piece of land on the Veramendi Land Grant. They donated a portion of it for the streets, cemetery, and public square of the new town, then sold town lots around the square and 12-acre farm lots just beyond it. John Drayton Pitts bought rich farmland east of San Marcos in the valley between the Blanco and San Marcos rivers. Family members followed, forming a long, narrow strip of farms leading to its name of Stringtown. Pitts prospered as a farmer, rancher, and breeder of fine racehorses. He and his family were active in San Marcos civic affairs and founded the Methodist Church. Prosperous farmers and ranchers began moving into town, establishing businesses and building fine homes in the popular Greek Revival and Victorian architecture. Residential expansion took over the farm lots just west of downtown. This area comprises today's historic district, which is featured on these walks.

Edmund Pendleton Reynolds, who arrived in 1867, worked diligently to promote education in San Marcos. In letters to his family back in Virginia, he expressed pride in the city and people of San Marcos. "I venture . . . there is not a more moral town in America than San Marcos. There is not one young man . . . who is a drunkard, and hard as times are we have but one habitual loafer." One wonders if this was really true or if Reynolds was a bit naive. In another letter he expounded on the fine climate, then said, "But, we can't all live in Texas, it would be too crowded." The first school in San Marcos, founded in 1869 by Orlando N. Hollingsworth, was a private coed school offering military training for boys. It became the Coronal Institute. Robert H. Belvin bought the school in 1871, then sold it in 1875 to the Methodist Episcopal Church. It closed in 1919.

Texas State University, San Marcos, formerly Southwest Texas State, sits on a hill overlooking San Marcos. Its distinctive Old Main was the original Normal (Teachers) School. This hilly campus is not conducive to walking unless you want a step-climbing workout. Its library holds the Southwestern Writers Collection. To visit the university, go up LBJ Drive. The guard at the gate will give you a free parking pass and campus map. Aquarena Center, the former Aquarena Springs, is owned by the university. Besides the popular glass-bottom boat rides over the springs, there's a large aquarium, a Wetlands Trail and interactive exhibits. Another trail winds past the Burleson homestead and the mission ruins. Still planned is a river Immersion Gallery built into the river itself.

Wonder World is a commercial park built around an earthquake-formed cave. Its 110-foot tower provides a fabulous view of the area. A train ride takes visitors through a wildlife petting park.

SAN MARCOS WALK I

Historic Hutchison, Belvin, and Burleson streets. 3.1 miles, flat except for one hill at Quarry. Park at intersection of Hutchison and Comanche. No public restrooms.

❶ Facing Comanche Street with your back to H-E-B, walk ahead on Hutchison.

Across Moore Street (no street sign—it's the traffic light), on the hill to the right, a marker commemorates the Coronal Institute.

❷ At Scott Street, Hutchison jogs right and becomes Belvin.

At the start of Belvin Street, on the right is a state marker. Across the alley on the left is a National Register Historic marker, first in San Marcos.

No. 715L (marker) was the 1909 home where Eliza Pitts Malone, daughter of Stringtown's John D. Pitts, lived after her husband, James L. Malone, died. All of the Pitts family moved into San Marcos.

No. 716R (marker) is the 1878 Victorian home of attorney Ossian T. Brown and his wife, Elizabeth Belvin Brown. Although he helped establish an electric generating plant, he had few electric fixtures in his home.

No. 727L (marker), the 1895 home of early settler George Thomas McGehee, incorporates several elements of Victorian architecture. McGehee was with the Texas Rangers in the Civil War, served three terms in the state legislature, and promoted local land enterprises. A self-taught engineer, he installed a pulley system to haul firewood from the basement to various floors and a cooling system that ran water through ice stored in the basement to preserve food.

No. 730R is the home Robert Belvin renovated after retiring as Coronal president.

He came here in 1870 from San Antonio, where he was a Methodist preacher, wholesale merchant, and head of a women's college. After he bought the institute he lived on the grounds for five years. When he sold the school in 1875, he kept 11 acres and this house.

No. 802R (marker) is the 1889 Victorian home of farmer and carpenter George W. Talmadge, a Union veteran who settled here among Confederate veterans without conflict.

No. 801L, an 1889 Victorian home, was bought in 1940 by the four Dodgen sisters, who remodeled it in the then-popular Colonial Revival style. The home sold in 1992 after all four had passed away.

No. 809, the charming stone cottage nestled under a magnificent live oak, was built by Dr. Alexander Gates Thomas, the first

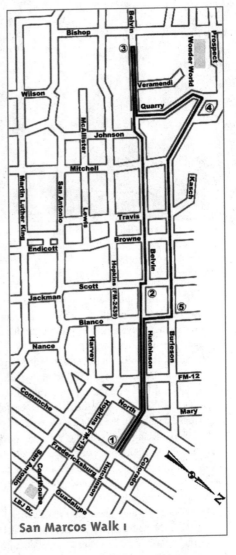

San Marcos Walk I

chairman of the English Department of the Normal School. His students helped him gather the stones. An avid collector of folklore, he entertained both locally and nationally renowned writers, including J. Frank Dobie and Carl Sandburg.

Among the Victorian houses in San Marcos is the Belvin Street home of George Talmadge, a Union veteran who got along well with his many Confederate veteran neighbors.

No. 819 is the John Montgomery home dating from 1909. Montgomery and his wife, Cecilia Cock, had a farm outside of town. One year, after a bumper cotton crop, they moved into town and built this home next to that of Cecilia's twin sister, Civilia Cock Earnest.

No. 833L, the 1892 Victorian home of Joseph and Civilia Cock Earnest, also nestles in the shade of a magnificent live oak. Earnest was a Texas Ranger during the Civil War, a merchant, and a cattleman.

No. 832R, the 1889 Victorian home of John Francis McGehee, is a gingerbread delight. To the right are the restored original barn and stables.

No. 903L (facing Travis) is the Victorian home that merchant Samuel R. Kone Jr. built in 1886. Kone came from Stringtown. His wife, Laura, taught art at Coronal. Their daughter, Florence, also an educator, lived here for 80 years. Herbert A. and Dorothy Yarbrough Jr. restored the house.

No. 904R, originally Victorian, had the three arches added later.

No. 922R is an 1880 "raised Louisiana Cottage" built for a Dr. Evans.

No. 227L N. Mitchell is the 1909 Colonial Revival home that merchant Isaac (Ike) Wood patterned after an antebellum mansion in Atlanta, Georgia. Wood was associated with Glover National Bank, which later became Wood National Bank. When William H. Crook, formerly president of the Baptist Academy, returned to San Marcos after serving in Australia as U.S. ambassador, he bought the house and named it Crookwood.

No. 1008R, set back from the street, is the barn restored by the Crooks in 1992 as lodging for their household help. As you approach Johnson Street, note the beautiful stained glass windows on the corner house.

No. 1030R is the 1919 Renaissance Revival home that noted San Antonio architect Atlee B. Ayers designed for banker Lloyd Gideon Johnson. After a fire on the second floor, the Johnsons moved. The San Marcos Masonic Lodge No. 342 used it from 1937 to 1990. Ron Graves authentically restored it as a private residence in 1992. The Burdick Coat of Arms is that of the home's present owner, Dick Burdick.

No. 1222R, with its lovely Ionic columns, was recently restored. The creek once marked the extent of the city limits.

No. 1236R is the 1891 home James L. and Eliza Pitts Malone moved into with their 16 children after leaving Stringtown. A Queen Anne Victorian, it was modified to Classical Revival in 1926 and restored in 1996. The live oak, its ancient limbs touching the ground, is outstanding. The Malones were the last of Stringtown's settlers to move into town.

➌ Unfortunately, the next street, Bishop, is too hazardous to walk up, so turn around and retrace your steps to Quarry Street. Turn left on Quarry.

This route winds around behind Fisher Hall and comes up on Prospect just past Wonder World.

➍ Turn right on Prospect, then right again on Burleson.

No. 1000 was the home of Col. and Mrs. R. M. Beechinor for many years. The red granite on the wall comes from the same quarry as that used to build the state capital.

On the left, just before Kasch Street, is an imposing yellow brick home. One of its several owners added the wall with his initial "G," and another added the Victorian spindle brackets.

Between Kasch and Browne on the right is the back of the John F. McGehee barn.

No. 724L Burleson was the 1890 Victorian home of Hays County Judge Edward Reeves Kone. He was first elected a county judge in 1878, then elected thirteen more times, not all consecutive, between then and 1906. After moving to Austin in 1911 as Commissioner of Agriculture, he sold the house in 1914 to Oran W. Cliett, a cotton grower and head of the volunteer fire department. One day, while Cliett attended a fireman's benefit across town, the back part of this home caught fire.

No. 702 was the 1890 home of James Gray Storey who established a farm on his arrival in San Marcos in 1848. After serving in the Confederate Army he resumed farming. The governor appointed him county judge but the Federal government removed him from office, citing his appointment as "an obstruction to reconstruction." In 1880, however, Storey was elected to the Legislature and, in 1888, was elected Hays County Clerk.

❺ Turn right on Blanco, then left on Hutchison back to start.

Down Hutchison from the H-E-B parking lot is First United Methodist Church, a beautiful example of Timbered Gothic Revival. The congregation organized in 1847. This 1893 building, third on the site, is the oldest church building in San Marcos and its pipe organ the first in the city.

SAN MARCOS WALK 2

Historic Hopkins and San Antonio Streets, Millie Seaton Collection of Dolls (tours by reservation: (512) 396-1944), courthouse square. 2.0 miles, mostly flat. Park at intersection of Hopkins and Comanche. Several restaurants around square and along walk.

❶ With your back to Comanche Street, walk ahead on Hopkins.

Hopkins was originally Fort Street, which led to a short-lived encampment on the river where men signed up with Captain Henry M. McCullough for the war with Mexico. (See Walk 3.) Look for 1920s concrete street markers that still exist at some intersections.

No. 225L W. Hopkins, originally the St. Mark's Episcopal Church rectory, is an 1899 Greek Revival with Victorian additions. As church membership dwindled it could no longer support a regular minister. In 1935 Archie Weatherford, a retired farmer and rancher, leased the rectory. His wife, Dorothy, had visited it often as a child. Her father, F. Sydney Smith, was active in the church, teaching Sunday school and conducting services when a traveling minister was not available. The church was torn down in 1955, but the Weatherford family lived in the old rectory for 50 years. It then sat vacant until lovingly restored by the present owners.

No. 316R (marker) is the 1902 Victorian home of John Matthew Cape, cotton grower and gin operator. He arrived in 1875, was postmaster from 1890 to 1911, and helped bring utilities to town. It was restored in 1985 for his great-grandson Don Emmis Jr., and has lately been a sorority house.

No. 326R, the 1883 home of Judge W. D. Wood, was of Victorian design (the oldest Victorian in San Marcos) until converted to Classic Revival, with

Ionic columns, in 1909. Judge Wood came in 1883 after retiring from the bench. He was active in local banking and land development.

No. 516R, the delightful 1890 Gothic Revival Fort Street Presbyterian Church, was restored in 1988 by architect Jeffrey H. Kester as home and office.

No. 716R is a 1900 Victorian home that until recently belonged to the Manskes, who ran a bakery and created the Manske roll, a super buttery cinnamon roll. Although the bakery no long exists, the roll is available at Gil's Broiler in the 300 block of LBJ Drive. The current owner of this house lived behind it as a boy and is now restoring it on his own.

No. 819L, the 1909 Colonial Revival home of Walter Hofheinz, has two distinctive leaded glass windows: the Palladian window on the second floor and the oval below.

No. 1117, a patchwork rock house like those seen in

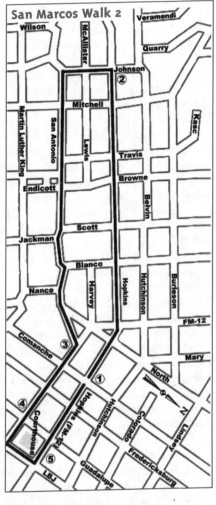

Wimberley, was possibly built by one of the Wimberley stonemasons.

No. 1104, across Johnson, is the 1908 house built for the widow Augusta Voges Hofheinz. Her husband, Daniel, was San Marcos's first hotel owner. This home also has two beautiful leaded glass windows and a leaded entrance door. Millie Seaton and her husband restored the home. As Millie's doll collection, now numbering around 9,000, eventually took over, the Seatons moved out and let their home become a museum.

② Turn left at Johnson, then left on San Antonio.

No. 1001R, with its magnificent live oak, is on land homesteaded by James F. Travis and his wife, Julia. He owned the Opera House on San Antonio Street in the 1880s.

No. 802L is the home that developer Ed J. L. Green built in 1909 and sold the next year to John R. Porters. It combines several architectural styles and has been a nursing home, funeral home, and training center for church seminars. The multitalented Green had an innate ability to make things succeed, amassing a great fortune and initiating many public enterprises, including the Water Power Enterprises, Electric Light Company, San Marcos Water Works, the first ice factory, Federal Fish Hatchery, First National Bank, and First Christian Church. He was an officer of the church from its organization in 1869 until his death in 1924. He also held county offices. An advocate of free public schools, he gave generously to the rebuilding of Coronal Institute after a fire destroyed it.

No. 714L, at the corner of Scott, still has its carriage step at the curb. This 1887 home was built by a doctor who sold it to a druggist, who ran his pharmacy from the front bedroom. One of the concrete street markers dating from the 1920s is on this corner.

No. 711R is a 1912 Classical Revival home built for Ignatius B. Rylander. Rylander arrived in San Marcos in 1867, served on the board of the First National Bank, as a trustee of the Coronal Institute, and as director of the First National Bank, plus helping establish electric power.

No. 621R is a 1868 Greek Revival with touches of Italianate built for Republic of Texas veteran Peter C. Ragsdale. Other than a portion of the Belvin house, this may be the oldest frame house in San Marcos. Another owner was trail driver William T. Jackman, who led 11 cattle drives up the Chisholm Trail before settling down as sheriff of Hays County. It is said he sometimes kept prisoners overnight in the basement of the house.

No. 620L is a delightful 1888 Queen Anne Victorian with a three-story octagon turret built by William Green and sold to Sam McGehee Heard.

On the right, where North Street bears to the left, is a nice old Victorian on an exceptionally beautiful lot, just waiting to be restored.

No. 411R, with the black iron fence, is the 1871 home grocer Basil M. Dailey built for his bride, Julia Manford. It was in the family until recently.

③ Just past here San Antonio Street makes an almost right-angle turn.

On the left is the former First Christian Church. Every Sunday after services Israel Donalson, who helped organize the church, stood at the door inviting strangers to dinner at his house.

The 1908 courthouse is the focal point of the main square in San Marcos.

❹ When you reach the square, cross to the courthouse side to better view the architectural details of the buildings around the square. Continuing along San Antonio Street, walk around the square, turn left on LBJ, then left again on Hopkins.

This courthouse is the fourth for Hays County. The first, built in 1861, burned in 1868. The second, of local soft limestone, was completed in 1871, then razed in 1881. The third, of harder limestone and designed by noted courthouse architect Frederick E. Ruffini, was finished in 1883. After a disastrous fire in 1908 most of it was razed. Some traces of the original are found in the base of this building. The distinctive black dome can be seen from afar. A mosaic Texas Star adorns the floor of the rotunda.

Nos. 136–144 is the Green and Faris Building begun in 1879 and completed in 1885, first masonry structure on the square and the first bank. At the corner of LBJ and San Antonio, the courthouse annex is in the beautiful 1909 Beaux Arts First National Bank Building.

Nos. 114–116 LBJ has a pressed tin front. On this and the next building, detail is highlighted with contrasting color, lending a distinctive look.

No. 139 Hopkins is Harper's Hall dating from 1873.

No. 127 is the 1885 Hardy Williams Building. Its round arches and cast iron columns are typical of commercial buildings of that period.

Nos. 109–111 was first the Glover and later the Wood National Bank.

⑤ Cross Guadalupe and continue straight ahead back to the start.

On the corner across Guadalupe is State Bank and Trust's original building. An unofficial plaque is "dedicated" to the Newton Gang, which held up this bank in 1923. According to the plaque, they used so much nitro they blew out the wall, sending coins flying across the street. Though they escaped, the Newtons did spend time in prison. On their release they lived comfortably on their ill-gotten gains, some to a ripe old age.

SAN MARCOS WALK 3

San Marcos Nature Center (open Tues–Sat, 10 a.m.–6 p.m.), River Trail and Cock House. On I-35 access road at Riverside Drive. The walk as described is just over 3.2 miles round trip and is not suitable for strollers and wheelchairs, but each section of the river corridor parks is accessible by car and is handicap friendly. The trails within each park are mostly flat. There are stairs from the river to Veramendi Plaza and the Cock House. Park in the Nature Center lot. Public restrooms at the Center and throughout the park. Picnic tables and barbecues along the walk. A delicious luncheon is served at the Cock House each Friday from 11 a.m.–1 p.m. (No map.)

San Marcos is justifiably proud of its string of city parks along the river, a Bicentennial project that united three small city parks. The park renovation was one of three projects that led to San Marcos being named an American Revolution Bicentennial City.

The greenhouse at the Nature Center was built in the 1940s on the grounds of the governor's mansion in Austin, then moved to the state cemetery in Austin. Renovations there necessitated another move. Word got to the San Marcos Parks and Recreation Department, which had plans for a nature center on the river. They accepted the old greenhouse, and the Crook family, Heritage Association, River Foundation, and Lower Colorado River Authority raised funds for its development.

The San Marcos River is a noted birding spot and home to unique plants and animals, including five endangered species. The Nature Center offers a variety of environmental education programs for adults and children, with indoor exhibits and outdoor gardens.

❶ Start the walk on the trail leading behind the Nature Center.

This first section of the river trail includes the wildlife habitat with native plants, ponds, and the Native Niche with a greenhouse and some smaller ponds with aquatic plants. The wetland trail is great for viewing dragonflies.

❷ The path comes out at Cheatham Street. To continue on foot, cross Cheatham at the crosswalks.

This is Rio Vista Park. The dam originally diverted water to the mills and cotton gins down river on Thompson Island. The area around the dam has changed from the first edition of this book. Now you will find beautiful ledges and rocks leading down to the river and the dam itself a series of ledges creating three small waterfalls. Just past the second pavilion, a footbridge leads to a tiny island where you can sit under the shade of bald cypress trees to watch the river flow by.

❸ The path ends at the railroad tracks. To continue on foot, cross the tracks, after checking in both directions to see that no train is coming, of course.

The trail ahead leads to the Playscape, one of the nation's largest. Townfolk raised $120,000 in cash and materials for construction. In November 1992, 4,373 adult and 1,398 youth volunteers spent six days, dawn to late night, putting it together. A concrete path is imprinted with names of fundraisers.

Next is Bicentennial Park. The trail leads along the river, where you'll find picnic tables and barbecue grills. On various walks I've stopped to chat with picnickers and scuba divers ("It's a slow, leisurely dive with lots of fish and crawfish." Members of the Heart-o'-Texas Chapter of the Good Sam RV Club help keep this section clean. The club plants a crape myrtle tree as a memorial to each of its members who passes away.

❹ The trail comes to a footbridge. To continue on foot, cross the bridge, go up the rustic steps, then down the paved steps, under the railroad trestle, then up the stairs on the left.

At the top of the stairs is Bicentennial Park. I've nicknamed it Plaque Park. You'll soon see why.

Among the plaques and markers you'll find here is one in a circle of crape myrtle trees that reads "We Love You, Lex." J. Lex Cook was a young STSU student killed in an auto accident. His friends petitioned to plant a memorial tree on campus but were turned down. They approached the Heritage Society and gained permission to place their memorial here.

Another is a commemorative marker for the River Walkway. Then, for the Bicentennial in 1976, the Heritage Society planted the Liberty Tree, and each Arbor Day since has planted another tree. Each has a plaque dedicating it to an outstanding citizen of San Marcos who died during the previous year. A historical marker commemorates Camp McCulloch, established on the river in 1846 for protection of the settlers during the war with Mexico. This encouraged settlement and boosted the economy of the growing town.

On the corner of Hopkins and C. M. Allen is the Charles S. Cock House Museum, the only rock house from settler days remaining in San Marcos and the first house here on the National Register of Historic Places. It is also a Texas Historic Landmark and Texas Archeological Landmark. Cock originally settled on a farm outside of town, but moved his family into San Marcos when he became active in city and county government. He was the town's second mayor. The Cocks had twin daughters, Cecilia and Civilia, wed in a double ceremony in 1870. Cecilia and her husband lived in this house before moving to her father's farm. Cock returned in 1884 and lived in the house until his death in 1897.

The house was restored by the Bicentennial Commission, later the Heritage Association of San Marcos. To raise money for its upkeep, luncheons are served each Friday by volunteers from local organizations and businesses. I was waited on one Friday by the city's head librarian. Lunches are tasty, filling and exceptionally reasonable, but the desserts are extra—and worth it. The stone portion of the house is Greek Revival with Victorian touches added in the 1890s.

❺ To return to the start, retrace your steps along the river trail.

Sisterdale

North of Boerne, east of Comfort at junction of FM 1376 and RR 473.
Population 63. One walk.

The Sisterdale settlement attracted one of the German "Latin Colonies," a group of intellectuals, also called "freethinkers," who studied in Latin and eschewed organized religion. The Latin Colonies survived only a few years. This educated group included nobility. Members immigrated, thinking they would farm half a day and study the other half. They knew nothing about farming and soon discovered survival would occupy most of their time. Nicolaus Zink came to Texas with Prince Carl of Solms-Braunfels, and in 1845 he surveyed and laid out the town of New Braunfels. In 1847 he settled in the valley where the two Sister Creeks join the Guadalupe River. Ottmar von Behr Sr., also from New Braunfels, arrived next in Zink's Settlement. The first post office was in his home. Behr developed a new breed of sheep by crossing German and Mexican lines.

The settlement continued to grow over the next two years with the arrival of the "Forty-Eighters," educated Germans fleeing the unsuccessful 1848 revolution in Europe. Ernst Kapp, a political activist and teacher in Germany, bought land here in 1850. Dr. Rudolf Wipprecht, who also immigrated for political reasons, joined him. They established the Hydropathic Institute based on cures with mineral waters. A Hermann Lungkwitz lithograph of the institute in the Comfort Museum illustrates some water cure processes. Early advertisements show such ones as the wet sheet pack, sitting bath, gymnastic exercises, and injection of water into the ears. Kapp became the first professor of languages at Texas A&M University. On a visit to Germany in 1865 he became ill and never returned to Texas. Many institute buildings still exist, but on private property not visible from the road.

In 1850 John Barlett described a visit he made to a log home in Sisterdale with "no floors or glass windows," furnished simply with a table, chairs, and a platform bed, but where "the walls were covered with books except one spot . . . that held 12 rifles." For want of closets and drawers, clothes hung on deer antlers.

The settlement's name changed to Sisterdale in 1852. According to the diary of Julius Dressel, the name came about "quite by accident." Dressel wrote, "Behr and I visited the Kapps who were already quite comfortable on the hill. After an interesting conversation with the professor about the influence of geographic location on the culture of people, . . . Behr brought the conversation to the naming of the settlement. He thought as long as we already had Bosom Hills, Sister Hills and Twin Sisters, we might as well continue with the feminine gender and call our settlement Sisterdale. . . This suggestion was greeted with undivided assent." Education was of prime importance. Each home had a library. A one-room log schoolhouse was built on the Kapp property in 1887. Men met here weekly to discuss literature, often in Latin. In 1893 a fourth, more permanent school was built of limestone near the road. The next one, north of town, was used until 1954, when the Sisterdale schools consolidated with the Comfort school system.

Sisterdale was the center of German Abolitionism and Unionism before and during the Civil War. The war ended the dominance of the Latin Colony settlers in Sisterdale. Most left due to hard times and hatred caused by the war, many joining Major Fritz Tegener's Union loyalists, the group massacred by

Confederate forces at the Nueces River (see Comfort Walk). Others formed a Confederate militia company; Kapp's oldest son was a captain. The Kapp property has had several owners. Some added buildings, others remodeled existing ones. In 1972 Dr. Samuel C. Woolvin and his wife, Valerija, purchased the property and restored the remaining buildings. They gave it the name Badenthal (Bathing Valley) to reflect its use as a water cure sanitarium and collected memorabilia, opening the schoolhouse as a museum.

While intellectual pursuits provided the social life for Sisterdale's settlers, American baseball filled that role in the early 1900s. Sesquicentennial plans at first included an old-timers' baseball game, but the remaining players from that "farmer boys' league" said they were too old.

Sisterdale had little growth until recent years. Subdivisions springing up around the Hill Country have not crept close to this tiny community—yet. The old cotton gin, now Sister Creek Winery, attracts tourists. Sisterdale Valley Historic District, on the National Register of Historic Places since 1975, begins a quarter-mile south of the Guadalupe River and runs north-northwest to the forks of the Sister Creeks. Sisterdale never incorporated. It never had a church. The town celebrated its 150th birthday in 1997 with a barbecue, demonstrations of old-time skills, a fashion show of historic clothing and, possibly, Sisterdale's first parade ever.

SISTERDALE WALK

Historic buildings, Sister Creek Winery. Just under a mile, flat on narrow paved road shoulder. Park in vicinity of Sister Creek Winery (open noon to 5 p.m. daily). No public restrooms.

The Sister Creek Winery, in the 1885 cotton gin, backs onto West Sister Creek. A steam-driven shingle mill, saw mill, and grist mill owned by Reinhold Kutzer also operated here. A San Antonian bought the property in 1985 as a weekend getaway and cattle ranch, building the stone house off to the left behind the vineyard. When running cattle proved more trouble than profit, the owner, a wine lover, began thinking of a vineyard.

By coincidence, or fate, his foreman, Danny Hernandez, developed an interest in winemaking when stationed in Germany during his army career. He enrolled in classes and learned the technical side of a winery. After planting their vines, the two went to work restoring the old cotton gin, installing new fixtures among the old implements. When you walk into the winery your olfactory system is met with a mixed aroma of old wood and fermenting grapes. After tasting some of Sister Creek's wines you can take a tour of the winery. I learned more on a tour of this intimate operation than on tours of large California wineries.

❶ With your back to the winery, turn left and walk along the shoulder.

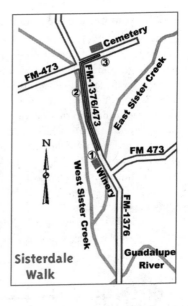

The first building on the left is the Marquardt Garage. Two Marquardt families settled here. Both ran garages.

The two-story 1887 stone house with a basement on the left, was built by stonemason J. Gottlieb Lorbeer.

Past the weathered outbuildings is the home August Langbein built. There are two theories about why so many doors face the street. Either rooms were added as more family arrived from Germany or separate store, post office, and stage stops occupied the home. Later Langbein built a store between his home and the dance hall. He was postmaster for 23 years and active in singing and shooting clubs and in political matters. Between the home and the river is a one-room stone building with rifle portholes that may have been built for defense against Indians.

Langbein built the frame dance hall about 1890. The old painted stage curtain depicts a pastoral scene of a church and stream and bears ads for the Kendall County Abstract and Title Company, Magnolia Petroleum Company and at least 30 other Boerne and Comfort companies. The dance hall was a location for the movie *Heaven and Hell* with Peter O'Toole.

❷ Where the paved shoulder ends (across from the RR 473 sign), cross the road to the old schoolhouse.

This 1893 building is the town's fourth school. The Sisterdale school was considered the finest primary school in Texas. Unfortunately, the museum created here by the Woolvins is no longer open to the public.

The first home of Nicholaus Zink, and the Kapp complex built around it and added onto by subsequent owners, are up the drive to the right. This is private property and is not open to the public.

The Sisterdale Cemetery is up the road to the left of the schoolhouse.

❸ With your back to the school, walk left back to the beginning.

As you walk back, look across the road for a glimpse of a stone building behind the dance hall. The narrow gun slots on this 1850s building indicate that it might have been a stronghold in case of an attack.

Next on the left is the Sisterdale Store and Tavern. The date it was built, 1954, is embedded in pennies next to a post. Inside the tavern, a wood mural depicts the history of Sisterdale. Hugo Schonewolf bought the curly pine back bar in 1919 for the dance hall across the street. In the other room is a small grocery store and tables for those who care to sit and enjoy a snack and cold drink. A fast-paced game of dominoes is usually in progress with owner Valerija Woolvin either watching or playing.

No. 1205 was originally a home, then a restaurant/post office, and is currently a home and post office.

No. 1203 was the Offer home. The post office was here for many years. The chimney, with its firewood box, is all that's visible of the original house.

29 Stonewall

Between Fredericksburg and Johnson City on U.S. 290. Population 469. One walk.

German immigrants settled near here along the Pedernales (pronounced PER-den-alus) in the 1840s. Maj. Israel Nuñez established a store and stage stop in 1870, and a post office in 1875. In 1882, when Nuñez moved both to the nearby Millville settlement, he changed the name to Stonewall to honor Confederate General Thomas "Stonewall" Jackson. Besides sheep and cattle raising, farmers tried fruit orchards. Stonewall is now the state's major peach-growing area and celebrates with a Peach Jamboree in June.

Stonewall's first famous native son was Emil Sauer, U.S. consul general in various countries and an author on international finance. The town's most famous native son, of course, is Lyndon Baines Johnson, 36th president of the United States, born here on August 27, 1908, the first child of Samuel and Rebekah Johnson. There are two LBJ parks in Stonewall. One is the LBJ National Historical Park Ranch District on the north side of the Pedernales River, accessible only on park service tours. It includes his birthplace, first school, and the LBJ Ranch, known during his term in office as the Texas White House. The other is the LBJ State Historical Park on the river's south side.

Lyndon B. Johnson's Summer White House near Stonewall is now restored and open to the public.

NPS PHOTO

The presidents' friends raised money to purchase property for this park with a visitor center, the Sauer-Beckmann Living History Farm, and nature trails.

Few early homes remain. Of interest are St. Francis Xavier Catholic Church, Winheimer & Sons general store (1906), Stonewall School and Trinity Lutheran Church—attended by the Johnsons—and its cemetery. All these may be seen along Ranch Road 1.

STONEWALL WALK

LBJ State Historical Park and Nature Trail (open daily except Christmas and New Year's Day from 8 a.m. to 5 p.m.), Sauer-Beckmann Living History Farm (open park days from 8 a.m. to 4:30 p.m.). Bus tours (fee) to the National Park from 10 a.m. to 4 p.m. One mile, flat gravel trails. Park in visitor center lot at LBJ State Historical Park (public restrooms). Closest restaurants are on Hwy. 290 in Stonewall, in Johnson City and in Fredericksburg. Map available at the Visitor Center.

① From the visitor center walk back to the Behrens cabin, then to the Sauer-Beckmann Living History Farm. (Rangers ask you to stay on the trails; cutting across land results in unnecessary erosion.) Markers identify trees and plants. After crossing the footbridge take the right fork.

The Living History Farm is the former home of Johann and Christine Sauer, who settled here in 1869 and added several stone buildings to their rock and log cabin. The Beckmann family bought the property in 1900 and added a new barn, a wood-frame room to the old house, and porches connecting it with a new Victorian house covered with fashionable pressed tin. Edna Beckmann Hightower sold the site to Texas Parks and Wildlife in 1966. After archeology and restoration, it opened to the public in 1975.

Today this is a living history farm where a "farmer" and his "wife" carry out the daily tasks of the early settlers. The farmer feeds and milks the animals, forges tools, and slaughters meat to make sausages. The farmer's wife gathers eggs, bakes, cooks a noonday meal for the park employees, and on Monday does the weekly laundry outside in an iron pot over a fire. On one visit I was invited by "grandmother," a park docent, to sit awhile and chat. As we rocked she told me about her mother's people, who came to Texas in 1847, settling in the Luckenbach area. After listening to her tales, as I walked back to my car I sensed the isolation settlers must have felt living here, far from neighbors, vulnerable to renegade Indian attacks.

Each December the public is invited to a holiday gathering. After a brief welcome at the visitor center and the arrival of Santa on a red fire engine, visitors load onto buses for a tour of the National Park. The tour ends at the farm, where you are invited to sample the sausage and baked goods the farmer and his wife have prepared. Along the short stroll back to the visitor center is a living crèche. It is a lovely evening.

② **To get back on the trail, face the vegetable garden and windmill, your back to the farmhouse, and turn left. The trail turns left at the mesquite tree. At the fork go left on the Texas Wildlife Trail. Go over the footbridge and turn left.**

Longhorn cattle and whitetail deer graze in the corral along here. A narrow trail follows the fence line.

③ **At the next fork (the Chinquapin oak tree), stay straight ahead and turn right through the wildflower field back to the visitor center.**

A statue of LBJ in a little plaza in the field points across the river to the LBJ Ranch.

Tarpley

West of Bandera on FM 470 at the intersection of FM 462. Population 30. No walk.

Tarpley is on picturesque, winding FM 470, midway between Bandera and Utopia, which inspired the local tee shirt slogan "Tarpley, Texas, Almost to Utopia." It gained its identity in 1899, when a post office designated Hondo Canyon was relocated a few miles down Williams Creek and renamed Tarpley after the son of the postmaster, John Prickett. Just east of what became the general store, rooms were rented to travelers in what was known as the Tarpley Hotel, a two-story board-and-batten house since lowered to one story. In 1902 a Baptist church farther up the creek followed the post office down to Tarpley. Its members dedicated their first building in 1911 and a newer one in 1949. However, Tarpley's population, estimated at 205 in 1930, continued to decline. The school closed in the 1950s, and the church fell into disuse.

As the community's fortunes improved, in 1971 a volunteer fire department was organized and a building erected between the Baptist church and the old school, now used as a community center. In 1978 the church was reorganized and its building repaired. Members are planning a large addition at the rear of the building.

While Tarpley may be known in the area for its good-humored annual Volunteer Firemen's Labor Day Parade and Barbecue (a goat was once paraded as "Miss Tarpley"), it has gotten some national attention as well. Some scenes in the 1975 movie *Race With the Devil*, starring Peter Fonda and Warren Oates, were filmed near Williams and Hondo creeks. And Tarpley is now the home of Mac & Ernie's Roadside Eatery, which has moved its original ordering/kitchen shack to become the entrance to new quarters just east of the main intersection (Fri. & Sat. 11 a.m.–4 p.m., 5–9 p.m., Sun. 10 a.m.–2 p.m., 830-562-3727). Offerings from Cabrito Burgers to Ancho Chili Honey Basted Quail to Mahi Mahi with Pineapple Aioli have drawn rave reviews from the likes of *Southern Living*, the Travel Channel, and the Food Network.

Some five miles to the southeast, off FM 462, is the Hill Country State Natural Area, opened in 1984. Most of its 5,400 acres were donated by the Merrick Bar-O Ranch with the requirement that it "be kept far removed and untouched by modern civilization, where everything is preserved intact yet put to a useful purpose."

31 Utopia

West of Bandera on FM 187 south of the intersection with FM 470.
Population 240. No walk.

Located in Sabinal Canyon in the northeast corner of Uvalde County, Utopia was originally named Montana and platted by Robert Kincheloe in 1884, eight years after the last Indian raid in the area. Kincheloe gave land for the school, churches and the community square. The post office moved in from Waresville, a mile south, settled by William Ware in 1852. When residents learned that Texas already had a town named Montana, they changed the name to Utopia. A book of stories by Mrs. W. L. Ames credits the naming to the postmaster, George A. Barker, who had come to the area to improve his health. Barker had taken swims in the Sabinal River before breakfast each morning, summer and winter, and became well. Welcome signs at the edge of town now call Utopia "a paradise."

Soon after Utopia was formally established there were 150 residents and two gristmills, a cotton gin, blacksmith shop, general store and three churches. The Gothic Revival style Methodist Church was built at 200 Cypress St. in 1892, after members raised $1,000 for lumber to start the building. The pecan grove at the rear is on the site of a brush arbor, where early camp meetings were held. Baptists shared the Methodist facility until they erected their own church at Johnson and Oak streets in 1912, replaced in 1952 by a new building. The Church of Christ stayed in what was left of Waresville until the church burned in 1902. Members reestablished their church in Utopia and held outdoor meetings in a brush arbor, now the site of the parking lot of the present brick church, built in 1985.

There was telephone service in Utopia by 1914. Annual rodeos began in 1929. Those are now major events, held usually the fourth weekend in June in the park at the southwest edge of town, beside a lake formed by the Sabinal River. Local history exhibits are displayed at the Sabinal Canyon Museum at Main and Jackson streets (Sat. 10 a.m.–4 p.m., Sun. 1–4 p.m., 830-966-3747).

The Lost Maples Cafe at 187 Main St. is famous for its pies, and has been enlarged in recent years. The original two-story frame part of the building dates from around 1900, and has also served as a Masonic lodge, doctor's office, drug store and school (Sun.–Thu. 7 a.m.–8 p.m., Fri.—Sun. 7 a.m.–9 p.m., 830-966-2221). Its name reflects that of Lost Maples State Natural area, a 2,200-acres park 14 miles north near Vanderpool, noted for its relict stand of bigtooth maples that add autumn color to the hills. Another recreation attraction that boosts tourism in Utopia is Garner State Park, on the Sabinal River 15 miles west.

32 Waring

East of Comfort, off I-10 at FM 1621 and the Waring-Welfare Road (Old No. 9). One walk.

Settlers around Waring came mostly from the British Isles. In 1860 Edward and Lucy Wentworth built a hand cut limestone home on the north side of the Guadalupe River where the San Antonio–Fredericksburg road crossed the New Braunfels–Comfort road. Later they added a two-story frame stage stop named Windsor. In 1880 Windsor got a post office designation with Lucy as postmistress. Edward had hopes of platting a town, but fate intervened.

On the south side of the river was Waringford, a settlement established by Robert Percival Maxwell Waring, a sheep rancher and native of Waringfield, Northern Ireland. In 1886, learning the railroad was heading their way, the two settlements competed for the depot. Waring, knowing the railroad favored an established town, donated land to build a school and a church. Whether because of this or because the river was easier to cross upstream from Waringford, that town got the depot. Although the town of Windsor never materialized, the Wentworths' home still stands on the hill across the river from Waring.

The railroad arrived in 1887. A favorite legend claims a porter on the train got tired of calling out "Waringford" and shortened it to "Waring," and the name stuck. This story held until recent times when a local historian, checking through county records, discovered the official name change came before the railroad did. Waring became a bustling freight and trade center. Wagon trains arrived with cotton, wool, hides, grain, and hay from the surrounding areas. They took back lumber, hardware, salt, foodstuffs, furniture, and anything else the farmers and ranchers needed. With no roads, these were arduous trips for the teamsters. Wagon tracks through the hills crossed creeks and boggy places where wagons could become stuck or break a wheel. When the river flooded the freight had to wait for the water to go down. The town soon boasted two blacksmith shops, a cotton gin, grist mill, barber shop, general stores, and, of course, a saloon. Like other Hill Country towns, it had its share of summer and weekend visitors seeking the healthy, cooler climate. Besides boarding houses and tourist cottages, later businesses included a cafe, butcher shop, garage, and confectionery that served ice cream.

The first blow to Waring's progress came in 1913, when Fredericksburg built its own branch railroad that met the Kerrville Railroad on the north side of the river. This brought an end to freighting by wagon through Waring, but the little town still prospered as a popular midpoint stop for gas and food on the all-day trip along Highway 9 from San Antonio to Fredericksburg. In the early 1930s Waring was once again bypassed when Highway 87 was extended from

Boerne to Comfort, creating a faster route to Fredericksburg. The post office discontinued mail by train in the 1950s and in the 1960s trains ceased to run altogether. Waring became the sleepy little town of today.

Waring residents like it that way, but with the increasing popularity of the Hill Country as a tourist destination and the growth of San Antonio, Waring could come to life again. The post office expanded in the late 1990s from the former Rust Texaco station to a shiny modern building. The Texaco station, attached to the former Highway 9 Cafe, is now the Waring General Store, a gift and snack shop long owned by caterer Don Strange. The cafe serves food on weekends, and attracts people from throughout the area for its Wednesday Steak Nite. For many years the only other business in Waring was Saur's Garage. It was joined a few years ago by a new business—Guadalupe Crossing Market, in the old butcher shop, featuring art, crafts, antiques, books and wine.

Waring has had many civic organizations, including the Central Shooting Club, Woodman of the World, Mendelssohn Gesang Verein (the singing club), Hermann Sons Lodge, the Waring Players, and the Thimble Club. At the Thimble Club's 60th anniversary in June 2000, two original members were living and one, Martha Rust, attended the celebration. The club got its start when the railroad's new section foreman moved here with his family. His wife missed the monthly get-togethers she and her friends had back home, so she started a group. Meeting at each other's homes they would visit while they did their sewing and mending. Because most women work now, the club's membership is dwindling, with membership hovering around 20. The Thimble Club meets the first Wednesday of each month—unless there is a flood or snowstorm and those living on surrounding ranches can't make it into town. Mail comes from Comfort, and local children go to school there.

WARING WALK

Church, school, depot, homes, and "monsters in the woods." About 1 mile plus side trip, flat in town, uphill side trip. Park by Waring General Store. Public restrooms in store. Nearby restaurants are Welfare Cafe and Po-Po's on the Waring-Welfare Road to I-10 West.

Note: Street signs are not plentiful, and some that exist do not correspond with street names on the hand drawn local map I used. This map should suffice. If not, Waring isn't big enough to get lost in for long.

❶ With your back to the Waring General Store, walk straight ahead on the Waring-Welfare Road.

At the start, across on the right is the Rust house. Next to it is the former Rust Hardware Store. The small white frame building, now Guadalupe Crossing, was the butcher shop owned by G. R. Edwards.

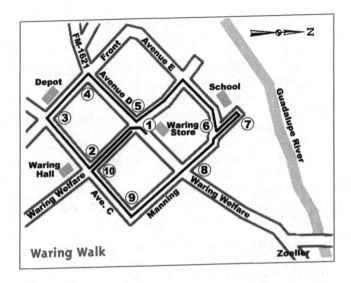

Waring Walk

Herman Rust arrived in 1898 at age 16. He worked in Mr. Anderson's blacksmith shop, bought the shop and became Waring's leading blacksmith. He later learned auto mechanics, opened a Texaco station, and had a Case tractor and implement dealership. After a fire, Rust and his sons Roy and Hilmar (Buster) built the Texaco station, now the general store. After he retired, his sons ran the station and garage. After 67 years as a family business, they sold it to Richard Saur. Buster stayed as mechanic and welder. Saur took on Freddie Blaschke as partner, and in 1980 they opened the larger shop across the street as R and F Auto and Welding.

② Turn right onto Avenue C at Waring Hall.

On the corner by Waring Hall sit two cast iron eagles. One is the original of a pair awarded to Rust as an outstanding dealer for 53 years. The eagles originally stood on a concrete pedestal in front of the Rust store. One morning, in the late 1940s or early 1950s, the town awoke to find one missing. They traced it to Pleasanton High School. With the whole base, up to the globe, set in cement, it would take a jack hammer to set the eagle free. Rust sold it to the school and used the money to buy another eagle.

Waring Hall, originally the Offer Dance Hall, was then, as now, the social center of Waring. The roof of the original 1910s building collapsed in the great snowstorm of 1985. That wooden structure still exists under the metal exterior built to support a new roof.

Between the fire station and the railroad tracks behind the depot was the Offer Camp Yard, where the teamsters who hauled freight stayed overnight. The tracks are gone.

When trains ran, mail was sorted on the train. You could send a message to any town ahead along the line on the morning train and receive your answer on the afternoon run. That's even faster than FedEx!

A spur ran off to the left to a rock quarry. Rock went to build the sea wall in Galveston and steps of the Bexar County Courthouse.

When Waring built the school he brought Agnes Robinson as teacher. They fell in love and married. Atop the hill ahead is the house he built for his bride, the upper part added in the 1950s. Agnes Waring was a talented musician as well as a teacher and played the organ in local churches. After Waring died while on a visit to Ireland in 1895, Agnes remarried and lived until two days before her 90th birthday. The house remains in the family.

❸ To take a side trip to look for "the monsters in the woods," walk straight ahead up the hill. The road goes on forever, so turn back whenever you're ready. To skip the side trip turn right at the depot.

Side trip:

A walk along this ranch road is not only pleasant, but for the sharp-of-eye it offers a great surprise. Every year around Halloween the Comfort Gallivanters, a Volksmarch group, sponsors a walk starting at Waring Hall. A member goes out before the walk and paints some of the deadwood along the way in whatever character its shape suggests to her. You may spot a dragon, alligator, snake, or owl. A dead oak tree had a bump that looked like big lips, so that's what she painted, plus big eyes with long lashes. A local woman's grandson, who asks to "Go look for the monsters in the bushes," calls that one "the Kissy Lady."

When the *Boerne Star* ran an article about "the dragons and monsters in the forest around Waring," people started calling and asking to "see those monsters."

From the depot:

After the depot closed in the early 1940s Herman Rust used it to store grain. Next, the Tomlinson family, who owned a ranch and dairy nearby, used it to mix ice cream base. After it sat neglected for many years, the Tomlinsons put it up for sale. A San Antonian saw the ad. Thinking it would be nifty living in an old railroad depot, he bought it over the phone, sight unseen. Much to his delight, when he tore "modern" paneling off the interior walls he found old timetables taped on the original walls, as well as initials etched in the wood. He immersed himself in Waring history and has spent many intriguing hours trying to connect the various initials with the people who might have carved them there.

The house across from the depot, originally much larger, was Lizzie's Boarding House.

❹ Turn right on Avenue D (FM 1621).

The stamped-tin building on the right was the Rust warehouse. A mold from this type was made of pressed tin to form concrete blocks.

Next on the right is the Rust house again. It is still in the family. The back end of the house is the original, built around 1908.

On the left-hand corner was Oscar Rechenthen's store and the post office. When Erhard Treiber bought it in 1946 the post office appointment passed to him. After the store closed in 1979, the post office stayed until 1985.

❺ Turn left at this point, then right onto Avenue E.

At the end of the block is the schoolhouse. Waring donated the land, and others supplied material and labor. The west wing is the original school (marker) with the original wood-burning stove. Tuition was $1 to $1.50 a month, in those days of large families a hardship for some. The last class graduated in 1954, and local children went to Comfort. The Thimble Club, charged with the school's care and upkeep, meets monthly here.

❻ Turn left, walking alongside the schoolhouse.

In the 1978 flood, the river backed up behind the school. The outhouse floated away, almost down to the ditch. The town had it restored.

Walk on down to the bluff. The town of Windsor stood on the hill across the river from here.

❼ Turn around and walk back along Manning Street.

The property for the church on the right was given to the city by Mr. Waring at the same time as the school. It is still in use.

❽ To take a short side trip down to the river, turn left. To skip the side trip, continue ahead.

Side trip:
The road leads down to a particularly beautiful view of the cypress-lined Guadalupe River. Until the bridge was raised recently, the road over the river was impassable in times of heavy rain.

To skip the side trip, continue on Manning.
Where the stone house now stands was the beautiful Victorian home, complete with gingerbread trim, porches, cupolas, and lightening rods, which

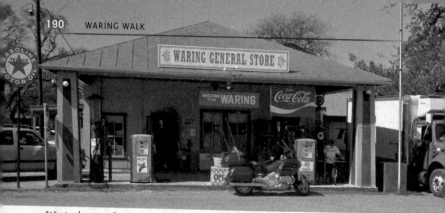

Waring's general store was built by August Offer in 1908.

Offer built for his family. In the 1960s the house burned. Fire, unfortunately, destroyed many of Waring's original buildings.

❾ Turn right on Avenue C.

On the left corner lived the prominent King family.

❿ Turn right on the Waring-Welfare Road.

The empty lot behind Saur's was the site of the Offer store. August Offer came to Waring in the 1890s from New Braunfels. After running several other businesses, he built the store here about 1908. The first floor of the stone building was a general store. Half of the top floor was a large meeting room and the other half an apartment of six rooms. There was a small building behind the store with cubbyholes for the mail. The stagecoach would pull up and stick the mail into the slots. In 1904 Offer built an electric plant to light his store, dance hall, and home.

The new post office is on the left. When I came through the first time the post office was a charming, small, old-timey affair at the Waring General Store where the gift shop is now. Postmistress Dottie Anders told me that though tourists like me found it "quaint," she sure appreciates having room for processing the mail. Waring may be small, but the post office serves the many ranches, farms, and new subdivisions in the area.

The Welfare Store/Texaco Station was an afternoon gathering place for some of the townsfolk. After they retired, Ray and Martha Rust still came by at 3 p.m. every afternoon for what was referred to as "tea time." The place really "jumped" on Saturday when the "city folks" stopped by.

You are now back at the center of town. The Walsh house next to the Texaco station is thought to be a Sears and Roebuck "kit" house, an early day prefabricated house.

33 Welfare

Just east of I-10 between Boerne and Comfort. Population 36. One walk.

I discovered Welfare in the early 1990s when a friend spotted the sign on I-10 and asked, "Why would anyone name a town Welfare?" We pulled off to find out. I especially like what J. Roy White wrote in *Hill Country Revisited:* "A place called Welfare so close to Comfort sounded strange, so I drove over . . . . The road went right through—or past—Welfare, and I found out that Welfare must need welfare, or comfort, or something."

When I first came upon it, Welfare was a sign on the road and an abandoned store with bright red geraniums poking between slats of gray, weathered steps. A few houses and a one-room schoolhouse sat on the hill behind. Driving by on a lovely spring day in 1999 I saw the store with a new coat of white paint and lace curtains in the windows.

First, because I know your curiosity must be piqued, here are the several stories about how Welfare got its name. Originally the settlement had the name Bon Ton or Boyton, meaning "Good Town." The name Welfare was in use as early as 1875, according to one historian. One story says it's a corruption of the German *wohlfahrt,* "pleasant trip." Another says it's a description of the surrounding rich fields where you could "fare well." I've also read that the word "Welfare" had a different, less negative, meaning in those days.

The settlement grew along the old Pinta Indian Trail—eventually Highway 9, the main route from San Antonio to Fredericksburg until 1932. Mail delivery by stagecoach began as early as 1846, with the first post office on the Gottfried Knoepfli ranch. When the San Antonio and Aransas Pass Railroad came through Welfare in 1887, the settlement grew. When the general store opened in 1890 the post office moved there. The store also was cafe, saloon, local gathering place, and lending library. Welfare soon boasted a depot, hotel, and cotton gin. Then, beginning in the early 1900s, Welfare suffered the same decline as the rest of the Hill Country due to drought and loss of the cotton crop to boll weevils. Further, in 1930 Highway 87 bypassed Welfare, the train ceased to run in 1970, and the post office closed in 1976.

Perry Laas and his wife, Alma, ran the store and post office from 1921 to 1976. In an article in the *Boerne Star,* Curt Littman related how the postmaster was paid per number of letters processed. Drummers (traveling salesmen) liked Laas and mailed from his post office to help him out. One day an inspector came by to find out why such a small post office had so large a volume. Tourists also liked to mail postcards from Welfare so they could say things like, "I'm in

Welfare, but not on welfare." The Postal Service had a mandatory age limit of 70 for postmasters but not for clerks, so to keep his job after he reached age 70 Laas took a demotion. The store remained closed until 1998, when Gabriele Meissner McCormick and David Lawhorn opened it as a cafe.

If you came off I-10 to Welfare you passed the Po-Po Family Restaurant. Po-Po's actually is in Nelson City, not Welfare, but that town no longer rates a road sign or even a dot on the map, nor have most people heard of it.

Rancher Edwin Nelson opened a dance hall in 1929 adjacent to his gas station. It held dances every two weeks, sometimes with an orchestra, or just a fiddle and guitar. Admission was 25 cents, and soft drinks were 5 cents. If you wanted something stronger, a shot of moonshine sold out back for 25 cents. Then along came the Depression. Times got so bad people couldn't afford the gas to get to the dance hall and it closed. In 1932 Edwin Houston, a rancher from across the road, bought the property and opened a restaurant. It is believed that in his search for a short, catchy name, while doing business in Mexico he decided to name his restaurant Po-Po after the volcano Popocatepetl. Houston sold out in 1934. It changed hands several times more, and Luther and Marie Burgon bought it in 1950. Under their ownership it became a popular family restaurant. On the Burgons' annual vacation they took to buying souvenir plates for the walls of the restaurant. Patrons continue to add to the collection, which now numbers well over 1,000 plates. In 1983 the restaurant again changed hands when Jerry and Jenny Tilley and their son David bought it. They brought dancing back with an outdoor sound stage and covered dance pavilion. In the mid-2000s Po-Pos changed hands again when sold to Sam Bournia.

After finding Welfare, your next question surely is: "Why, if this is all there is of Welfare, does it rate an exit sign on the Interstate?" For one thing, it is the location of the popular Don Strange Ranch, where many a Texas-size party is catered. It is also, to quote a local old-timer, "a great place to live," with new homes, belying any resemblance to "welfare," being built all around Welfare.

WELFARE WALK

A scenic country walk along Poehnert Road to an 1880s home. 2.4 miles from Poehnert Road turnoff; long, gradual upgrade on narrow paved road with good shoulders, okay for strollers, but if you're in a wheelchair you might check it out first. Park at Poehnert Road turnoff (look for long row of mailboxes). Please respect the privacy and property of the residents by staying on the road. No public restrooms. Eat at Welfare Store or Po-Po's.

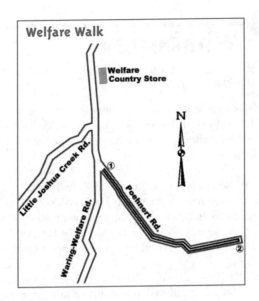

❶ Walk up Poehnert Road.

This road is pronounced PAY-nurt. At the start of the walk I heard cries of peacocks to the right. A friendly donkey greeted me in a field to my left, following me to the end of his fence line. Cattle, horses, and goats are other livestock you'll see. Watch for deer and jackrabbits.

At the end of the road ("Kendall County Maintenance End" and "Private Lane" signs) are the home and barns of the Frederick August Poehnert homestead in a grove of live oak trees with vast pasture land behind. The home has been added onto. Two Poehnert families settled in Welfare, the other, cousin Johann Heinrich, on the Waring-Welfare Road between here and Po-Po's. Both were stonemasons. Frederick August went by August. He married Auguste Kleimstein. One child was August. How confusing!

❷ Turn around and retrace your steps to the start.

On the return walk your sight line will present different, and quite spectacular, views across the Hill Country.

Wimberley

Northwest of San Marcos on FM 12 at the intersection of FM 2325 and FM 3237. Population 3,797. One walk.

The early history of Wimberley was not written about momentous events for there were none. Wimberley's early history was written through the way its people lived on its hills and in its valleys. —Dorothy Wimberley Kerbow, *Clear Springs and Limestone Ledges.*

In 1854 William C. Winters moved his family to the small trading post of Glendale at the confluence of the Blanco River and Cypress Creek. He built a rock home on the hill overlooking the creek and bought the town's mill. Glendale soon became known as Winters' Mill. After Winters' death his son-in-law, John Cude, took over the mill, and people started calling the settlement Cude's Mill.

Pleasant Wimberley arrived in Texas in 1847 with some of his siblings and their families. They gathered a herd of longhorn cattle and settled in Blanco County, where they also raised stagecoach horses. Wimberley bred his Percheron stallions to native horses, resulting in animals of "such size and stamina they could gallop all day, sending the old stagecoach rocking and reeling as it bounced across creeks, streams and hills." But life was dangerous and Wimberley's wife, Amanda, begged for them to move to San Marcos where, she heard, it was both beautiful and safe. In 1874 Wimberley set out along the Blanco River to look for a new home. Arriving at Cypress Creek, he followed it to Cude's Mill. Thinking this beautiful place near San Marcos would please Amanda and provide a good living for his family, he bought 200 acres between the river and the creek including the mill and the Winters' home. Cude's Mill then became Wimberley's Mill. In 1880 the San Marcos postmaster decided Wimberley's Mill needed its own post office. He submitted the name as "Wimberleyville" to the postmaster general in Washington, D.C., who dropped the "ville." When John Will Pyland bought the mill in 1907, the town broke tradition and left the name alone.

As a mill town and trading post Wimberley served the surrounding farms and ranches. Anyone else, as longtime resident Raymond Czichos once put it, "discovered Wimberley because you got here accidentally. The first time someone would drive onto the very colorful square, . . . you knew you had just discovered something nobody else knew about."

❷ Walk around the square starting on the left side.

The Cypress Creek Cafe is a fine representation of the "patchwork" rock buildings constructed by James C. Lane, John E. Harris, and other local stonemasons in the 1920s and 1930s.

The Old Mill Store is new. The first section's facade features a parapet with typical early overhanging eaves. Charles Roccaforte designed it for the Steve Klepfers, who hope to see the square restored to its earlier look.

The last rock house, at Oak Drive, is the James C. Lane home. Lane used some of his vast rock collection to build this 1934 house that incorporates pieces of petrified wood, quartz, and stalactite. Wimberley's first telephone switchboard operated from a front room here.

Susie Brooks Danforth, fondly known as "Miss Susie," was the town's most beloved teacher. She lived in several houses around the square during her 101 years. Not only did she teach, she continued to learn, receiving her last degree at age 56, at the same time her 21-year-old daughter received hers. They taught together in a two-teacher school. Before and after her marriage Miss Susie taught in Texas and Oklahoma but always came back to Wimberley. She served for a short time as the town's telephone operator. The school forced her to retire from teaching at 63, later hiring her back as principal. During World War II she taught and drove the school bus. At 95 she was called upon to substitute teach. Her autobiography, *One Hundred Years in Wimberley*, is full of stories of early years.

No. 303, on the right just past Oak Drive, dates from around 1900, maybe earlier. In the 1940s Mrs. O. T. Egger ran the switchboard from here. There were no home phones then. When you needed to make a call you came here. The lines weren't good so you had to shout. Consequently everyone around heard your conversation.

Later, when phones were in homes, calls still went through the switchboard. The operator knew everything. She'd say, "You don't need to call the X's. They've gone to San Marcos to buy groceries." Or, "No, M.F. hasn't had her baby yet." She handed out advice, like telling a young man, "I wouldn't bother calling Y for a date. She turned you down last week. Why don't you try some of the ones who want to go out with you?"

❸ At this point turn right and continue past the shops.

The buildings along the north side of the square and those down below at creek level all date to more recent times. Originally homes on this side of the square had lawns sweeping down to the tree-lined creek.

❹ Go down the walk between the shops to creek level. Turn right toward FM 12.

Originally the mill was on this side of the river, powered by the force of the water in the creek. After it washed away in 1856, Winters rebuilt on higher ground across the creek, digging a millrace to power the mill.

❺ At FM 12, turn left. Stay on the left side of the street. Cross the bridge over Cypress Creek. Walk through the park and behind the bank.

Across the creek is a small park. Beyond it, the Ozona Bank nestles into the former mill site. Builders preserved many old-growth trees, making it difficult to tell where the park ends and the bank parking lot begins.

A short trail leads along the creek from the park behind the bank building to River Road. Use of native rock and wood for the bank created a modern building that fits appropriately into its historic surroundings.

❻ Cross River Road and turn right, crossing FM 12 at the light. Walk up the short hill to the Visitor Center.

In front is a wildscape and herb garden maintained by Keep Wimberley Beautiful and watched over by Mrs. Meriwether, the "garden lady." Behind the Visitor Center is the Wimberley Community Center, home to the Wimberley Art League's gallery; the Senior Center; and a 280-foot mural painted by Wimberley native and nationally recognized artist James Buchanan "Buck" Winn for the old Pearl Brewery in San Antonio. Adjacent to the Center is the Patsy Glen Bird Sanctuary.

North of the Visitor Center is the newer, commercial section of Wimberley. In 1997 the property between the Senior Center and Millrace Lane below, including the historic Winters-Wimberley home, went up for sale. Local citizens raised money to purchase five acres that would save the house and provide a buffer zone for the town's historic district. The Senior Center is the steward of record for the property.

❼ Take the path leading from the Visitor Center down to the Winters-Wimberley House.

Wildflowers line the path. A weathered sign marks the remains of a former outhouse. Besides his mills, Winters was known as a maker of fine black walnut furniture. The black walnut fireplace mantels inside the home replace the originals, which had been removed. The floor is 150-year old longleaf pine from New Orleans. The Wimberley Institute of Cultures has restored the home for use as a meeting place for cultural, educational and social programs. It is not open for touring.

❽ Continue down the path to the Senior Center Thrift Store.

This thrift store helps support activities of the Senior Center. It has a great variety of stuff at very reasonable prices.

❾ Continue past the Thrift Shop and through the parking lot to Millrace Lane. Turn left.

At the start of Millrace Lane, on the left behind a more modern house, is the house Wimberley's son, Zack, built for his wife. When first married they lived with his parents. One day, the story goes, Zack got home to find Mary coming down the hill with a suitcase, declaring she could no longer share a house with his mother. He promised if she would not leave he would build her a new home. This is the house, built of sturdy cypress and pine. When a retired schoolteacher bought the property she put a new roof on the old house but built a new house for herself.

Directly across the lane is the Harris Camp. Many years ago, Clarence Burdett fell in love with a woman who loved camping. To woo his lady-love, he built her Camp Waloa. Later the Harris family from Austin bought the property. Besides running a camp for children, Mrs. Harris made and sold bread and herbal teas. It is now private property. From the gate, on the right you can see the rock house Burdett built. Mrs. Harris swam in the creek every day until she went into the local nursing home in 1999.

Up the lane, the gully on the left is a partially filled-in portion of the millrace that supplied power to the mills. It ran three-quarters of a mile from a dam below the Blue Hole to a millpond where the Senior Center is.

Farther up, at the log fence, the millrace widens and deepens, more like its original size of 5 feet across and 16 feet deep. Dug by pick and shovel, the dirt was loaded onto steer hides and hauled out by donkeys. This portion is designated historic by the Texas Historic Commission. Look for a post showing its designation also as a State Archeological Landmark.

❿ Retrace your steps back to RR 12. Turn left across the creek.

Across the creek, the road curves to the left. The first building was the store of John Henry Saunders, who built the first local water system, using a wooden tank into which he pumped creek water. A former teacher, he established a school system. He had a reputation as a wise counselor and at times took in travelers, the aged, and the down-and-out. As a surveyor he drew the first map of Wimberley and could substitute as doctor. He added to the store in 1890.

Note that date and the initials "JHS" on the left side of the building above the porch roof. The more recent porch was designed by San Antonio architect O'Neil Ford, who told the owners they needed a place for old-timers to sit and mothers carrying babies to rest. He used square-cut cedar posts to keep the feeling of the old square.

Two doors up is the 1870s wood frame Saunders home (marker), the oldest home on the square. Its original open dogtrot design was later enclosed and the porch and other rooms added. John Henry, his wife, and 13 children lived here until 1903.

⑪ When the shops end, continue ahead on Old Kyle Road.

On the right a short way up is the John R. Dobie house, on both state and national historical registers. Originally a dogtrot built by Charles S. Cock in 1892, the home was purchased by John R. Dobie in 1899. The Dobies owned the property around the Blue Hole (farther up the road) for some 90 years. The Blue Hole is the deepest spot on Cypress Creek and the town's favorite swimming hole. A family could swim and picnic all day for 25 cents. The city acquired the Blue Hole and its surrounding land in 2005. A trail leading to the swimming hole begins at the square near Old Kyle Road and runs along Cypress Creek. It's a lovely additional walk to enhance your Wimberley visit.

⑫ At the cemetery, enter at the second entrance.

A marker at the second entrance gives some history. Walk to the end of the drive, then directly down from the back of the storage house. Here you will find the pink granite gravestone of Pleasant and Amanda Wimberley that reads, "For Whom the Town was Named." The move here did indeed prove to be healthy for the Wimberleys, for in spite of the hardships of pioneer life, Amanda lived to be 78 and Pleasant to be 96.

⑬ Retrace your steps to the square.

The Square is one of those rare places that takes needs of shoppers into consideration, with shady porches and benches for resting and people watching. As you sit with an ice cream cone or refreshing drink, let your imagination take away the cars and asphalt. Imagine instead a dirt or gravel square with horses and buggies. Watch out, though. Here comes a herd of cattle (or horses, or goats) being driven to the railhead in San Marcos.

Hill Country History and Architecture

Some 15 million years ago, an upthrust of the earth in what is now central Texas formed the Edwards Plateau. The tiers in which its hills rise above the fault zone prompted Spanish explorers to call them *balcones,* or balconies, giving it the name Balcones Escarpment. Interstate 35 follows its eastern boundary. Erosion by streams cut forward as well as downward across the plateau, forming a deeply eroded area to the southeast. This is the Texas Hill Country.

Lipan Apaches, Tonkawas, and Comanches—considered "less than friendly" by their neighbors—were the major inhabitants of the Texas Hill Country when Spaniards arrived. In the late 1600s and early 1700s, Spain encouraged settlement of its territory north of the Rio Grande River and established missions to help keep the French in neighboring Louisiana.

Anglo-Americans came to Texas in large numbers after Mexico won independence from Spain in 1821. Mexico offered land grants if they accepted Mexican citizenship. But when Americans began to outnumber Mexican Texans, the authorities attempted to stop immigration from the United States. As Antonio López de Santa Anna seized power, tensions increased. In 1836 Texans won independence as the Republic of Texas and encouraged further colonization. During the 1840s significant numbers of Americans, English, and Europeans—especially Germans—arrived.

This was a time of economic and political unrest in Germany. With overpopulation and crop failures plus over industrialization, farmers and workers could barely earn a living. Revolutions shook Central Europe. Dissatisfaction grew especially among the educated. Then came reports of a new land across the sea. In 1831, Johann Friedrich Ernst brought his family to fertile farmland between Galveston and San Antonio. He wrote home of land rich in game with soil needing no fertilizer, a climate with no winter, and no need for money. One needed to work only three months a year. The letter was published in newspapers throughout Germany, sparking emigration and leading Ernst to be credited as the father of German settlement in Texas.

Increased interest in emigration led nobles to form organizations to ensure safe passage and settlement of immigrants, thus reducing restlessness of displaced workers and removing the furor of the highly educated while also developing new trade markets for the German aristocracy. Most important of the organizations was the *Adelsverein*, also known as the German Emigration Company or Society for the Protection of German Immigrants in Texas. Organized in 1842 by five princes and 16 noblemen, this group sent Prince Carl of Solms-Braunfels to Texas as general commissioner. The Adelsverein in 1844 bought, sight unseen, a huge tract between the Llano and Colorado rivers in West Texas. The society, poorly organized, misinformed, and underfinanced, discovered their tract was far inland, had poor farmland, and was in the territory of the hostile Comanches. For a way station the Adelsverein bought land just north of San Antonio at Comal Springs and named the place New Braunfels. Prince Carl built a new port near Galveston he named Carlshaven, later known as Indianola. It was a major Texas port until it was wiped out by hurricanes in 1875 and 1886. He built warehouses for supplies but no living accommodations. The first wave of immigrants arrived in December 1844 and had to camp out on the beach. The next March Prince Carl led them by wagon train to New Braunfels.

When the next group of immigrants arrived they found the United States at war with Mexico, and all forms of transportation confiscated by the army. Further, the society claimed it had run out of money, leaving the new arrivals stranded on the beach. Already exhausted after a three-month ocean voyage, their health failed and they became vulnerable to epidemics. More than a thousand died of starvation and typhus. Those who survived made the 200-mile trek by oxcart and on foot to New Braunfels. Along the way, heavy rains caused carts to mire in the mud, resulting in delays. Hundreds more died. Arriving three months later in New Braunfels, they found the Guadalupe River too high to cross and had to wait for it to recede. A monument in New Braunfels is dedicated to the casualties of the ordeal.

John O. Meusebach, practical and well educated, took over leadership of the bankrupt society. Under his guidance immigrants received better support. In 1846 Meusebach led 120 settlers on to a second way station he named Fredericksburg for King Frederick of Prussia, the highest-ranking nobleman in the Adelsverein. Meusebach secured peace with Comanches by negotiating an 1847 treaty, still unbroken.

Arriving in Texas that year was Dr. Ferdinand Ludwig von Herff, whose family was to play an important part in the history of the Hill Country and San Antonio. He, too, extolled Texas as a place where colonists through work and industry could become self-supporting and respectable citizens in a short time. Echoing Ernst, Herff said the climate was healthful, land and provisions were cheap, and little work and time were required to make a crop. Many envisioned a "New Germany" in Texas. The short-lived democratic revolutions of 1848–49 in the German states brought many more immigrants to Texas, especially intellectuals. In the first five years of settlement more than 7,400 immigrants arrived. By 1860 another 20,000 came. They spread throughout the Hill Country along a corridor from New Braunfels to Mason down the old Indian trail later referred to as Upper Emigrant Road. By 1887 the population of much of the Hill Country—particularly in the river valleys of Gillespie, Comal, and Kendall counties—was predominantly German. Immigrant groups established their own subcultures. In the Llano Valley, German Methodists were against dancing, drinking, and card playing. In the Pedernales Valley, German Lutherans and Catholics enjoyed their traditional dance halls and beer gardens. The Guadalupe Valley, primarily in Comfort and Sisterdale in Kendall County, attracted utopian, freethinking agnostics—the Latinists, educated in universities where they were taught in and conversed in Latin.

Intellectuals in particular possessed few skills necessary for pioneer life. The first years were hard as they found hunger, disease, drought, and hostile natives. An old German adage prescribes for the first generation, death; for the second, deprivation; for the third, bread. Some immigrants passed through these phases in one lifetime.

Though the Hill Country's semiarid climate and thin layer of soil made the new land difficult for farming, settlers proved to be good builders, carpenters, stonemasons, furniture makers, and iron and leather workers. Some discovered that cattle, sheep, and goats fared better on the land than crops. Eventually the Hill Country became one of the nation's major sources of wool, and it remains the largest producer of mohair. The white angora goat is the mascot of Fredericksburg High School.

Many families had both a town lot and an outlot for farming. Because of the distance between the two, they came to town on Saturday, sold their produce, shopped, and stayed overnight to attend church. Some built small "Sunday Houses" on their town lots, while others camped on church grounds. In *Yesterday in the Texas Hill Country*, Gilbert J. Jordan remembers, "There was no work or play on Sunday; however, I was never able to figure out how this keeping the Sabbath holy jibed with all the work done by the women in preparing and serving the Sunday meals."

At the time of the Civil War most Germans in Central and Southeast Texas were deeply involved in the cotton industry, and as the Civil War approached they supported secession of Texas from the United States. Many Hill Country Germans, however, were against the war. Not only would it take the army away from the forts that protected them, they opposed slavery. This led to persecution, and sometimes lynching, by their neighbors. Many fled to Mexico, others served in the Union Army, and repercussions lasted for many years.

By this time the character we associate with the Hill Country was set. These hardscrabble years of early settlement remain reflected both in memory and in the natural and built environment, offering visitors—especially those who slow down and walk—a distinctive travel experience.

ARCHITECTURE

Especially appealing today is the Hill Country's distinctive architecture, which divides easily into phases reflecting frontier settlement, the antebellum South, and American Victorian. Fredericksburg may be the most architecturally significant Hill Country town because of its size and the number of early buildings extant. Comfort, though smaller, also displays a particularly fine array of early styles.

German immigrants' first shelters were little more than huts of poles and grasses chinked with clay and moss, like the Mexican *jacal*. Then came one-room cabins of round logs chinked with mud and rock that could be erected quickly with little more than an axe. Where timber was in short supply, the local soft limestone was cut into building blocks hand-quarried with chisel and hammer, leaving tool marks recognizable today. Two-room homes were often connected by an open space called a dogtrot, a style quite suitable to the Hill Country. The open hall caught the breeze and helped keep rooms cool. In good weather it provided extra living space, in bad weather a place to hang out the wash, in the winter a storage space for meat and other foodstuffs.

Germans introduced *Fachwerk* construction, with diagonal braces extending from corner to corner of the square timber frame and space between timbers filled with stone, sun-dried mud bricks, or wattle and daub. A coat of lime plaster could cover the walls. As time passed, log homes were often covered with shingles and had limestone block additions. Stone homes were sometimes plastered over for a more "refined" look. Tall cypress trees found along rivers and abundant cedar also provided building material of superior strength and resistance to rot. Many cypress floor boards laid on packed earth 150 years ago have never warped and show little sign of wear. Cypress water tanks are still watertight.

Often a home started with one room, with perhaps a sleeping loft/storage room above reached by an outdoor stairway to conserve interior space. This is the style of Sunday Houses, the small dwellings farmers and ranchers used when they came to town on weekends to conduct business and attend church. Large fireplaces provided for heating, cooking, and curing meat. In towns, homes were set close to the street to allow maximum space in back for a garden and outbuildings. As they prospered, settlers built larger and more substantial homes. Greek Revival, popular from the 1830s to 1860s, is recognized by side gabled rooflines, a narrow line of windows along the top and sides of the entrance door, and entry porches supported by columns. The porch might be one or two stories high and just cover the entrance, or it might run the length of the house as in the southern antebellum homes. American Victorian styles gained popularity from the 1860s through the early 1900s as arrival of railroads made light, factory-milled lumber available. It is identified by mansard roofs, steep gabled rooflines, asymmetrical floor plans, turrets, decorative brackets, spindles and scrollwork, shingles, bays, and wraparound porches. Doors, windows, and trim were mass produced. Kits could be ordered from Sears and Roebuck for a complete house.

Commercial buildings of wood or limestone often had living quarters over the store reached by an outside staircase. Cornices of tin pressed to imitate stone often decorated the roofline. Churches and public buildings were first built of log or wood, but they frequently burned and were eventually replaced with substantial stone edifices.

The Author

Diane Capito grew up taking family walks in her hometown of Kansas City, Missouri. She explored Southern California and Mexico on her own and in walking groups. She ended up in San Antonio, Texas, where she co-authored *San Antonio on Foot* and organized a series of neighborhood walking tours, finding time in between for freelance writing for a variety of newspapers and magazines.

She approached *Walking Hill Country Towns* with typical enthusiasm and diligence. She planned the routes on her own, researched points of interest and had others both test the walks and check her information. The result is this unique walking guide to the charming towns of the Texas Hill Country.

Not long after completing revisions for this second edition, Diane Capito died unexpectedly in 2009 in Berkeley, California, where she had moved several years before. Her youthful energy and zest for new horizons belied her chronological age of 78. Future updates of her work will be maintained by the publisher.

Bibliography

A Portrait of Blanco, Early History and Buildings of an Old Texas Town. Blanco: Blanco Historical Commission, 1998.

Alexander, D. B. *Texas Homes of the 19th Century.* Austin: University of Texas Press, 1966.

Baker, T. Lindsay. *Ghost Towns of Texas.* Norman: University of Oklahoma Press, 1986.

Biesele, Rudolph Leopold. *The History of the German Settlements in Texas, 1831-1861.* San Marcos: German-Texan Heritage Society, Southwest Texas State University, 1987.

Brandimarte, Cynthia and George Kegley. *Archeological and Historical Investigation of the Old Marketplatz in Fredericksburg, Texas.* Austin: Archeological Resource Evaluation Associates, 1990.

Carpenter, Bonnie. *Old Mountain City.* San Antonio: Naylor Co., 1970.

Comfort at Work, A History of Comfort's Business Buildings, The Comfort-able Years, 1854-1979. n.p., n.d.

Comfort Heritage: "Unser Fortschritt" Our Progress. Comfort: Comfort Heritage Foundation, 1990.

Danforth, Susie Brooks. *100 Years In Wimberley.* Austin: San Felipe Press, 1976.

Edwards, Walter F. *The Story of Fredericksburg, Its Past, Present, Points of Interest, and Annual Events.* Fredericksburg: Fredericksburg Chamber of Commerce, n.d.

Emmett, Chris, *Texas Camel Tales.* Austin: Steck-Vaughn Co., 1969.

Estill, Julia. *Fredericksburg, Texas.* Fredericksburg: Fredericksburg Publishing Company, n.d.

Flach, Vera. *A Yankee in German-American Texas Hill Country.* San Antonio, Naylor Co., 1973.

Hanna, Edith Margaret. *The Indigenous Architecture of Fredericksburg, Texas.* Master's thesis, North Texas State Teachers College, 1942.

Heritage of Blanco County Texas. Blanco: Blanco City News, 1987.

History of Bandera County. Bandera: Bandera County Historical Association, n.d.

Hunter, J. Marvin, *Pioneer History of Bandera County.* n.p., 1922.

Hunter, J. Marvin Jr. *100 Years in Bandera, 1833-1953.* n.d., n.p.

Jardin, Earl Jr. *Country Historian Notebook 16,* no. 1 (Spring 1994).

Jordan, Gilbert J. *Yesterday in the Texas Hill Country.* College Station: Texas A&M University Press, 1979.

Jordan, Terry. *Texas Graveyards, A Cultural Legacy.* Austin: University of Texas Press, 1982.

_____. *Texas Log Buildings.* Austin, University of Texas, 1978.

Gregory, Rosemarie Leissner and Myra Lee Adams Goff. *New Braunfels, A Pictorial History.* New Braunfels: Sophienburg Museum and Archives, 1993.

Kiel, Frank W. *Guadalupe River Valley Discovered, A Self-Guided Cassette Tour.* n.p., 1998.

Kimball, Allan C. *Texas Family Adventure Guide.* Old Saybrook, CT: Globe Pequot Press, 1997.

Kowert, Elise. *Historic Homes In and Around Fredericksburg.* Fredericksburg: Fredericksburg Publishing Co., 1990.

_____. *Old Homes and Buildings of Fredericksburg.* Fredericksburg: Fredericksburg Publishing Co., 1977.

Kerbow, Dorothy Wimberley, comp. *Cedar Whacker, Stories of the Texas Hill Country.* Austin: Eakin Press, 1988.

Knopp, Kenn. *German Immigration to America, Book 1.* n.p., 1999.

Lich, Glen E. *The German Texans.* San Antonio: University of Texas Institute of Texan Cultures, 1981.

McAlester, Virginia, and Lee McAlester. *A Field Guide to American Houses.* New York: Alfred A. Knopf, 1997.

McIlvain, Myra Hargrave. *Six Central Texas Auto Tours.* Austin: Eakin Press, 1980.

McInnis, Kathryn Cage. *Solid Lace and Tucks, Memories of a Girlhood in the Texas Hill Country 1892-1918.* New York: Vantage Press,1983.

Metz, Leon C. *Roadside History of Texas.* Missoula, MT: Mountain Press Publishing Co., 1994.

Moore, David. *Fredericksburg Historic Resource Survey.* Austin, n.p., 1983.

Moore, Melba McFarlin, and Bernice Smith West and William W. West. *Blanco City Heritage.* n.p., 1996.

Morris, Eleanor S. *Country Roads of Texas.* Castine, ME: Country Roads Press, 1994.

Murphy, Lloyd, comp. *A Tour Through Comfort History.* n.p., 1984.

Neidhardt, Ralph, and Bill Pellerin. *Bicycling the Texas Hill Country.* 2nd. ed. Houston: Texas Bicycle Map Co., 1993.

Penniger, Robert. Fredericksburg, *Texas: The First Fifty Years.* Fredericksburg: Fredericksburg Publishing Co., 1971.

Perry, Garland A. *Images of Boerne, Texas.* Boerne: Perry Enterprises, 1982.

Ransleben, Guido. *A Hundred Years of Comfort in Texas.* San Antonio: Naylor Co., 1974.

Rivers, Ranches, *Railroads and Recreation, A History of Kerr County Texas.* Dallas: Taylor Publishing Co., 1984.

Saul, Jeanette Hunter. *Inklings of the Past in Bandera County.* vols. 1 and 2. n.p., 1976.

Schutze, Albert. *Diamond Jubilee Souvenir Book of Comfort, Texas.* n.p., n.d.

Spearing, Darwin. *Roadside Geology of Texas.* Missoula, MT: Mountain Press Publishing Co., 1991.

St. Clair, Kathleen and Clifton St. Clair. *Little Towns of Texas.* n.p., 1982.

Stovall, Frances et al. *Clear Springs and Limestone Ledges, A History of San Marcos and Hays County.* Austin: Nortex Press, 1986.

Swanson, Eric R. *Geo-Texas, A Guide to the Earth Sciences.* College Station: Texas A & M University Press, 1995.

Syers, Ed. *Backroads of Texas.* Houston: Gulf Publishing Company, 1979.

Tyler, Ron, ed. *The New Handbook of Texas.* 6 vols. Austin: The Texas State Historical Association, 1996.

Von Boeckmann-Jones. *Pioneers In God's Hills, A History of Fredericksburg and Gillespie County People and Events.* Austin: Gillespie County Historical Society, 1960.

Watkins, Clara. *Kerr County, Texas 1856-1976.* Kerrville: Hill Country Preservation Society, n.d.

Watriss, Wendy and Fred Baldwin, with Lawrence Goodwyn. *Coming to Terms: The German Hill Country of Texas.* College Station: Texas A&M University Press, 1991.

Watt, Don, and Lynn Watt. *Fredericksburg, Texas, Living with the Past.* Fredericksburg: Shearer Publishing Co., 1987.

Acknowledgments

Where to start? So many wonderful people contributed to this book, either directly with personal interviews and assistance or indirectly through their published and unpublished works.

Just plain "Thank you" seems inadequate for the help and guidance given by librarians and library volunteers, members of heritage and conservation societies, and local historians who guided my way. Thanks also to the owners of historic homes and buildings whom I met by chance as I walked and who took a few moments to relate history and anecdotes—you exemplify the friendly, neighborly ambiance of the Hill Country.

Special thanks go to the following who gave of their personal time and effort in interviews, walking me through a town's history, and/or reading the manuscript for accuracy: Claire Smullen Billingsley, Fred Bartel, Tom Call, Bettie Edmonds, Morris Edmondson, Margaret Evans, Everett Anthony Fey, Mary Giberson, Pete Glosson, Theresa Gold, Syd Hall, Odis Hohmann, Elizabeth Hudson, and Stanley Jones, Bill and M.F. Johnson, Kenn Knopp, Virginia Kohls, Gregory Krauter, Dr. Lance Lambert, Bill Meyer, Mary Jane Nalley, Minnie Nelson and her sisters (the Harper sisters), Josephine Parker, Louis Postert, David Rice, Barron Schlameus, Barbara Schutt, Frances Stovall, Ann Miller Strom, John Tiff, Carl Wait, Bernice West, Linda Wiles, Dr. James Wilson, Jane Wood, Barbara Barton Younts. If I left anyone out, my apology—and thank you.

Special thanks also for time, effort, and helpful feedback to the following members of the Selma Path Finders Chapter of American Volkssport Association who tested the walks for me (in July and August!): Ed Bruetsch, Martin Callahan, Frank Chappell, Phyllis Eagan, Pat Gunter, and Darlene Oner.

Thanks to the members of my critique group for help and encouragement. And to the friends who encouraged, supported, and put up with me over the three years it took to pull this book together: I couldn't have kept at it without you. Many, many thanks.

Special thanks to Xonia Kargl and Sarah Nawrocki for catching misplaced commas and modifiers, and other grammatical errors, and suggestions for improvements in the text. Very special thanks to Virginia Ford for her patience and efforts in creating the maps.

Acknowledgments for the Second Edition

Many of the local contacts who helped with the first edition of *Walking Hill Country Towns* once again answered questions that arose as I revisited all the walks for this update. Again, I extend grateful thanks to all of you. Additional thanks go to some new contacts: Pam Sullivan in Wimberley, Julie King and Melani Howard in San Marcos and some others whose names, phone numbers, and emails were scribbled on scraps of paper not kept. I meant no disrespect for your generous time and effort checking information for me, it's just that I didn't think ahead to an updated Acknowledgments. So if you helped and are not listed, I extend an apology and many thanks.

Between the time of the first edition and my move from Texas to California, I did a series of San Antonio and Hill Country walks for the North East Independent School District's community education program, having been recruited by Mary M. Fisher. A core group of walk buddies emerged from this series. This group came through for me when it was time for a new edition. Since I couldn't be in the area long enough to rewalk all the walks, Ginny Ford, who also did the maps, and various walk buddies drove me slowly through the walks, leaving me free to look for any changes. So special thanks go to Ginny and to walk buddies Valerie Crosswell, Arlyn Krug, Yvonne Richardson, Donna Romero, Laurie Stiteler, and Jeannie Townsend, as well as to Maverick Publishing's Lewis F. Fisher for his encouragement, guidance and editing throughout the process.

Walks in two new towns, Marble Falls and Leakey, were added to the new edition. For invaluable help on the Marble Falls walks thanks go to Jeannie Townsend, who spent several days there with me, then followed with further research on her own; to Yvonne Richardson and Arlyn Krug for verifying the accuracy of the Marble Falls walk; and to Marble Falls residents, librarians, and historians who gave of time and effort answering questions and supplying additional research: Ollie Ann Baker, Billy Becker, Betsy Engelbrecht, Mary Jackson, Patricia Craig Johnson, Jane Knapik, Fran McSpodden, Kerri Roberts, Elizabeth Schnelle and various others along the way who offered tidbits of information. Extra thanks also to Ollie Ann Baker for letting us stay in her B&B. For Leakey, thanks go to Yvonne Richardson and Arlyn Krug, for additional research and input; to Laurie Stiteler, for checking the walk for accuracy; to Leakey historians Susan Knight and Darlene Buchanan Sharp; and to others who provided interesting stories.

Index